ADVENTURES OF A RAILWAY NOMAD
HOW OUR JOURNEYS GUIDE US HOME

"Adventurous, bold . . . full of twists and surprises."
— Chris Brady, *NY Times* bestselling author of *A Month of Italy*

"Hilarious, inspiring, and beautifully written. Karen McCann proves that you can head off on an adventure at any age. Sixty is the new twenty." — George Mahood, bestselling author of *Free Country*

"Karen's storytelling is, if possible, even more enticing than her astonishing journey." — Alicia Bay Laurel, bestselling author of *Living on the Earth*

"Warmth, wisdom, and humor . . . I loved this book and laughed out loud on more than a few occasions." — Susan Pohlman, author of *Halfway to Each Other*

"A thoroughly enjoyable whistle stop tour of Europe's roads less traveled . . . never a dull moment." — David & Victoria James, authors of *Going Gypsy: One Couple's Adventure from Empty Nest to No Nest at All*

"In Karen's new book, she and her husband tackle an adventure via rail, showing that no matter your time and place in life, you can grab the train by the locomotive and head out into the great unknown."
— Ryan, author of *Jets Like Taxis*

DANCING IN THE FOUNTAIN
HOW TO ENJOY LIVING ABROAD

"I loved this book ... I must have laughed aloud at least once in every chapter." — *Lonely Planet*

"A warm, humorous account . . . She makes shopping for a screwdriver sound like a grand adventure." — Rolf Potts, *Vagabonding*

"With wit, humor, and insight, McCann . . . tells an engaging and realistic tale of how someone can create a modern life very much their own in a new and unfamiliar country." — Johnny Jet, *johnnyjet.com*

"McCann's wacky sense of humor will have you smiling on every page." — Rita Golden Gelman, author of *Tales of a Female Nomad*

"Karen McCann's engaging style and sense of humor are both refreshing and immediately evident. In fact, I find them reminiscent of British author Peter Mayle and his romps in France, but with a bit more substance." — *Spain Expat*

"A delightfully well-written true-life adventure story ... warm, inviting, immediately charming, and constantly entertaining. Her narrative was so good I found myself wanting to hear more about Cleveland! Now THAT's good travel writing!" — Chris Brady, *NY Times* bestselling author of *A Month of Italy*

Adventures of a
RAILWAY
NOMAD

HOW
OUR JOURNEYS
GUIDE US
HOME

KAREN MCCANN

CAFÉ
SOCIETY
PRESS

Published by
Café Society Press
Hartland & Co.
1100 Superior Avenue East, Suite 700
Cleveland, OH 44114

ISBN 978-0-9850283-3-6

1. Travel. 2. Rail travel

www.enjoylivingabroad.com

For my mother,
Helen English Keating,
who taught me the joy of adventure
and the comforts of home.

Books by Karen McCann

MEMOIRS

Dancing in the Fountain
How to Enjoy Living Abroad

Adventures of a Railway Nomad
How Our Journeys Guide Us Home

TRAVEL GUIDES

Pack Light
Quick & Easy Tips for Traveling Everywhere with the Right Stuff

101 Ways to Enjoy Living Abroad
Essential Tips for Easing the Transition to Expat Life

Contents

CHAPTER 1

The Experiment

"Well, it's been nice knowing you," said my friend Enrique, when I told him about The Experiment.

"We *do* expect to return alive," I pointed out.

He just rolled his eyes the way people from Seville do when they're too polite to say, "You crazy Americans . . ."

The Experiment was born on a battered ferryboat off the coast of Portugal, on a rainy spring day when anyone with any sense was staying dry at home. But this was the only chance my husband and I would have to visit a beachcomber we knew who lived on the tiny island of Culatra, so there Rich and I sat, surrounded by islanders who were returning from the mainland with sacks of potatoes, tins of fuel, piles of paperbacks, and various other lumpy bundles stacked about their feet. Rain drumming on the roof made the drafty cabin almost cozy, and I was lulled by the rocking of the boat, the homey smell of damp wool sweaters, and the buzz of a dozen conversations as friends gossiped over the heads of the small children in their laps.

"I miss this," Rich said suddenly. "We need to go on the road. We need another adventure."

I stared at him in disbelief. How could he *say* that? We were *living* a grand adventure. More than a decade earlier, a few years after Rich had taken early retirement from a demanding corporate career, we'd fallen in love with southern Spain. As a writer, I could work anywhere, and we began spending more and more time in Seville and finally moved there, renting a flat in the city's old quarter "for a year." We were still there, although we returned for part of each year to the area of California where I was born, because I knew that America was something you had to stay in practice for, and I didn't want to lose my touch.

During our years in Seville I'd struggled mightily to learn Spanish, make friends among locals and expats, and adapt to a life that was foreign in a thousand tiny, tricky ways. Now, after some spectacular social and linguistic pratfalls, I'd finally (more or less) gotten the hang of our adopted home. My life was settled, comfortable . . . and in danger of growing dull. Come to think of it, there had been entirely too many moments lately when I'd found myself moving through Seville on automatic pilot. Oh my God, Rich was right. We needed to shake things up a little.

"I'm in," I said. "Absolutely. Where shall we go?"

The conversation began to fizz with possibilities. Cambodia. Russia. Argentina. Iceland. Cuba. All we knew for sure was that we wanted to go somewhere that we'd never been before.

That narrowed the field considerably. During the twenty-five years of our marriage, wanderlust had taken us to more than forty countries. Although we were lucky enough to have seen some of the world's great cities, we preferred smaller, more offbeat destinations — a tributary of the Peruvian Amazon, an African village, Thailand's hill towns. We'd accepted volunteer work assignments to help international charities sort out struggling microenterprises in developing or postwar nations. Rich and I were always trying to find ways to get further *"out there"* — that is, off the tourist track, past the boundaries of commonly known routes, to the cultural equivalent of places where, in ancient times, the maps would have been marked, "Here there be dragons."

I thought with pleasure about all the times I'd climbed into some wheezing old boat and headed upriver with the wind in my hair and birds darting overhead, having only the haziest idea where I was going, but sure that something astonishing lay just around the next bend. Memories flooded in: baking bread with the village grandmothers in a farmhouse on the Chechnya border; opening a tent flap at dawn to catch my first glimpse of the Himalayas; being served the brains of a pig on the point of a knife in the Republic of Georgia. I'd learned when, where, and why it was advisable to shake out my shoes in the morning to dislodge any scorpions, to watch the trees overhead for leopards, and to stay on the path to avoid stray land mines. I'd bathed in rivers with the locals calling out cheerfully, "Don't poke your hands under the dock — that's where the electric eels live!"

A montage of increasingly disagreeable bathroom scenes flickered through my mind, culminating in a certain Guatemalan hut so gruesome that afterwards I simply threw away my shoes. I remembered trekking at high altitudes, the long, breathless days followed by sleepless nights in bitter cold that easily penetrated two sleeping bags. Come to think of it, I hadn't slept on the ground since 1996. I doubted it had gotten any more yielding since then. I knew my joints hadn't.

With a small shock, I realized that activities I'd undertaken without a moment's hesitation in my twenties, even my forties, raised new questions now. I was active and healthy, but there was no getting around the fact that I was in my early sixties (a *sexagenarian*!) and I'd lost my taste for traveling rough. I no longer considered it romantic — or worth the aches and pains in the morning — to sleep on the ground, in a bamboo hut, or on the floor of a rice barge. But I hadn't lost my love of adventure, my desire to get far enough *out there* to feel the spine-tingling zing of being truly alive.

"What do you think?" said Rich, his face alight with eagerness. "Asia? South America? Mongolia?" It was the kind of conversation where no dream seemed too outlandish.

"We'd have to spend a fair amount of time flying," I pointed out. The conversation deflated for a moment as we both contemplated how much we'd come to loathe the tedium of modern air travel.

"I know," he said, brightening. "We'll go by train. Not to the other side of the world, but around Europe. How about Eastern Europe? You can get to some really remote areas with a Eurail pass."

"Civilized travel to uncivilized places." I was nodding thoughtfully.

"We could go right out our front door and walk to the train station. And from there . . ."

I found myself grinning. "From there we could go anywhere in Europe. Hopping on and off trains, wandering like nomads . . ." Then my grin faded a little, and I said, "You don't think we're getting soft, do you? I'm wondering whether we can still have adventures if we're traveling in a civilized manner."

"Only one way to find out."

"It would be a sort of experiment," I mused. "To see if we can still get *out there* and have adventures while traveling in a way that makes sense at our stage of life."

When I was young, I'd thought nothing of throwing a few spare clothes in a backpack and hitting the road. I'd climbed mountains, slept rough, and eaten fried flies just to see if I could do it. Fortunately, having done all that in the past, I didn't feel obliged to prove it all over again now. I knew sexagenarians who were still trying to keep up with twenty-somethings, often ones they'd just married, and it was rarely an edifying spectacle.

No, I wasn't interested in the adrenaline rush of strenuous physical challenges, but I did want some excitement and the kind of experiences that would show me a new side of the world — and, perhaps more importantly, of myself. Young travelers *expect* to come home changed. Every journey is a quest. While their hopes of returning a worldly-wise, unutterably cool sophisticate and sexual virtuoso may not be fully realized, exposure to the world usually broadens horizons and rubs off a few rough edges here and there. Middle-aged travelers, on the other hand, frequently just want to come home rested. In the midst of demanding lives, the last thing they want is another mental or physical challenge.

Friends of my own generation often like to sit around swapping rollicking stories about coming of age in the 1960s. No doubt some of the details have been embellished over the years, but my memories of the era and of my own youthful escapades confirm that it's a miracle any of us made it through our teens and twenties alive, out of jail, and with a reasonable portion of our brain cells still functioning. As they recount tales of long-ago road trips, my friends often turn wistful, as if such derring-do was well beyond them now.

I don't believe that.

Just because you celebrate a particular birthday doesn't mean you have to restrict yourself to motor coach vacations and cruises to nowhere. Unless you have a significant physical impediment — which can happen at any age — the chances are pretty good that you can still choose to travel independently if you want to. Lots of my more sensible friends prefer the comfort and convenience of organized group tours, which obviously have huge practical advantages. I respect their choices but don't feel obliged to travel that way myself solely because I'm entitled to a particular number of candles on my cake.

As I thought about the proposed train trip, it was clear to me that spontaneous, independent travel *was* possible at my age and could be done without sacrificing all shreds of comfort and security. The real question wasn't whether I could go, but why I wanted to. What did I hope to get out of this trip? A diversion? A few novel experiences to refresh my repertoire of travel tales?

Yes, I thought, that was part of it, but mostly I wanted to shake up my inner life a little. Like those youthful travelers, I wanted to come home from the journey changed. I wanted to be surprised into new emotions and new perspectives. I hoped that getting *out there* would alter the way I looked at the world and my place in it. But at the moment I had only the haziest idea how or where we'd need to travel in order to make that happen, if it happened at all.

Echoing my thoughts, Rich said, "What would that kind of trip look like?" And we began to sketch out possibilities.

By the time the Portuguese ferryboat drew near the island, we'd laid out some key criteria for our upcoming trip, soon to be known as "The Experiment."

1. We would travel in a relaxed manner, by easy stages.

2. Trains would be our principal mode of transportation, although ferries and an occasional taxi or bus would be acceptable when necessary.

3. Our itinerary would not be fixed; we'd have a general idea of the route but leave ourselves open to diversions and detours.

4. We'd go as far *out there* as possible, seeking authentic experiences in remote, off-the-tourist-track places.

5. We wouldn't make reservations far in advance but would use the Internet to book comfortable, conveniently located, affordable lodgings a day or so before our arrival in any new place.

6. Our luggage would be just one small suitcase and maybe a day-pack each.

7. If at any time it got to be too much for either of us, we would give in gracefully and go home.

Possibly the biggest stretch for me was item three: no fixed itinerary. Although in my youth I'd favored unstructured travel, during the decades since then, as Rich and I had journeyed to more and more remote corners of the planet, I'd become a bit of a fiend about nailing down logistics. I didn't want to arrive in a remote village — or even an airport — in, say, Kenya or Bosnia-Herzegovina and try to explain in sign language that we were there to help a handicraft cooperative, our driver was a no-show, and we had no idea where to go next. Hoping to forestall any such moments, I would type out our itinerary, the flight schedule, reservation numbers, transportation arrangements, addresses of hotels and guest houses, local contacts, emergency contacts, home office contacts, and anything else I could think of. Then I'd make two copies, carrying one with me at all times while stowing the backup securely in the depths of my suitcase.

Traveling back and forth so often between California and Spain, we'd naturally relaxed these standards, but this would be the first time we'd ever set out on a major trip with nothing whatsoever organized in advance. I was sure it would be good for my soul; I wasn't quite so certain about my nerves.

Rich and I were still discussing The Experiment as we followed the other passengers off the ferry and onto the old wooden quay. We'd traveled to Culatra to visit Jan, a German who'd retired there some twenty years earlier to live on the beach in a whimsical cottage he'd covered with gifts from the sea: shells, sun-bleached oars, bits of driftwood he'd carved into mermaids. He seemed to enjoy passing the time of day with random visitors, and I'd chatted with him a few times while I was in southern Portugal taking painting classes from a Dutch artist at a British-run art school.

The year before, while I was struggling to improve my skills in the art of portraiture, Jan had agreed to let me take a series of photographs of him that I could use as the basis for a painting. The resulting work shows Jan in his customary garb: nothing but a bathing suit and, rather incongruously, a wristwatch. It wouldn't have surprised me to discover it was broken and that he wore it to remind himself of the pleasure of being retired, saying to himself, "My watch doesn't work anymore, and neither do I."

"We could learn a lot from Jan," I said, as Rich and I slogged across the soggy sand toward his cottage.

"You want to spend your days half-naked on a beach collecting driftwood?"

"God, no. But here's someone who has really learned how to slow down."

I was there to bring Jan copies of a postcard featuring his portrait, which I'd used to promote a recent exhibition of my paintings in California. As I expected, he roared with laughter at the idea he was famous — at least briefly, in a very small section of the San Francisco Bay Area — and seemed quite pleased to receive a handful of the postcards.

On the way back to the mainland, and for the next several weeks, Rich and I spoke of little else but The Experiment. When we mentioned the plan, expat friends seemed to think it all sounded like great fun, while Enrique and other Spanish *amigos* seemed seriously worried that we wouldn't survive the trip.

"Eastern Europe? Really? *Why*?" my friend Tonio asked in bewilderment and distress. "Those are the most dangerous countries in Europe. Besides, in Eastern Europe the people are very poor. Conditions are very bad. There's nothing to see."

But it seemed to me that Central and Eastern Europe offered, if anything, almost too many points of interest from which to choose. I bought a map of Europe and taped it to the kitchen wall, and Rich and I began to circle possibilities: Lake Como, Zurich, Kraków, Sofia, Bucharest.

"We can go to the Carpathian Mountains," Rich said excitedly one morning, drawing a big circle on the map.

"Which are where, exactly?" I asked, squinting blearily at the eastern section of the map as I sipped my tea.

"Transylvania," he said.

"Sounds like fun. I'm only sorry we won't be there for Halloween."

We had decided to leave in June of the following year. Departing any sooner was impossible, as I was in the final stages of writing *Dancing in the Fountain*, a book about our lives in Seville. Rich was thrilled to have thirteen months to do the planning, which he considers nearly as much fun as the journey itself. He threw himself into researching train routes, possible destinations, travel clothing and gear, apps for the iPad and iPhone he soon acquired, and special software for keeping track of it all. I helped out when I could, but I didn't enter into this phase of the planning as fully as he did, being too wrapped up in making the final edits on my book. Our dinner conversations tended to go like this:

RICH: Did you know that the Wieliczka Salt Mine outside of Kraków was in continuous operation from the thirteenth century until 2007?

ME: Cool. Do you think I ought to add a Reading Group Guide to the back of the book?

RICH: Sure. The mine has dozens of statues, three chapels, and an entire cathedral carved out of salt.

ME *(realizing that he's been speaking)*: What?

RICH: *Salt.*

ME *(handing him the salt shaker)*: Here.

Occasionally we did manage to put our heads together and make a few critical decisions. During the summer of The Experiment, we would forego our usual visit to California and travel from early June through August. We would keep our route loose and our days unhurried, spending at least two or three nights in each location, with train travel of no more than about three hours at a stretch. Like nomads, we would keep moving ever onward to greener pastures.

Whenever I found myself in the kitchen, I'd peer at the wall map, reading the names of strange and exotic cities, places I couldn't even pronounce, let alone imagine: České Budějovice, Žilina, Košice, Nyíregyháza, Sighișoara.

A picture gradually formed in my mind, something akin to the Grand Tour that young gentlemen used to take to add the finishing touches to their cultural and social education. I'd read all sorts of novels about nineteenth-century travelers leisurely making their way around the continent, bearing letters of introduction to friends of friends who would provide them with an entrée into the local social scene. I wanted to meet people — locals, expats, fellow travelers — as often as possible along the way. It would make the trip more interesting, providing fresh insights and, with luck, a bit of colorful commentary for my blog. I began to send out feelers to some of my international friends, to see if anybody could write letters of introduction on my behalf to residents of any of the locales on our tentative itinerary.

"And if that doesn't work," said Rich, showing me his iPad screen, "I've found a group called Rent-A-Friend."

"What, they thought 'Escort Service' was too subtle?"

"No, no, it looks legit. Really."

Peering at photos of the rentable friends — mostly young people, it's true, but with nothing remotely glamorous or come-hither in their appearance — I had to agree that it seemed unlikely that these friends came with benefits.

"I'm sure it's just a guide service," he said.

"Maybe keep them as a backup?" I suggested.

Rich bookmarked the link and made a note in his electronic files. In the months following our decision to embark on The Experiment, his research and planning files had rapidly grown to Biblical proportions, containing links to everything from navigational apps to high-functioning travel clothing to esoteric points of interest in the most obscure corners of Eastern Europe. In times of stress (about which you'll be hearing a lot more later), I could always turn his thoughts to a more cheerful direction by murmuring the magic phrase, "I saw an app today that might interest you . . ."

If the idea that we might be biting off more than we could chew crossed either of our minds, we certainly never mentioned it to one another.

CHAPTER 2

Get Ready, Get Set . . .

I'm not saying I was jealous, but when Rich first brought home an iPad to help with trip planning, he was holding it in his lap all day, taking it to bed every night, and occasionally getting into spats with it when it exhibited annoying behavior. But I didn't get seriously worried until he started buying it gifts. "Look what I can get for it," he'd say, showing me yet another app he'd bookmarked for his new darling. "This one can ask for directions in a hundred languages. And it's only ninety-nine cents!" I was just grateful that they didn't sell a high-priced diamond necklace app. (And if they did, I could only pray Rich would never find out about it.)

But I have to admit that his app obsession paid off, as our iPad soon became capable of performing all sorts of clever tricks, from doing currency conversions in the blink of a pixel to displaying the timetables of every train system in Europe, complete with details about connections, intermediary stops, maps, and the local name for stations. And thank God it did; I, for one, would never have figured out on my own that Glavna Železnička Stanica was the rail hub of Belgrade, Serbia.

Rich began using this new iRail app to find routes and calculate travel times between possible destinations, and we spent hours standing in front of the map on our kitchen wall, tracing the network of black lines snaking across the continent. Eventually we began roughing out a route that made a giant, irregular loop from Spain through France, Italy, Switzerland, Germany, Austria, the Czech Republic, Poland, Slovakia,

Romania, Bulgaria, Serbia, Montenegro, and Croatia, then back again through Italy, France, and Spain.

Then one day it occurred to me that those dotted blue lines arcing across the Mediterranean represented ferries. Instantly I imagined myself leaning against the ship's railing in the moonlight, a light breeze fluttering the long skirts of my chiffon evening gown, the kind Ginger Rogers wore on ships in the old black-and-white films. Like many of my generation, I found my perceptions of life were largely filtered through the lens of Hollywood's movie cameras. To me, the words "train travel" instantly evoked images from *The Lady Vanishes, Murder on the Orient Express, Silver Streak*, and countless others. It was going to seem awfully tame if I didn't encounter at least one corpse during the trip. When it came to ships, the only film that sprang to mind was *Titanic*, which hardly seemed auspicious. But upon reflection, I felt fairly sure we didn't have to worry about icebergs while crossing the Mediterranean in summertime.

"What about taking the ferry from Barcelona to Italy?" I suggested. "We could bypass France altogether, zip right over to the port of . . ." — I double-checked the map — "the port of Genoa, then start heading northeast."

Rich loved the idea, and we scratched France off our list and penciled in the ports of Barcelona and Genoa. Narrowing down our destination countries, even by one, helped some, but there was still an amazing amount of territory under consideration. In my eagerness to get *out there* and explore unknown lands, I now found myself contemplating a host of ex-Soviet nations about whose geographic boundaries and cultural heritage I was very hazy indeed. The old names kept popping up in my mind, and more than once I referred to visiting Czechoslovakia, a country that, in my saner moments, I was fully aware had ceased to exist in 1993.

One of the first apps added to our collection was a translator to help us navigate the various languages we would encounter in all these countries. I had high hopes our new translator app would make it easy to communicate with the locals, at least well enough to locate our hotel and order a meal. Once we actually got on the road, however, I discovered that it was entirely too awkward to pull out an iPhone, open the app, type in the phrase I wanted, and then ask cab drivers and waiters to squint at the tiny screen in order to read it. And it was abundantly obvious that there was no way they were going to take the time to tap in any sort of reply, let alone one that was spelled correctly enough for our translator to transform it into English. In the end, the most successful approach turned out to be a mixture of English, hand gestures, learning a few key words in the local language, and — I know how old-fashioned this sounds! — writing things down in a small notebook.

That notebook turned out to be the most useful single item we brought along on the trip. Rich carried it everywhere with him, tucked into his shirt pocket with a slender pen clipped to the cover. Since his handwriting is so illegible that even he has trouble reading it, it was my job to print in large, clear letters anything we'd need to ask people: hotels we were seeking, trains we wanted to catch, local dishes we had a hankering to try. Of course, when we got to places that used the Cyrillic (кирилица) alphabet, things got a bit more complicated. But more about that later.

During our trip preparations, Rich spent a lot of time researching the kinds of accommodations we might expect to find, especially in the more obscure destinations we were considering. We'd learned the hard way that we never feel at home in soulless, cookie-cutter hotels and prefer to seek out colorful little offbeat places whenever possible. But these take time to find and, being small, they tend to fill up rapidly, so they need to be booked well in advance. That posed something of a problem on our train trip, since we were determined to maintain a spontaneous, nomadic spirit and avoid set timetables. We agreed it was okay to book a few days in advance, but no more than that — and no less. I'm always reading stories by travel writers who simply arrive in a city and amble blithely about, almost instantly discovering a suitable, affordable, and amusing place to pass the night. In my experience, the process tends to involve hours of trudging around, dragging suitcases up and down hills and hotel steps. On the rare occasions when I've done it, I find the whole process so tedious and exhausting that eventually I reach the breaking point and fling myself headlong into the next available hotel, however dull and/or overpriced it might be.

In his quest for last-minute lodgings with character, Rich was thrilled to discover an app for Airbnb, the online system for arranging private, informal (and some say questionably legal) rentals of anything from someone's guest room to an entire apartment or house. Rich also bookmarked the site Hostelworld.com, as he'd been reading that hostels had recently become the hot new lodging option, even for people like us who were long, long past qualifying as "youth." I was skeptical, but I told Rich I'd stay anywhere, as long as we had a private bathroom and no bedbugs.

"It'll be *fine*," said Rich. "Besides, if we do wind up someplace awful, it will just give you that much more to write about on the blog." How right he turned out to be!

I was relieved to notice that all the lodging websites converted the prices into the currency of our choice and would let us pay online via credit card. There would be no need to calculate, on the fly, whether 10,878 Hungarian forints was a good price for a single night's stay. (Yes, it was, being a modest forty-nine dollars.) Getting off the well-worn tourist path meant that many countries on our list — the Czech Republic, Romania, Bulgaria, Serbia, Croatia, and of course, Hungary — did not use the familiar euro but maintained their traditional currencies. Fortunately, cash in local currencies would be readily available to us from bank machines along the way. And with luck and Rich's new exchange rate calculator app, we would have a pretty good idea of what we were actually spending.

That app, I fervently hoped, would help us avoid ridiculous errors like the one that occurred back when Italy was still on the lira. At the end of a long and exceedingly jovial dinner with friends at a restaurant in Milan, Rich lost track of the decimal places when signing the credit card receipt and left a tip larger than the bill itself. He wondered why the waiters kept shaking his hand, begging him to come back soon, and giving every indication of being willing to carry him out of the restaurant on their shoulders if he'd like. Two hours later, he sat bolt upright in bed, exclaiming, "Wait a minute! That tip— !" He hunted around in his wallet until he found the receipt and then sank back against the headboard with an anguished groan. But of course, there was nothing to be done. Our new currency app, which included both a converter and a calculator, would (we hoped) help us avoid a repeat performance.

Rich began to work up budgets for food, lodging, and various other trip expenses. We had always been thrifty travelers, preferring modest accommodations with character, funky little eateries, and public transportation or, whenever possible, walking. Our itineraries usually included a few splurges, such as a night or two at a better hotel; these were offset by ultracheap accommodations elsewhere, such as the longboat driver's home in Bangkok, where we slept on a mattress on the floor with the centipedes. We weren't planning anything quite that down-and-dirty on this trip, but we knew that the food and accommodations in most of our destinations, especially in the farther reaches of Eastern Europe, would be pretty affordable.

People who don't travel extensively sometimes get the impression that long journeys have to be insanely expensive. They calculate the cost per day of their honeymoon in the Caribbean or last business trip to New York, multiply that times thirty or sixty or ninety days, and gasp at the total. But travel doesn't have to be lavish and pricey. In his classic book *Vagabonding*, Rolf Potts writes about watching Charlie Sheen play a hyperambitious character in *Wall Street* who says, "I think if I can make a bundle of cash before I'm thirty and get out of this racket, I'll be able to ride my motorcycle across China." Watching this scene, Potts recalls, "I nearly fell out of my seat in astonishment. After all, Charlie Sheen or anyone else could work for eight months as a *toilet cleaner* and have enough money to ride a motorcycle across China."

Like so much else in life, the cost of travel is determined by the choices we make. Basing the numbers on our style of travel — simple, comfortable, safe — Rich went to work with his calculator. In the end, backing out all the expenses that we would have anyway, such as groceries and occasional nights out, he figured the three-month trip would cost us, out of pocket, about thirty-five hundred dollars apiece. Luckily, we wouldn't have to go out and scrub toilets to afford that kind of outlay. Rich's pension, my book sales, and the rents we were charging for the Seville apartment and cottage in California were enough to cover it. And as a travel writer, a large portion of my expenses would be a tax write-off, which helped as well.

Along with his ever-growing collection of apps, Rich was saving zillions of articles, blog posts, links to websites, and snippets of information that might someday come in handy — if only we could find them again. Eventually that led him to Evernote, an app for organizing electronic files. I never warmed to its clunky navigation and utilitarian graphics, but it did provide a solid structure for corralling information into retrievable form.

Although destinations and trip logistics dominated the Evernote folders at first, we were also accumulating a lot of information about health and safety on the road. We had a keen interest in this topic, having suffered through our share of medical crises, often in places where the local health care system was of such dubious quality that we were better off relying on our own resources.

For instance, there was that time in Mexico when my normally sensible husband ordered a plate of shrimp at our rural, inland hotel. As he popped the last glistening morsel into his mouth, he got the first inkling that he was in trouble. Serious trouble. Four days later he was still in active torment, unable to keep down anything but Coca-Cola and crackers. When I walked into the village that morning to postpone yet again an excursion we'd scheduled before the disaster struck, the tour operator convinced me it was time for a professional to take charge of the case. When I got back, I sat down beside the bed and said, "Rich, I've got the name of a local doctor who speaks a little English . . ."

At the prospect of receiving medical treatment from an unknown doctor in a remote Mexican village, Rich instantly sat up exclaiming, "NO! I'm feeling a *lot* better." In minutes he was dressed, within hours he was walking around, and the next day we resumed our journey. Sometimes a good scare is the best miracle cure.

While we were doing our health and safety research for the train trip, I happened to have lunch with a travel blogger I know, and we naturally started swapping road stories about medical crises we'd faced. She confided, "I once had to have emergency eye surgery in Thailand. It only cost me seven dollars and turned out fine. So I don't really see why I would ever need health insurance while I'm traveling." I gave her full marks for courage — and luck — but personally I wouldn't want to risk my vision on a seven-dollar medical procedure. Rich and I carried plenty of health insurance, and for this trip we also bought evacuation insurance; the $350 price tag seemed hefty until we compared it with the astronomical costs of international medical evacuation flights, which can easily run into six figures. I would hate to sustain that kind of hideous financial blow on top of whatever other calamity was in progress.

So far, neither of us has landed in the hospital on one of our trips (and yes, I am knocking wood as I type *that*), but we have dealt with all sorts of minor emergencies, and Rich is famous for his comprehensive travel medical kit. One afternoon we spread its contents out on the kitchen table to see what might prove useful and what could safely be left behind. We set aside, among other things, the snakebite kit, the dental kit, and the syringes. (Yes, syringes. Luckily we've never needed to get an emergency injection in a village clinic that had run out of clean needles, but we've heard stories of people who have, motivating us to carry a few with us on our more rugged adventures, just in case.) By the end of half an hour, we'd whittled the kit down to the bare necessities.

It now included the oral antibiotic Cipro, the topical antibiotic Gold Bond ointment, insect repellant, After Bite (in case the little devils got through the repellant), Citrucel, Ex-lax, Imodium, the anti-nausea suppository Promethegan, echinacea, Advil Congestion Relief, Sudafed, the sleep aids Quietude and melatonin, the homeopathic hangover remedy Drink Ease, the allergy medicine Cetirizina Cinfa, Compeed protective strips for blisters, Nick Relief, and such basic supplies as a thermometer, paracetamol (known in the States as acetaminophen), Advil, Band-Aid strips, butterfly closures, Omnistrip wound closure strips, gauze, and a tiny roll of first aid tape.

Always in hot pursuit of more and better ways of keeping us safe on the road, Rich now began to focus serious attention on our security measures. And here he was, as they say, "in his salsa." In addition to the "be prepared" attitude instilled during his childhood years as a Boy Scout, he'd recently developed a keen interest in the science and art of sleuthing. Two years earlier, he'd announced that he wanted to become a consulting detective. I *assumed* he was kidding, but since then he'd spent hours taking online courses in foiling pickpockets, following people, picking locks, and spotting the microexpressions and verbal evasions that indicated people were lying. It had become nearly impossible to keep him in the dark about holiday and birthday gifts, and I had completely abandoned any ideas about ever throwing a surprise party for him.

When we started planning our railway journey, Rich naturally took the lead in researching security measures. I knew he was no fan of the travel wallets worn on a string around the neck or, worse, the waist pouches that conveniently concentrate essential valuables in one easy-to-snatch location.

"They just say 'rob me!'" Rich commented over lunch one day. "Remember when our tour guide in Peru had his stolen in a bar?"

I nodded absently, my thoughts on a blog post I was writing. I didn't give trip security another thought until the day a package arrived and Rich excitedly reported that it contained his RFID-blocking Rogue wallet. His *what*? That's when I asked him to sit down and tell me exactly what kinds of security measures he had in mind.

He explained that the microchips in many credit cards emit a radio frequency filled with your personal and financial data. Apparently tech-savvy thieves using a "skimmer" could access this data from up to thirty feet away, right through clothing, wallets, and even cars. Luckily Rich had found a company that made a special, ultraslim credit card wallet lined with paper-thin metal sheets to block the transmission of your radio frequency identification (RFID) info. I asked Rich whether these were the same people who instructed you to put aluminum foil on your head to block gamma rays from space aliens, but he assured me this was the real deal.

The RFID-shielding wallet was cleverly designed with a curved bottom edge that matched the shape of the pockets in Rich's new, eight-pocket travel trousers, fitting into the inner depths as snugly as a hand in a glove. The curved shape was great for security but made it tricky to extract the wallet every time he wanted to pay for a coffee. Not surprisingly, the sight of my husband rummaging at length inside his trousers garnered some pretty strange looks from waiters and fellow diners. Eventually Rich decided to reserve the wallet for our rare credit card purchases and began securing his cash with a rubber band, as advised on a travel blog he'd read. While this method had obvious cost and space advantages, wrestling a rubber band on and off a wad of grubby, flimsy bills is a fiddly sort of business at best, and Rich found it nearly as time-consuming — although less alarming to bystanders — as fishing around inside his trousers. By the time we reached Genoa, he was only too happy to purchase an inexpensive money clip, which he used for the remainder of the journey.

My own security concerns were simpler. In travel situations, I often find that carrying a purse feels akin to posting a sign on my back saying "Hey, thieves! Over here! An American with cash and credit cards! Act now!" Instead, I decided to stow my valuables in the inner sanctums of a high-tech, seventeen-pocket travel vest, one craftily engineered to hide the pockets behind a sleek exterior. At least, it was sleek until I stuffed the pockets with daily essentials; anything more than a few euros and a comb left me looking distinctly chunky, but I figured it was a small price to pay for foiling those dastardly pickpockets.

Having devised ways to secure our personal effects, Rich began studying ways to protect our electronics. We'd be taking the iPad (for all those apps and general navigation), a small laptop (so I could keep up with my blog, website, and social media), two iPhones, and various cords, chargers, hard drives, and other e-accoutrements. Rich bought lightweight padlocks for our suitcases and the daypack and a tough little cable for securing our bags to fixed objects whenever they were left alone in our lodgings.

Rich's final safety backup was (you guessed it) another app. We'd had several long discussions about how much information concerning our whereabouts should be disclosed to the general public via my website and blog. I'm hardly in the category of writers famous, glamorous, or controversial enough to attract stalkers or other undesirable attention, but it seemed sensible not to write things like, "Boy, did we spend a bundle on our laptop. Well, I'm done posting for now, so in five minutes we'll be leaving Room 234 in the Grand Hotel on Fourth Street to take a two-hour walk in downtown Belgrade . . ." In the end, we decided that my social media posts would only describe places we'd been and not identify where we were at the moment or where we'd be heading next.

But we did want a few people to have (as my consulting detective put it) real-time information on our current whereabouts. So Rich acquired an app called TrackMyTour that lets you mark your stops on a map and add notes and photos. As our head of security, Rich would fill in the details about our lodgings, how long we planned to stay, and where we'd be off to next. A few close friends agreed to monitor our progress and, if Rich suddenly stopped posting this information, to send in the cavalry. Their intervention would likely be far too late to be of any practical help to us, of course, but at least they'd know where to search for our bodies.

I tried to take comfort from that thought.

CHAPTER 3

Expect Delays

The first bombshell to derail our plans was the breathless announcement that my youngest brother was getting married. Amid the general rejoicing rocketing around the family via phone and email, a small, ignoble part of my brain was busy thinking, "And I bet they pick a date right in the middle of our train trip." Which, of course, they did, eventually announcing that the happy occasion would take place in late June on a beach in Oregon.

Luckily, as that was nearly a year in the future and The Experiment called for spontaneous, reservation-free travel, Rich and I didn't have a lot of bookings or timetables to unravel. The wedding would push our departure date back a month, from the first of June to the first of July. No big deal, really. We could use the extra time for further trip research.

But by Christmastime, we had to admit that we simply couldn't continue stuffing facts into our exhausted brains. I came to realize that on a trip this long and varied, it was utterly impossible to retain significant amounts of information about every place I might visit. It made far more sense to wait and look up information shortly before arrival, when it would be fresh and pertinent and I'd have some chance of remembering it. Twenty minutes on Google and I'd be in possession of all the essential information about must-sees and try-to-avoids, without the headsplitting effort of trying to retain hundreds of facts about dozens of cities over many months.

It gradually dawned on me that perhaps I had been trying too hard to control The Experiment. Too much research and too many random details buzzing around in my head could undermine the spontaneity. I reminded myself that adventures are by their very nature unpredictable, often arriving unexpectedly and involving lots of dizzying detours and course corrections. When you overplan an adventure, the only thing you really accomplish is giving God a good laugh.

I knew all that in my head. In fact, I was spending lots of time thinking about flexibility, spontaneity, and taking nothing for granted when I was utterly blindsided by the next revelation that disrupted our plans.

At first, it seemed such a minor problem. In April, Rich began complaining about pain in his right leg. I responded in my usual compassionate way by telling him to man up and walk it out. When it became clear that it was more than just a pulled muscle, he started visiting doctors and physical therapists, first in Spain and then, as May and the run-up to the wedding rolled around, in California. Intensive physical therapy and daily exercises made no difference whatsoever.

Things got seriously scary for a while as California doctors tested Rich for all sorts of possible diagnoses, ranging from grim to truly horrific. Eventually (*¡gracias a Dios!*) all the results came back negative. That was certainly cause for rejoicing, but we still didn't know what was wrong. The prevailing theory among our physicians, physiotherapists, massage therapists, yoga instructors, nurses, friends, neighbors, and bartenders was that Rich had some weird form of sciatica (an irritation of the sciatic nerve, which runs from the spine down through the legs), or possibly piriformis syndrome (which occurs when the piriformis muscle compresses the sciatic nerve, with similar results). But our primary care doctor wasn't convinced. He kept scratching his head and saying, "Hmmm. Interesting . . ." All we really knew for sure was that Rich's leg hurt abominably when he walked for more than fifteen minutes, forcing him to sit down and rest for a while before continuing.

Was it psychological? Could he possibly be having second thoughts about our nomadic railway journey? Was The Experiment over before it had begun? Rich assured me that he was as eager as ever, and judging by the wistful glances he kept casting at our suitcases whenever he was in the attic, I was inclined to believe him.

One afternoon, while Rich was in the doctor's office having more tests, I began chatting with one of the physician's assistants about the proposed train journey. "You know," she said, "there's no reason your husband can't go on that trip. We can give him medication to mask the pain, and he should be okay as long as he doesn't walk much or do any lifting."

Doesn't that sound delightful? I pictured myself playing Sherpa, hauling our bags on and off trains and dragging them up endless flights of stairs, while Rich stared off into space in a drug-induced stupor, repeatedly asking me where we were now and how long he'd have to wait for his next pain pill. To add to the fun, there would be the constant worry that this unidentified problem would suddenly flare into something much, much worse, most likely in some obscure village where there was no doctor and no train due in or out for days.

Call me crazy, but I felt we'd better stick around California long enough to get a diagnosis — and, with luck, an effective treatment plan. Rich felt he would enjoy the trip more if he had the use of both legs and all his mental faculties. Go figure. So with the all-too-familiar feeling of frustration that we'd come to call "delay-jà-vu," we canceled our flight back to Spain and resigned ourselves to spending at least another month in the San Francisco Bay Area.

Yes, I know, spending time in the Bay Area isn't exactly hardship duty. People flock there from all over the world to enjoy the wonderful scenery, amazing food, and zany culture and to bask in the electronic glow of the most advanced technology and commerce on the planet. But it's one thing to vacation there and quite another to be trapped by circumstances in a place that you have, off and on throughout your life, called home.

I am one of those rare birds, a fourth-generation Californian. My great-grandparents arrived by covered wagon in the nineteenth century, and the vast majority of my relatives still live in the Golden State. My parents had a harder time settling down and passed something of their restlessness on to me. By the time I moved to Seville, I'd lived in nineteen places in five states, to say nothing of two overseas work assignments lasting for months. So where was home? One of the seven towns in which I grew up? I decided early on that "home" was wherever I was currently living, and my first task upon arrival was to put a metaphorical stake in the ground, claim the place as my own, and begin building a life there. To me, it had always been an exclusive commitment; I was a one-town woman, and there was no point in looking back at my past or flirting with other locations that might throw out lures in the future.

When Rich and I fell in love with Seville and decided to move there, I gave the city my customary, all-in allegiance. We came back to the States to sell the Ohio home we'd cherished for twenty years, and although it's never easy to leave a house where I have been happy, we were giddy with excitement about our adventure in Spain. We agreed that we would spend time in the United States every year, mostly in California visiting our various relatives. We wanted to be part of their lives, and as Rich pointed out, sooner or later there would probably be some crisis, such as a health issue or family emergency, that would require a longer stay. Did we really want to face that kind of high-stress situation while camping on our relatives' sofa beds?

We invested in a home in San Anselmo, California, a small cottage that we're easily able to rent out while we're away. I felt that I couldn't afford to let myself get too attached, knowing every visit was temporary and we'd always be leaving again soon. However, over the years and almost despite myself, I'd come to feel the same sense of belonging in both San Anselmo and Seville. For the first time in my life, I found myself thinking of two different places as home. Did dividing my time mean dividing my loyalty, I wondered? By committing to both, was I less than fully committed to either one? No matter — I resolved simply to enjoy my time wherever I found myself.

But that summer, anxious over Rich's physical condition and itching to be off on our nomadic railway adventure, I found it impossible to settle into my San Anselmo home with any real pleasure. It was like reading a very, very good book in an airport departure lounge; each minute passed pleasantly enough, but I wanted, with every fiber of my being, to be elsewhere doing other things.

In late June we duly traveled north to attend my brother's wedding. It was lovely, held on a vast, sun-drenched beach on the Oregon coast, and Rich managed the long walk across the sand and even some dancing with grace and not too much grimacing.

Returning to San Anselmo, we took lots of short walks that usually ended with a rest in the town's new park, a gift from our most famous resident, filmmaker George Lucas. The centerpiece was a large fountain presided over by life-sized bronze statues of Indiana Jones and Yoda — both of whom, as discreet plaques proclaimed, were "created in San Anselmo" in the early 1970s. George Lucas brought Harrison Ford to see it, and although I wasn't around that day, I heard all about the visitation from wide-eyed residents.

"I said to my friend, 'Who is that old, bald guy with George Lucas?'" one woman told me. "And then we were, like, 'Oh my God, that's *Harrison Ford.*'"

As Indy himself said in *Raiders of the Lost Ark*, "It's not the years, honey, it's the mileage." I knew what he meant. Rich and I had covered a lot of territory since we'd met in the eighties, and for a long time traveling to exotic places and living in a foreign land had kept us feeling almost as young and vital as Indiana Jones. Four years earlier, at my husband's sixty-fifth birthday party, I'd put up a photo of Indy next to one I'd taken of Rich in the Amazon, in which he was looking very much the dashing ruffian in a battered hat and a week's growth of beard; below the two photos I wrote, "Twins separated at birth?"

But now, sitting on one of the new park benches admiring the statues, Rich and I talked about feeling as if time was finally catching up with us. When you're young, even middle-aged, it's easy to shrug off most physical ailments as temporary setbacks that can surely be overcome with time and modern medical know-how. But Rich was now in his late sixties, an age at which every new diagnosis makes you wonder if this is it, the one that's going to get you — the ailment that is going to grab on, refuse to let go, and drag you down into old age. In his more pessimistic moments, I caught Rich looking at the statue of Yoda as if wondering whether he should start identifying with the wrinkled figure with the cane instead of the bold adventurer. Were Rich's travel days over? These were lowering reflections indeed.

But like his movie heroes, Rich has never been one to sit around and wait for fate to overtake him. He now flung himself into every possible form of therapy, including massage, yoga, more walking, less walking, yet more physical therapy, and several new sets of leg exercises. Since we were in countercultural Marin County, I was surprised that no one suggested shamanic drumming or medical marijuana. One yoga teacher did try to convince us that a wheat-free diet might do the trick, but there Rich drew the line.

Meanwhile — and I am by no means comparing this to Rich's sufferings — I had to find a cheerful (or at least not hideously depressing) way to announce to my blog, Facebook, and Twitter readers that the trip I'd been writing about for so many months was being postponed.

"I don't suppose you can do it without mentioning my leg," Rich said gloomily.

"Not entirely; what other reason could I give? I do have another unmarried brother, but I'm not sure Steve would be willing to march up the aisle just to provide me with something else to blog about." So I told my social media world a little about what was happening and that Rich and I would be on our way as soon as we could.

And then a really wonderful thing happened. A fellow named Francis, whom I've never actually met in that other realm we sometimes refer to as "real life," shared this sage advice from his father in a comment on my Facebook page:

"Never chase a missed train . . . get a pastry and wait for the next one."

This is such perfect wisdom that I could only assume Francis's father was a Jedi master or one of the more advanced mystics. We all know it's utterly useless to chase missed trains, boats that have sailed, and planes that have taken off without us or been canceled altogether. Yet that seldom prevents us from running down the platform, shouting curses at the retreating taillights, stopping only when we realize that we've lost not only our transportation and our mental equilibrium but the last shreds of our dignity as well. Finding a café and sinking our teeth into a warm, flaky pastry — or pursuing some other simple, pleasurable activity that enables us to be present to the moment — has a way of putting life back into proper perspective.

Halfway through the pastry, you begin to wonder: Is your life really going to be that much worse because you missed that connection? You never know.

Many years ago, when Rich and I were heading to the tiny Himalayan Buddhist kingdom of Bhutan, we discovered that by one of those weird coincidences, our friends Blyth and Russ happened to be on the same flight. Two weeks later their departing flight, scheduled for just one day after ours, was delayed by bad weather, and a Bhutanese acquaintance of theirs, knowing that our friends ran a small publishing company, offered to introduce them to the publisher of Bhutan's main newspaper. The publisher had recently received the king's blessing to establish the first Internet connection between this isolated mountain kingdom and the outside world, and our friends volunteered to return later in the year to provide him with a computer and the training to run it. Since then, Blyth and Russ had made more than a dozen trips to Bhutan, often bringing along groups of travelers, and their circle of Bhutanese friends widened until it included an introduction to the king himself.

I'm not suggesting that every missed flight leads to the chance to hobnob with royalty; I'm just saying you never know. The Buddhists have an oft-told story about this. A farmer buys a splendid horse, and when all the neighbors praise his good fortune, he says, "You never know." The horse breaks out of his corral and disappears, and the neighbors commiserate with the farmer about his loss. He says, "You never know." The horse returns, accompanied by several mares. Rejoicing from the neighbors. The farmer says, "You never know." The farmer's son attempts to train the horse, is thrown off, and breaks his leg. Condolences from the neighbors. "You never know," says the farmer. The army sweeps through the area, conscripting all able-bodied men; the farmer's son is left behind because of his broken leg. There's more, but you get the idea.

Unless you're a highly evolved spiritual being like that farmer or Francis's dad, you can't count on keeping your cool every time your plans get turned upside down. But in an emergency, it's hard to go wrong placing your faith in the healing power of pastry. That summer, I took Rich out for a lot of pastry (thank God he didn't adopt the yoga teacher's wheat-free diet!) and cups of coffee.

Did you notice how I casually mentioned having coffee, as if it were an everyday occurrence? That summer marked the return of coffee to my life after a fifteen-year absence. I've always adored coffee — the flavor, the aroma, the energy boost, the whole fuss and tradition of making and serving it — and I drank plenty of it in my younger days. But then in my forties, when I was working as the health editor of a magazine, I began reading all sorts of articles about coffee's potential hazards, and eventually I virtuously gave it up in favor of tea. But that summer in San Anselmo, I threw caution to the winds and began drinking coffee every morning. I wasn't surprised to find that it helped me cope with stress and power through some difficult days, but I was absolutely astonished to discover that I wasn't turning into a jittery insomniac. In fact, I was sleeping better at night than I had in years. By day, it gave me the get-up-and-go to do what needed to be done. And by mid-July, that meant having a heart-to-heart with Rich about our options.

The conversation took place on a park bench, where he'd had to stop and rest after walking for a scant fifteen minutes. "Traveling through Eastern Europe at this pace is going to take us a while," I said. "I can't decide if we should cancel the trip or extend it to six months."

"I don't want to cancel," he said. "If this is the way things are going to be from now on, I'm just going to have to adapt. I do *not* want to give up and stay home for the rest of my life."

"Fine with me," I said. "I'm willing to see the world at a more leisurely pace. But I think we should stay here in California until we've explored all the treatment options. If we have to delay the train trip another month, or six months, or a year, that's not as important as getting you mobile again. What's next on the list? Didn't you get a referral to an acupuncturist or something?"

He nodded without much enthusiasm. "Yeah. This afternoon. Just what I need, another new therapy."

But to my astonishment, he came waltzing home afterwards announcing he was pain free for the first time in months. After a few more sessions with his acupuncturist, followed by some esoteric muscle-manipulating chiropractic treatments, Rich had a new bounce in his step and was able to walk for an hour or two at a time.

"That's it," he said. "I'm booking tickets back to Seville, and we are going on this railway trip."

"You don't think we should wait around a little longer and see if the improvement is going to last?" I asked. "Maybe go in for a few more sessions?"

"No. I am done with all that. I have exercises to do every day, and that is just going to have to be enough. We're leaving next week."

Suppressing my mental reservations and feelings of trepidation, I agreed we should rebook our flight to Spain for the last week of July. With a few days in Seville to recover from our jet lag and pack, we could start the oft-delayed train trip the first week of August. Of course, by that time, I was taking all timetables with a pinch of salt, a dash of pepper, and some Tabasco sauce.

San Anselmo was full of road work that summer, and every day I passed a huge, lighted sign that read, "Expect delays." We adopted that as our motto. I wondered what would delay us next. It might be anything — an alien invasion, total worldwide economic collapse, another brother announcing imminent nuptials — but surely something was about to throw another monkey wrench into the schedule.

I reminded myself yet again that the best adventures don't start smoothly, at a convenient time, or according to plan. They arrive unannounced, at awkward moments, and you have to be ready to dash out your door, fling your pack across the gap, and jump on the ferry as it's pulling out of the harbor, as I'd once done as a teenager crossing the Adriatic. I had understood that lesson at nineteen, and wasn't about to forget it now, just because I was a sexagenarian.

So we made arrangements to fly back to Seville and (I fervently hoped) proceed from there to begin The Experiment at last.

When the day of our flight came around, and we were strapping ourselves into our seats, Rich said, "Remember: expect delays."

"You never know."

And we were off.

Disembarking into the staggering heat of high summer, I remembered all the reasons we usually leave Seville during the hottest parts of the year. No matter, we were on our way at last and nothing — I fervently hoped — was going to stop us now.

And incredibly, nothing did. The next few days were spent unpacking, doing laundry, and repacking. Our evenings were passed agreeably in the company of various *amigos* who hadn't managed to flee to cooler climes. And before I knew it, we were handing over copies of our apartment keys to neighbors who would be checking on the place while we were gone, in the short interval until the subletters would arrive.

We left on a sultry August morning, walking out our front door with our little rolling suitcases and strolling to the train station twenty minutes away. Rich insisted his leg was fine, *fine*. But I noticed he was favoring it by the time we arrived.

"Let's sit down and have some breakfast," I suggested. We had half an hour before we needed to board, and in all the predeparture excitement, we hadn't managed to eat a bite. It was far too lovely a morning to go indoors, but unfortunately, we could only find one outdoor option.

"Seriously? This is the first road food on our grand adventure?" said

Rich, as we went to the McDonald's counter and collected drinks and sweet rolls. "A McCoffee?"

"Look at it this way," I said. "It's the first outside-our-comfort-zone experience of the trip."

I knew there would be plenty of other small, unwelcome surprises in the days ahead. Being an optimist, I expected mostly good times, but I was braced for the occasional grisly meal, ghastly smell, cold room, hard bed, and unfriendly stranger. I knew that we would visit places where great suffering had taken place, and that I'd feel moments of anxiety, sorrow, and anger. Adventures, I reminded myself, were all about going beyond the boundaries of ordinary life, sometimes in ways that weren't entirely comfortable. Those times provided the contrast that made the rest of the adventure so sweet.

As if to offer itself as a metaphor, the McPastry was surprisingly good, fluffy and warm and comforting. If I ever missed a train at this station, I knew where to come to regroup. The coffee, on the other hand, was dull and dispirited, especially compared to Seville's usual robust brews. But hey, it was coffee. Being newly reunited with this beloved beverage, I wasn't inclined to be too picky.

Rich swallowed his last mouthful of McPastry and rose to his feet. "It's time."

We gathered up our things, walked downstairs, and boarded the high-speed train that would whisk us northeast to Barcelona in just five hours.

We were on our way at last. The Experiment had begun.

CHAPTER 4

Recombobulation

The workers of Barcelona are fond of pulling themselves together in the morning with a *cigaló*, a small, dense cup of espresso enlivened with a shot of brandy. This eye-popping kick-start to the day firmly upholds the twin pillars of the local character: the *seny*, or common sense, of coffee mingled with brandy's *rauxa*, the chaos and creative madness that gives so much zing to Barcelona and the rest of the Catalonia region.

Disembarking at the Barcelona railway station in the late afternoon, Rich and I decided to forgo the *cigaló*, but we did stop at the station café to kick-start a new tradition of our own. One of our favorite travel bloggers, Wandering Earl, says that whenever he arrives in a new place, he immediately sits down at a café, right in the airport or train station, and has a coffee.

"As travelers," writes Earl, "we tend to be taken advantage of most when we are tired, disoriented and unfamiliar with our surroundings, which is exactly the state we're in right after landing in a new destination. So why not relax for 20 minutes instead of immediately trying to figure out how to get into the city? Enjoying such a rest allows you to take a few deep breaths, observe your surroundings and to clear your head before stepping out into the unknown. You can also ask the staff at the café for reliable information about transportation and you can read the signs around the airport from your table without looking completely lost. Then, when you feel ready, you can calmly and confidently (you won't be so overwhelmed anymore) head off into the city."

Over the next three months, Rich and I came to appreciate the deep wisdom of Wandering Earl's advice. After the discombobulation of travel, relaxing for twenty minutes over a coffee at the station café was a great way to recombobulate.

Now, sitting in the Barcelona train station with a decaf cappuccino, I took some deep breaths and tried to get my head in the game. I wasn't particularly worried about Barcelona — we'd visited several times and always liked the city — but I was feeling a bit shell-shocked after months of delays and uncertainties. And I was by no means convinced that Rich's recovery — which was only partial at best — would endure for three months without a serious relapse.

But as I kept reminding myself, this was an adventure, which meant accepting some risks and doubtful circumstances along with the fun and excitement. And as we'd said in composing our guidelines for The Experiment, we could always call it quits and go home if need be. In the meantime, we'd enjoy the trip for however long it lasted; we'd keep moving forward in easy stages, and see how far *out there* we could get. Even if that was just Barcelona.

After twenty minutes at the café, I did feel calmer and more composed — thank you, Wandering Earl! I was ready to face Barcelona and whatever followed.

A few days earlier we'd made online reservations at a small, inexpensive hotel in the heart of the old quarter. After the taxi deposited us by its front door, I discovered it had a great location on a lively little plaza, a charming exterior, and rooms that were cramped and drably utilitarian. But of course, the most urgent question on my mind was: were there bedbugs?

As you may have heard, the world is in the midst of a bedbug apocalypse. These hideous parasites have become an unstoppable, planetwide menace since the ban on DDT. A cross between a deadbeat roommate and a vampire, the bedbug lolls around all day in sloth and squalor, burrowing deep into sheets, mattresses, and bed frames. At night it creeps out to feed on human blood, leaving behind red welts like mosquito bites, only less itchy and often in neat rows of three. It can survive three hundred days without a meal, but when it does eat, it gorges itself until it swells to alarming proportions. This makes it irresistibly attractive to the nearest male bedbug, which will urgently insist on mating, even if the swollen bug doesn't happen to be female. You can imagine the kind of psychological and social stress that causes in the colony.

Infestations have increased dramatically in recent years — up by 500 percent in the United States, according to some reports — and even the most advanced chemical weapons have failed to slow their advance. Specially trained dogs have been brought in to sniff out bedbugs, but with success rates ranging all over the place from 11 to 80 percent, the canine solution has not proved quite as reliable as anyone hoped. Cockroaches are said to eat bedbugs, but even New York doesn't have enough cockroaches to deal with the problem.

Friends who've had these unwanted bedfellows tell long, grisly tales involving toxic sprays and sleeping for weeks on plastic-wrapped mattresses to make sure the little bloodsuckers were really gone — only to discover they weren't, and the whole process had to start over. How does all this misery invade the sanctity of your home? Usually a few bedbugs hitch a ride in a suitcase or electronic device that's been with you on the road.

Rich, who had of course researched this critical health and safety issue in depth, showed me pictures of brown bugs about the size of a grain of rice and the light brown egg casings they leave behind. "We'll just check the bedding and mattress seams of every place we sleep," he said blithely. And, like coffee at the train station, this became a ritual upon our arrival anyplace new. In our Barcelona hotel room, we peeled back the sheets and peered into the mattress seams. Nothing was moving, and eventually we decided that the tiny gray and black specks were lint, not eggs or spoor.

"Bedbug check complete," Rich announced.

Bedbug authorities warn that even after you've inspected the premises, you should never put suitcases on the bed or the floor, because you never know what might be lurking there unseen. However, these authorities obviously weren't staying in tiny, bare-bones rooms like ours, with no spare tables or luggage racks. What did they expect us to do, sit up all night holding our suitcases over our heads? Instead, we set them on the floor, attached them to the radiator, and headed out the door in search of some dinner.

As we passed through the small lobby, I noticed a sign for a free walking tour of downtown Barcelona the next morning. I love free tours, which are one of the best ways to explore a city, even if it's not your first visit. You usually get the liveliest and most knowledgeable guides, who are highly motivated by hopes of earning good tips and luring you into taking additional (paid) tours. I usually tip almost as much as I would pay for a standard tour, so I don't really save much money, but it's nice to feel I can adjust the amount to reflect the quality of the experience. I've found that people who go on free tours tend to be slightly less conventional, so the casual conversations struck up during the morning can be pretty interesting and sometimes lead to going out together for a post-tour lunch. When I made inquiries at the front desk, the receptionist phoned the guide and arranged for him to come collect us the next morning.

In the meantime, Rich and I left the hotel in search of dinner and most definitely a glass of wine, stepping outside into the hubbub of one of the world's best-loved cities. The exuberant architecture of Antoni Gaudí and others, the colorful street life, and a reputation for world-class food had made Barcelona the fourth most popular tourist destination in Europe, after London, Paris, and Rome. The number of annual visitors had skyrocketed from 1,700,000 in 1990 to just over 3 million in 2000 to 8 million now, bringing in nearly 20 million euros — 27 million dollars! — *a day*. Civic leaders were so busy counting the money that they didn't have time to listen to residents' complaints that the city was becoming overrun with foreigners and somebody should do something before it was too late.

It was hard to reconcile this booming Barcelona with the one I'd first seen at nineteen, during the last days of the Franco era. In my memory, the city was perpetually gloomy, with gray skies, nearly deserted streets, and rifle-toting *Guardia Civil* in their traditional *tricornios*, the shiny black patent leather pillbox hats with a flare at the back like a nun's wimple. Those hats might (okay, it totally did) look silly to outsiders like me, but even as a teenager I wasn't foolish enough to mock a man with a gun, especially in a country where sexism wasn't just an attitude, it was the law. At that time, Spain's legal code still required a woman to have *permiso marital*, her husband's permission, to get a job, spend money she had earned, own property, or travel. Divorce, contraception, and abortion were illegal, but prostitution was not. (So it wasn't as if girls couldn't earn a living . . .)

During that long-ago trip, I was traveling with a friend from my art class at the university. Having studied the madcap architecture of Antoni Gaudí, we looked up the address of one of his landmark works, the Casa Milà apartment house, and went over to pay homage. The building was a masterpiece of inspired lunacy, its exterior a rippling, undulating sea of stone with wrought iron balconies like twisted wrecks of snagged seaweed. It must have caused quite a sensation when it was finished in 1910, and although it was looking a bit worse for wear by the time we saw it in 1972, my friend and I were awestruck. We stood gawking on the sidewalk until a resident returning home kindly offered to let us inside for a look.

He escorted us to a small, rickety elevator, which groaned, shrieked, and shuddered with the effort to heave itself eight stories closer to the sky; Gaudí may have been an architect of genius, but he wasn't much of an engineer, it seemed. I stepped out onto a rooftop that was a marvel, a forest of gigantic chimney pots in fantasy shapes, some looking like helmeted warriors, others like weird, twisted, organic chess pieces. I lingered as long as I could, so dazzled that when the time came to leave, I didn't even object to risking the ride back down in Gaudí's elevator. I only managed to pull myself together just in time to thank our benefactor profusely for the rare treat.

My second visit took place in 2003. There I was again, standing in front of the same building, only this time I was with Rich and a hundred other tourists, all ready to fork over twenty euros, about twenty-six dollars, for the privilege of visiting Casa Milà. It was now an official UNESCO World Heritage Site — that is, one of about a thousand places on the planet designated as culturally or geographically spectacular by the United Nations Educational, Scientific, and Cultural Organization. Casa Milà was now preserved as part of the patrimony of humankind and had become one of the most beloved cash cows of the tourist industry. We were herded into a vastly improved elevator, which whisked us upward with nary a shudder or creak and disgorged us onto the rooftop. The towering chess pieces and helmeted warriors were as outlandish as ever, but it was hard to recapture my sense of wonder when jammed elbow to elbow with a chattering throng. I shuddered to think what the crowds at Casa Milà must be like now, ten years after my last visit.

The next morning, our guide arrived at the appointed hour — well, not more than fifteen minutes late, which by Spanish standards represents an almost unseemly degree of punctuality. Duncan was an Irish architect thrown out of work by the economic crisis; he'd lived in Barcelona for three years and was ready to provide our small group with a colorful account of the city's history, culture, and politics.

Pointing out a Catalan independence flag flying from a balcony, Duncan spoke passionately about the desire — and the moral right — of this autonomous section of Spain to separate from the rest of the nation. Catalan had been an independent kingdom, with its own language, laws, and customs, from the ninth century until 1714, when it was overwhelmed by Spain's military might and forced to bend its knee to King Philip V. Many Catalans still view Spain as an occupying foreign power and feel it is past time to get rid of their unwelcome overlords once and for all.

"I think independence is going to happen in the next twenty years," Duncan told us.

Really? The issue had been hotly contested for centuries, and as recently as the late seventies to early nineties, the flaming rhetoric had ignited into violence, even terrorist attacks. Times were more peaceful now, and with the latest polls showing that the number of Catalonians favoring separation from Spain had risen to just over half ("a majority" crowed the headlines), talk of independence through legal means was in vogue.

Coming from a nation that fought a revolution for its own independence, I couldn't help but feel some sympathy for Catalan's desire to shake off the oppressor's yoke. But there were some practical difficulties. For one thing, there was no provision for secession under the Spanish constitution, making it nearly impossible to accomplish without plunging the country into another civil war. As Duncan was talking, I was looking at a wall covered with bullet holes from executions held during the last civil war, back in the thirties. To me, the possibility of independence through genuinely peaceful means seemed as remote as ever.

Duncan also spoke of the sad prevalence of domestic violence here, in the country that had coined the term *machismo*. To be fair, Spain's track record was far from the worst in Europe, let alone the world. But there had recently been a huge scandal over a staggeringly offensive remark by a Spanish politician, who'd said in a public meeting, *"Las leyes son como mujeres, estan para violarlas"* (Laws are like women, they are there to be violated). The public outcry was rightly focused entirely on the politician's appalling attitude toward violence against women. But his comment didn't exactly speak well of his reverence for the law, either. The politician was forced to resign within hours, claiming he was leaving for personal reasons; I guess he wanted to spend more time with his wife, in the unlikely event that she was still speaking to him.

The streets were crowded and noisy that day, and every few minutes Duncan's words were drowned out by blaring trucks, barking dogs, and once, a religious zealot with a German accent who considered himself divinely appointed to explain to us just how far we had strayed from the path of righteousness. Finally Duncan led us away through some side streets to a small plaza.

"We should be better here," he said. "It's one of the quietest plazas in the city."

Then the shouting began.

Just around the corner out of sight, a man was bellowing at the top of his lungs, a diatribe so heated it seemed likely to scorch the paint off nearby buildings. The theme, as best I could make out, was, "That's it, I've had it, you've gone too far this time, you've always been like that," and so on. When he paused for breath, a woman's voice answered, a searing reply that was too rapid and colloquial for me to follow. Their fury was escalating so rapidly that if this had been a nation where firearms were legal, I'd have been listening for the sound of gunshots.

Duncan's face creased in a worried frown. "I really don't want to get into this," he said. "Let's hope they don't—"

Then the woman's shouts turned to screams, and Duncan took off, running around the corner to intervene in the fray.

I heard him say something in a low voice to the couple. Then the man shouted, "I've been wanting to kill her for twenty-five years!"

Thinking that maybe more witnesses might make the man hesitate to commit actual murder — and naturally curious to see what kind of street crazies we were dealing with — I followed Duncan around the corner for a look. The perpetrators turned out to be an ordinary, well-dressed Spaniard of about sixty and his tiny, white-haired mother, who must have been eighty-five. Duncan, doing his best to insert himself delicately between the combatants, repeatedly asked the woman if she wanted him to call the police. She scoffed at the idea, waving his offers aside to continue the verbal brawl with her son. Finally she turned and stomped over to a nearby door, unlocked it, and went inside, followed by her son, still shouting and gesticulating. Through the open window over our heads, we could hear the hostilities continuing at full volume.

"Well, it's *usually* a quiet plaza," said Duncan. "I think we'll find another spot to continue the tour. As I was saying about domestic violence . . ."

Although we'd witnessed a bit more of Barcelona's famous *rauxa*, or mad chaos, than I'd expected during a morning tour, living in Spain had taught me that life's high and low points were often enacted in the streets, especially during the steamy summer months. Barcelona's public spaces were rich with baroque fantasy elements; on that trip alone I saw a fire juggler, a tightrope walker, an old opera diva offering singing lessons in a street booth, wild graffiti, human statues, mimes, a marijuana museum, and some truly astonishing tattoos. Every street corner and café seemed to offer up a small vignette: pierced and tattooed teens flirting shyly, firebrands arguing politics over cheap beer, families gathering for leisurely meals at long tables, old couples sipping wine in the twilight, mothers and sons threatening to kill each other . . .

Duncan's route ended, inevitably, at a cozy bar, and many people from our tour group decided to restore themselves after the morning's exertions with a nibble, a pint, and a few hours of talking about the local culture, economy, art, and politics.

"This is why we travel," Rich said, after we'd passed around our cards and kissed our new friends goodbye. "To learn about other cultures. And to think we got embroiled in a near-murderous domestic dispute on our very first day!"

"Obviously we can't expect to be that lucky all the time," I said. "But I do feel the trip is off to a promising start."

During the rest of our stay, however, between the sweltering heat and relentless crush of tourists in the streets, Barcelona failed to exert its usual charm over us. We passed the next day strolling about our favorite neighborhoods and trying without success to find a remembered restaurant, which seemed to have disappeared, taking an entire plaza with it. Rich was handling the walking well, although at times he became rather tight-lipped and white-faced and suggested we stop for a coffee *now*.

As we sat over a second coffee that second morning, he said suddenly, "I need to express a concern."

Oh God, I thought. What now? Hideous possibilities flooded my brain in a femtosecond. His leg was horribly worse. He'd been waiting for the right moment to tell me he had some gruesome, invariably fatal disease. War was breaking out back home (in Seville, the States, or both) and we were trapped in Barcelona for the duration . . .

He took a breath and continued, "I don't want the trip to be all about your blog, to the point where we spend six hours a day in our hotel room, with you hunched over the computer typing away and me with nothing to do."

Was that all? For a moment there, I'd been really worried. I almost laughed in relief, but then I saw that he was very serious, so I replied firmly, "That's *not* going to happen."

"Yes, but I know you. You spend tons of time at your desk every day."

"Sure. Back home. I love writing. But I told you when we planned this trip that it was an adventure first and material for the blog second." He still looked skeptical, so I added, "I mean it. How much time did I spend on the computer this morning?"

"An hour. But—"

"I rest my case, Your Honor."

"Okay." He dropped the matter then and didn't allude to it again. Rich had always been very supportive of my blog, so I knew he wasn't so much jealous of my time as worried that I might get caught up in the writing process and fail to fully engage with the trip, shortchanging us of the experiences we'd come so far to seek. I had no intention of letting that happen.

I had once read an interview in which Stephen King spoke of writing for many hours every single day, and I'd wondered how he ever found new things to write about if he never went out and *did* anything. Maybe his fertile imagination provided enough raw material, but I write about experiences that have touched me in some fresh way and made me feel more alive. Neither my life nor my blog would be particularly interesting to me, let alone others, if I didn't go out and *do* stuff all the time. As someone once said, "The unlived life isn't worth examining."

No, I knew I could keep my writing within reasonable time boundaries, but I was a little less certain of the photography part of the process.

With an endless need for more images on my blog, website, and other social media, I can easily snap 150 photos on a good travel day. I'm always thinking, "How often am I likely to have the chance to photograph a fire-eater?" or "They'll never believe *that* tattoo's typo if I don't get a shot of it."

But taking the pictures is only the beginning. I then have to sort through them, discard the duds, and play with the rest to see which ones might be coaxed into really sparkling. I run every shot through iPhoto, cropping, enhancing, straightening, boosting the yellow a smidge to warm up the light, sharpening the definition, bringing up detail in shadows and highlights, and so on. In just a couple of minutes I can take an image from "uh" to "ahhh."

Why go through all that? "When people look at my pictures, I want them to feel the way they do when they want to read a line of a poem twice," said photographer and film director Robert Frank. I'll never be in Frank's league, but I'm going to keep on trying to produce photos that capture a glimpse of the delight I felt when I saw that subject for the first time.

But as much as I enjoy fussing with my photos, I realized that Rich was right. No matter how many I took each day, I couldn't let the sorting and editing expand into hours that should be spent *out there* exploring the world. On the other hand, I needed well-tweaked images to post on social media every day and my blog once a week, so I would have to stay on top of the task. I resolved to be very efficient and start each morning editing photos taken the day before, making a strenuous effort to finish the task before Rich was through skimming the news headlines on his iPad.

I carried out this plan the next morning, racing through culling and editing 140 images before breakfast. Whew! What a sprint! I would become ever more ruthless as the trip went on, making snap decisions to dump marginal shots, rapidly tweaking the most promising, and tossing the best into my "ready to post" file — all before my morning coffee. Like writing on a deadline to fit a specific word count, I think the discipline made me work smarter as well as faster.

So I felt as if I had one area of my life under better control. But for the most part, there still seemed to be more *rauxa* (chaos) than *seny* (solid ground) in my days. As we packed up our things to head down to the harbor and board the ferry to Italy, I reflected on the many unknowns: our route and the destinations along it we'd visit, where we'd stay, whom we'd meet, the effect of so much travel on the well-being of Rich's leg, how long we'd last on the road. Would we encounter bedbugs? Were there really nefarious thieves out there just waiting to snatch data from my non-RFID-protected vest pockets? And most of all, what kind of adventures would we have?

It would take a lot more than a twenty-minute cup of coffee — or even one of those eye-opening *cigalós* — to grapple with those questions. After being out of whack for months, I was nowhere near recombobulated yet.

CHAPTER 5

Fakes: the Good, the Bad, the Deeply Worrying

The ferry from Barcelona to Genoa was evidently under the mistaken impression that it was really a transatlantic luxury liner. It was huge and sported acres of royal blue carpeting, glittering chandeliers, and polished brass. Uniformed attendants were strategically deployed throughout the ship to bow, glance discreetly at the tickets, and wave us on until we arrived at our private stateroom. We'd splurged on the accommodations, which included a double bed and private bath, and it was all far more elegant than I'd anticipated. I began to wish I'd packed one of those Ginger Rogers chiffon evening gowns to fit in with the posh ambiance.

I needn't have worried. No one was the slightest bit interested in socializing with us, or indeed, acknowledging that we existed. Almost everyone on the ship was a Moroccan teetotaler, and the quietly festive little family groups occupying the lounges kept to themselves so completely that Rich and I began to feel invisible. Waiting in line to board, we had encountered a trio of young Americans, but when we'd addressed some casual remarks to them, their brief, crushingly polite replies made it clear they would rather be thrown overboard than be caught chatting with anyone their grandparents' age. Clearly, striking up shipboard friendships was going to be a total nonstarter.

I recalled a story about my grandmother, the silent film actress Ramona Langley, taking a ship to Europe once when she was low on funds. "She was traveling steerage," my mother told me. "There she was, in her fur coat, sitting on her suitcase, looking absolutely gorgeous." This

I could easily believe; she was a stunner well into old age, and she was likely in the full bloom of her forties at the time of this tale. "The instant the captain laid eyes on her," my mother continued nostalgically, "he insisted that she come up and dine at his table every night."

Sadly, there was no such Cinderella story for us on our voyage. Rich and I never even saw the captain, and we ate our meals in the cafeteria, where the choice of options ranged from bad to worse; even the pasta was dismal.

It was a long voyage, nearly eighteen hours. We had boarded at midday, and following the demoralizing lunch in the cafeteria, we'd headed back to our stateroom and spent the better part of the afternoon and evening watching movies on our computer. We went to bed early, and at eight o'clock the next morning, we arrived at the port of Genoa.

Nearly every website promoting Genoa starts off by pleading, "Please don't rush through here on your way to Florence or Rome. No matter what you've heard about us, we really *are* worth a visit! Really! Please say you'll stay!!!" I may be paraphrasing a little, but that's definitely the gist. Apparently Genoa is a place where the newly arrived depart again as quickly as possible for more glamorous — and less dangerous — destinations.

"Genoa? Last time I was there, it was full of prostitutes and muggers," commented a friend upon learning that Rich and I were planning to take a ferry to this hotbed of sin and skullduggery. "Especially down by the docks." Yikes!

Docking at Genoa early that August morning, Rich and I were on high alert and felt lucky to get down the gangplank and across the wharf with our lives and our wallets. Half an hour later, we were well on our way to falling in love with the city.

After stopping for coffee and recombobulation at a modest waterfront café, we strolled along wide, silent boulevards lined with magnificent old palaces and grand hotels, surrounded by charming, if slightly gritty, little back streets. We weren't mugged or propositioned even once. Genoa, it turned out, had been making heroic and successful efforts to reduce the number of nefarious cutthroats per capita and to clean up its act across the board. Apparently no one outside the city had read the memo on this, as visitors continued to stay away in droves, much to the frustration of those in the hospitality industry. They kept pointing out, to anyone who would listen, that the city was now safe, historic, charming, and filled with all the elements of a major tourist destination — except, of course, actual tourists.

An hour's walk through the city brought us to the bed and breakfast we'd booked through Airbnb. It was on a narrow back street, more of an alley really, and was reached by climbing up a very long, steep staircase to the third floor. Rich, whose leg had begun to protest, set his jaw and made the ascent without complaint. Our hosts were warmly welcoming, immediately ushering us to seats at a table in a tiny breakfast room filled with other guests.

Sitting in that breakfast room, it took us less than five minutes to ascertain that our fellow guests, all European couples, were focused on their private conversations and were about as eager to talk with us as the young Americans on the ferry had been. We could hardly wait to push back our chairs and go to our room.

It shouldn't have come as a surprise — we'd seen the pictures of it on the Internet — but the staircase that led up to our attic room was a zigzagging nightmare of irregular steps, all of which would have to be negotiated in the dark of night if one of us needed to use our bathroom, which, while technically in our room, was situated at the bottom of the stairs. I made a mental note not to drink too much during our stay.

The room itself was charming, with a steeply sloping ceiling and a dormer window overlooking the street far below, where men in sleeveless undershirts sat on wooden chairs in doorways and old ladies in black dresses gossiped over the little fruit and vegetable stand.

"Well, I'm glad to see they got the memo from central casting," said Rich. It did indeed look like a movie set for an Italian film; I half expected to see subtitles appear along the lower edge of my view.

After a short rest, we were ready to head out to explore the city further. Our hosts handed me a map and assured us that the worst of the rats, prostitutes, and thieves had (mostly) been rousted out of the old quarter, and it was safe to walk just about everywhere now, even down by the docks. Well, maybe not at night . . . Of course, it was a city, and naturally we should always be careful . . . With these dubious assurances ringing in our ears, we set off for the heart of the city.

We started, of course, with the cathedral. Many years of living in Spain and exploring the neighboring countries had taught me that the cathedral is the heart of any medieval or Renaissance city, and its treasury serves as an accurate indicator of the community's wealth during its heyday. Giving the Church expensive relics and other sacred objects was a common way to court favor in heaven — and, not incidentally, among the powerful and influential men of the cloth on earth.

In Genoa, which grew wealthy during the Crusades and spent the next five hundred years as one of the world's leading financial centers and busiest ports, the Church's treasures were very upmarket indeed. The cathedral alone housed the actual platter on which Salome carried the head of John the Baptist after his decapitation, a splinter of the True Cross, and the Holy Grail. Not everyone is 100 percent convinced of the authenticity of these sacred objects, especially now that we know the Holy Grail was actually found by Indiana Jones, but nonetheless it's an impressive collection.

The crown jewel of this vast treasure trove, housed under the high altar itself, is the Ark of the Ashes of St. John the Baptist. You may recall that John the Baptist was the one who dressed in camel hair, lived on wild locusts and honey, baptized his cousin Jesus in the Jordan River, helped him launch his ministry, and wound up having his head cut off and served on a platter at the request of Salome after her famous dance. All in all, he led a very colorful life.

His afterlife was pretty vivid too. He was buried in Samaria, dug up in the year 362, partially burned, divided up, and carried off to various destinations, such as Jerusalem and Alexandria. His head, after many adventures, is now resting comfortably in the Umayyad Mosque in Damascus, in the Basilica of Saint Sylvester the First in Rome, and in the Residenz Museum in Munich. The Knights Templar also held one at Amiens Cathedral in France for a while, and yet others have been reported in Antioch, Turkey, and in a parish church in Tenterden, Kent.

In addition to his six heads, John the Baptist apparently possessed at least three right hands, which are now variously enshrined in the Serbian Orthodox Cetinje Monastery in Montenegro, the Topkapi Palace in Istanbul, and the Romanian Monastery of the Forerunner. Yet more of his skeleton has turned up in Calcutta, in Egypt, in Nagorno-Karabakh in the Lesser Caucasus mountains, and, as recently as 2010, in a Bulgarian church undergoing renovation.

So are the ashes in the Genoa cathedral *really* those of St. John the Baptist?

Does it matter?

Every year when they carry the Ark of the Ashes through the streets of the city in a grand procession, the citizens of Genoa know — if only for a moment — what it's like to be touched by glory. That feeling is real, even if the ashes might be fakes. Growing up Catholic, I was surrounded by saints and relics and miracles. Since then, I've become something of a skeptic, but I've always been grateful for my early childhood training in believing impossible things. The world would be a drearier place without it.

All the same, if someone offers to sell you a sliver of the True Cross or the actual Holy Grail, I'd demand a *lot* of authentication.

Rich and I visited the altar where they keep the Ark of the Ashes, then set off to see more of the city. Genoa's old section, one of the largest in Europe, stretches for one and a half square miles, and we strolled about it until we eventually found ourselves at the harbor, where we saw a sign for a modestly priced walking tour the next day. It was meant to be a group tour, but naturally, this being tourist-deprived Genoa, we were the only ones who showed up for it.

Our guide, a quiet woman named Loredona, escorted us through the streets, providing a steady stream of mildly interesting information.

Genoa was the birthplace of Christopher Columbus, violin virtuoso and composer Niccolò Paganini, and pesto sauce. It was the sixth largest city in Italy, held the title "European Capital of Culture" in 2004, and had been nicknamed *la Superba* (the Superb), presumably by the city's desperate hospitality industry.

The highlight of the tour was an olive oil tasting at a small *olioteca*. Having lived for nearly ten years in agricultural Andalucía, Rich and I were able to hold our own in a discussion of the rival merits of regional varieties, and pretty soon our hostess, Francesca, was fetching stools so we could sit down for a more leisurely sampling. She kept bringing out more kinds of olive oil she wanted us to try, and finally, with the air of one bestowing a magnificent treat, she ran to get some special twenty-five-year-old vinegar so she could drizzle it over slivers of Parmesan cheese. The flavors were wonderful, but the real pleasure was sharing them with someone who took such obvious delight in savoring the essentials of Mediterranean life.

After we'd kissed Francesca and Loredona goodbye at the door of the *olioteca* and started off down the little street, Rich turned to me and said, "You remember that old barbershop Loredona showed us?"

"Sure. Why?"

"I think I need a haircut."

"Can you find it again?" I asked, thinking of the maze of back streets we'd traversed for nearly two hours. Rich shot me an affronted look. "Sorry," I said. "Of course you can."

Rich has the enviable ability to glance at a map of just about any city in the world and grasp its intricacies in about five minutes. Istanbul? Hong Kong? Tangier? Child's play to my husband. I, on the other hand, am so notoriously bad at finding my way about that when we lived in Ohio, friends giving me directions would start by telling me which way I should turn out of my own driveway — and I lived on a dead-end street. They were kidding, but only sort of. Now I watched in awe as Rich threaded his way back to the barbershop with unerring accuracy and a spring in his step.

"How's the leg now?" I asked.

"Good," he said. "Surprisingly good. Pain-free, in fact."

Hmmmm. Could it have been psychological after all? Did he just need to get on the road to loosen up whatever was causing the tightness and pain? I've often noticed that in the excitement of travel, many of my minor aches and pains seem to disappear. Was he in recovery? Denial? Indiana Jones mode? Time would tell.

We arrived at the barbershop just as it was closing, but the proprietor, a tall, bearded man with sandy-gray hair, kindly agreed to give Rich a trim. The place was barely big enough to hold three old-fashioned barber's chairs and the row of minute sinks, counters, and cabinets that stood along one wall, littered with a jumble of scissors, combs, bottles of hair tonic, old magazines, and cloth towels. The ceiling and walls were lined with art deco stained glass in gorgeous shades of turquoise and gold, framing enormous old mirrors. A tape deck was playing the drinking song from Verdi's *La Traviata*, and the barber hummed along as he picked up a comb and some manual clippers and went to work. There was no hurry or fuss, just a man who loved cutting hair the old-fashioned way while listening to opera.

One of the things I love about Italy is that unlike most places, it actually lives up to my mental images of it. Over the years, I've hung around Italian-American neighborhoods such as San Francisco's North Beach, Boston's North End, and Cleveland's Little Italy; attended many Italian operas; and, of course, watched movies such as *The Godfather, Romeo and Juliet, Under the Tuscan Sun, La Dolce Vita, A Room with a View, Tea with Mussolini, The Italian Job, The Bourne Identity, Moonstruck,* Sophia Loren love triangles, Fellini's baroque fantasies, and countless others. Each movie has its own cultural perspectives, no doubt skewed by the personal views, faith, experiences, prejudices, and dreams of those who made them. But there are two elements that just about all of them treat with tremendous love and reverence: music and pasta.

Whatever you think of the Mafia (and I, for one, am not a big fan of that organization in a general way), you can't help but be touched by the scene in *The Godfather* in which Clemenza teaches young Michael Corleone how to make tomato sauce when the men go to the mattresses in preparation for a mob war. And what about Julia Roberts sublimating other urges by slurping up a plate of spaghetti in *Eat, Pray, Love?* Couldn't you just taste the red sauce and Parmesan? Spaghetti isn't just food; it's family, comfort, and identity. As Sophia Loren once put it, "Everything you see I owe to spaghetti."

My own love affair with spaghetti and Italian culture began with the scene in *Lady and the Tramp* in which Tramp's human friend Tony sets up a table in the alley and the two dogs eat pasta under the stars to lush accordion music. When I was five, I thought Tramp pushing the last meatball over to Lady with his nose was the most romantic thing I'd ever seen.

Our Genoa bed and breakfast was on a Lady and the Tramp-style alley, and one evening, when a café set out a few tables under the stars, Rich and I sat down and ordered wine and big plates of pasta with *pesto Genovese*. The scene felt so romantic that I was only sorry I hadn't ordered meatballs so I could push the last one over to Rich with my nose. (Rich has expressed tremendous gratitude that I didn't attempt this, especially in public.)

Even without meatballs, I found that sitting in that back alley on a sultry night, sipping rough wine from stemless glasses, and eating plates of pasta held a certain kind of enchantment. There was a shimmering sort of *rightness* to the moment, the feeling that my five-year-old self and my current self and all the people I'd been in between were all present and enjoying this enormously. I felt, with deep satisfaction, that in that moment I was the kind of grown-up that my five-year-old self had hoped to become.

I wound a little more pasta onto my fork and thought about one of my favorite quotes from Joseph Campbell in *The Power of Myth:* "People say that what we're all seeking is a meaning for life. I don't think that's what we're really seeking. I think that what we're seeking is an experience of being alive, so that our life experiences on the purely physical plane will have resonances with our own innermost being and reality, so that we actually feel the rapture of being alive."

Filmmaker Federico Fellini put it more simply: "Life is a combination of magic and pasta." Fellini's magic and Joseph Campbell's rapture were what we'd set out to find when we'd first dreamed up The Experiment all those months earlier in Portugal. Our entire nomadic railway adventure was designed to take us far enough *out there* — off the tourist track, away from prepackaged experiences, into the unknown — to feel the magic and the shivery excitement of being alive.

Rich leaned back in his chair and said, "So where shall we go next?" And that brought me down from my lofty thoughts with a thump. Genoa had offered an agreeable setting enlivened by a few sparkling moments, but after three days we were ready to move on. And that meant we had to make a decision that we'd been putting off for some weeks.

We'd originally planned to head north, since Rich had long wanted to see the legendary beauty of Lake Como and was curious about why Zurich was so often rated the most livable city on the planet. But lately I had grown keen on an alternative route that would eliminate both those stops, taking us east to Verona and then north to Munich. Rich was still voting for the more roundabout Lake Como–Zurich route.

"This trip is meant to be an *adventure*," I objected after we'd rehashed those arguments sitting over the last of our wine in the alley café. "There's nothing particularly adventuresome about Lake Como or Zurich."

"Everybody says they're great," he pointed out. But I could tell he was weakening.

"Yes, and they said Genoa was dangerous and dull. What do *they* know? If we start heading northeast now, we'll get to the Czech Republic that much sooner. And that's where we're going to start feeling like we're really getting *out there*."

During the months we'd stood in our Seville kitchen tracing railway lines on the wall map, I'd come to view the Czech Republic as the turning point in the journey, where we would start to leave behind the relative familiarity of Western Europe for strange and enigmatic lands. In my childhood, the countries that now make up Central and Eastern Europe had been cut off from the rest of the world behind the Iron Curtain, and to me they still seemed mysterious, challenging, even a little sinister. Definitely *out there*. Just thinking about what lay ahead made my spine tingle. And from the gleam in his eye, I could see Rich was starting to feel the same way.

After a bit more discussion he finally said, "Oh, what the hell," and reached into his ever-present backpack for the iPad. "Let's see what trains are running to Verona tomorrow."

Arriving in Verona the next afternoon, we found it beautiful, hot, and jammed with vacationers in flowered shirts and sensible sandals. Wikitravel points out that compared to nearby Venice, "the number of tourists per square meter is lower," but as there seemed to be at least four tourists inhabiting every square meter we were attempting to pass through, that was cold comfort. "I miss Genoa already," I said to Rich as we elbowed our way along the sidewalk, attempting to avoid running over any exposed toes with our rolling suitcases.

Having managed with only one day's notice to book a spacious studio apartment in the heart of Verona at the height of the August tourist season, we felt we were in no position to complain overmuch about such minor deficiencies as a lack of air conditioning and a malfunctioning fan. My first act upon arrival (besides, of course, checking for bedbugs) was to unpack and do some laundry. I figured with the room temperature somewhere around 90 degrees Fahrenheit, our clothes would be dry in no time.

People often ask me how I can live for months out of one small suitcase; mine measures just twenty-one by thirteen by seven and a half inches and weighs a mere four pounds. I always explain that it's really quite simple. The first step is, of course, to lower your fashion standards a little and buy truly practical clothes. There's a great assortment of lightweight, fast-drying, wrinkle-resistant, and fairly stylish apparel on the market these days, so we can all leave behind must-iron cotton shirts and jeans that take three days to dry.

So what *do* you pack for three months on the road? On this trip I took two pairs of slacks, two pairs of light trousers suitable for yoga or the beach, two tank tops, two T-shirts, one long-sleeved T-shirt, two collared shirts, a dress, a light sweater, a fleece top, my seventeen-pocket vest, a rain jacket, a nightgown, a light robe, and five days' supply of socks and underwear. I had one excellent pair of walking shoes, sandals, waterproof flip-flops, and some flats for dressier moments. A hat, scarf, and a few bits of cheap jewelry completed my wardrobe.

The second secret to living out of a suitcase is being prepared to do laundry constantly. You've probably seen ads for that ExOfficio underwear with the slogan "17 countries . . . 6 weeks . . . One pair of award-winning underwear. (Okay, maybe two)." I don't know who gives awards to underwear, but these have earned my vote. They are comfortable, breathable, and dry so quickly you probably could survive on just two pairs if you had to. But I don't advise going overboard as one blogger did, writing about how he'd worn a single pair continuously, without washing them, for weeks at a time on the Appalachian Trail. Eeek! I can only assume he did it as the result of losing a bet or in an effort to get in the *Guinness World Records*.

Call me old-fashioned, but I favor hygiene over that kind of efficiency — and over the method recommended in this Wikihow travel article: "Socks and underwear can easily be washed when you shower before bed — put them on the shower floor (avoiding the plughole), and agitate them with your feet as you shower. Shampoo is a mild detergent that also works on washable fabrics, and you can rinse as you step out."

This is a horrible idea on so many levels. While I admit that I have not personally tested it, I feel certain your socks and underwear are not going to achieve even basic standards of cleanliness from being trampled by your dirty feet in the less-than-immaculate water sluicing off your body onto a shower floor on which yet more grime could be lurking. But that's me; feel free to try it if you like, and let me know how it works out.

The Wikihow author was right on one point: shampoo can do double duty as laundry soap. Some friends who are permanently on the road told me about Lush shampoo, which comes in solid, lightweight bars and can wash just about anything from your socks to your body to (my friends assure me) your pet's hair as well as your own. Arriving in Verona, I took out my trusty Lush bar and got to work on our laundry while Rich did battle with a clothing rack that seemed curiously reluctant to stand on its own four feet. He emerged victorious, and pretty soon our wet things were draped over its wooden rods, steaming in the room's sultry heat.

There's nothing like hanging laundry or performing other activities of daily living to make a place feel more like home. This was the first apartment we'd stayed in during this trip, and it felt luxurious to drape our wet clothes someplace besides the shower stall and to know that later I could make simple meals in the kitchen and work on my computer while sitting in a proper chair at the dining table instead of propped up in bed. This was the first time I'd done any serious writing while on a long journey, and I realized, with a small shock of surprise, that I really had joined the ranks of the new breed of location-independent workers sometimes known as digital nomads.

I used to think such terms applied only to people like our friends Lindsay and Ross, who have jobs they can do entirely via laptop and smartphone, allowing them to move every three to six months to a different part of the globe, just for the fun of it. But it seems increasingly clear that we're all becoming digital nomads, using our devices to stay connected to the larger world when we're at home, and to keep working wherever we go. Being a digital nomad doesn't mean being on a permanent vacation; on the contrary, people like Lindsay and Ross are almost never untethered from work and other responsibilities. Like most young couples, they live in modest rented apartments and work hard five days a week. "The difference," Lindsay once told me, "is that at the end of the day, when we walk outside, it's always someplace new and exciting."

"Let's go check out Verona," Rich said after the laundry was hung.

And off we went to explore a city that was new to us and would, we hoped, prove exciting or at least interesting.

People flock to Verona to admire the beauty of its Roman, medieval, and Renaissance architecture and to hear classic opera sung in the Roman Arena, where the two-thousand-year-old acoustics are so fine they didn't bother to put in even minimal sound boosting equipment until 2011. We bought tickets for the current production, which was *Nabucco* (short for Nebuchadnezzar), the Bible-based opera that established Verdi's career as a composer.

Sitting on the ancient stone seats, Rich and I listened to the soaring perfection of the voices that carried easily through the night air, even to our nosebleed section. People who had sprung for the better seats closer to the stage were given candles, and as the brilliant sunset faded to darkness, the glow of hundreds of tiny flames added a touch of magic to the scene.

Visitors to Verona rightly rave about the opera at the arena, but for sheer popular appeal, nothing could come close to the city's top must-see attraction: the balcony where Juliet enacted her famous love scene with Romeo. Of course, it is no more Juliet's real balcony than 221B Baker Street in London is the real home of Sherlock Homes because — and I think you can follow my logic here — they are both *fictional characters*. But that doesn't keep lovestruck teenagers (and a lot of people who are old enough to know better) from making romantic pilgrimages to the site.

The balcony itself is (appropriately enough, considering Juliet's fate) an old sarcophagus that someone stuck onto a thirteenth-century house in 1936. That was the year Hollywood director George Cukor made a hit movie of the play starring Norma Shearer and Leslie Howard, and in the blast of publicity following the film's release, enterprising publicists in Verona decided to create the "real" Juliet's balcony as a tourist attraction.

It succeeded beyond their wildest dreams. The balcony, situated in a small courtyard off a main street in the town center, is constantly mobbed with visitors, many of whom leave love notes, trinkets, graffiti, and wads of chewing gum formed into little hearts. Some believe that leaving such tokens of affection at the site (I almost wrote "shrine") will make their love everlasting. A legend (which I suspect was also created by the Verona tourist board) suggests that caressing the right breast of the bronze statue of Juliet in the courtyard brings luck, and as you can imagine, that breast is now polished to a high sheen. For four euros (about five dollars) you can tour the house, which contains a few bits of Renaissance furniture and the bed from the Franco Zeffirelli movie. There's always a giggling girl posing on the balcony while her boyfriend stands below snapping her picture. If he's also busy declaiming "Hark, what light by yonder window breaks?" it's impossible to hear him over the cacophony of conversations in a dozen languages.

Each year thousands of people write letters addressed simply to "Juliet, Verona" in which they ask for advice about their love lives. I find this absolutely astonishing. Would you ask *any* teenager — dead or alive — for long-term relationship advice? And there's no getting around the fact that Juliet didn't manage her own affairs with any marked degree of success. The part about the union lasting "till death do you part" would have been a lot more impressive if she and her husband hadn't both committed suicide during the first year of their marriage. But of course, all that is moot, because Juliet never existed and is not the one answering these letters; a team of volunteers responds to them, sending each writer a handwritten note offering counsel and encouragement. The letter writers are asking *complete strangers* to tell them how they should conduct their romantic adventures. It boggles the mind.

Yet I am obviously in the minority for thinking that the Juliet craze is wildly irrational and more than a little exploitative on the part of those promoting it. Hordes of visitors clearly get a tremendous kick out of gazing at Juliet's balcony, leaving their chewing gum hearts, fondling the statue, and asking people they've never met to tell them how to deal with their sex partners. Like the Genoans basking in the glory of carrying St. John the Baptist's ashes through the streets, Juliet's fans seem exalted by this contact with the woman who has defined star-crossed romance since 1595. And why shouldn't they? If the line between fact and fantasy blurs for a moment, where is the harm?

Everyone chooses to suspend disbelief occasionally and for a variety of reasons, some of which are even sensible. Back in medieval times, it was hard to be certain what was true; everybody knew magic and miracles existed, recordkeeping was dubious at best, and no one had ever heard of DNA or carbon dating. And I can understand how modern lovers, raised on a diet of infotainment that erodes critical faculties, might let go of common sense long enough to indulge in a brief, personal fantasy while on a European vacation. But when professional travel writers lose the ability to make the distinction between fact and fiction, I find it deeply worrying.

On a website that describes itself as "the world's leading resource for researching, finding and booking the best travel experiences worldwide," an entry on Verona attractions reads, "None of us care that it's very possible that Romeo and Juliet were only figments of Shakespeare's imagination." *Possible?* Heaven give me strength! You're not *sure?* In that case, you might be interested in a sliver of the True Cross I just happen to have for sale . . .

[CHAPTER 6]

The Devil's Footprint

Few places could have been less fanciful or romantic than the Ludwigs-vorstadt neighborhood of Munich, where we found ourselves a couple of days later. "The area may look initially a bit raunchy to visitors due to the presence of a number of adult stores, gambling halls and strip clubs," Wikitravel informed us. "However, it is perfectly safe and a good bet if you are looking for authentic Asian and Middle Eastern restaurants." I wasn't looking for exotic cuisine in Germany, nor was I initially keen on the neighborhood, but in the end, Rich and I agreed that as long as it was safe, Ludwigsvorstadt might make a refreshing contrast to our days in Verona surrounded by lovesick honeymooners armed with heart-shaped wads of chewing gum.

A young German filmmaker had agreed to let us rent his apartment while he took off to his girlfriend's place for the duration. The photos he'd posted on the Internet showed big, sunny windows and bright, contemporary furnishings. Our only hesitation had been a casual, almost throwaway line toward the end of the description that mentioned the presence of "a very shy cat."

Although I do not worship cats as a species, as some of my friends do, I have liked some individual cats a great deal, finding them pleasant and amusing company. I prefer them in small doses — unlike my Aunt Beverly, who had eleven cats running free in her house (along with a family of raccoons). To sit down anywhere in her home required peeling a feline off the furniture, claw by claw; as a result, those cats and I never really warmed to each other. The shy cats I'd known tended to retreat to the tops of closets and undersides of sofas, doing their best to appear invisible, which struck me as a more livable arrangement.

"We may never even see this cat," I said. "But I suppose it might be fun to have a pet around for a few days."

"It says here all we'd have to do is feed it once a day. That doesn't sound like too much work."

How naive we were!

The moment we arrived at the apartment, which was situated in a soulless concrete block overlooking a construction site and a sex club, we were assaulted by the smell. The cat litter box occupied half the floor space in the minute bathroom, but the overly perfumed scent of fresh litter, with something nastier lurking underneath, permeated every inch of living space. The apartment was clean except for the fine film of cat hair clinging to every surface. The animal himself, a large brown and black creature known as "Kitty," sprawled on the dining table, glaring at us with disgust.

We got a much warmer welcome from the human who let us in. Since the filmmaker was tied up on a project, his friend Mike met us at the apartment and provided a wealth of information about the flat, the neighborhood, and the city. Like most Germans, he spoke excellent English, and when I complimented him on his language skills, he explained he was part Canadian on his mother's side. Learning that I was a travel writer interested in meeting locals, he arranged for us to join him and his mother for breakfast at a beer hall in two days' time.

After Mike left, I read over the note our host had posted in the kitchen. Along with various instructions about windows, laundry, and keys, he advised visitors to deposit the cat droppings in the toilet, or simply leave them where they were "if you can stand the smell." As I could hardly stand the smell now, I resigned myself to a close acquaintance with that cat box. I glanced over at Kitty, who had turned his back disdainfully and was licking himself. "Your servant, sir," I said.

The next day, Rich and I took a free walking tour of the city, led by an exuberant British woman named Liz. Naturally she took us to the cathedral, which was popularly known as Frauenkirche, meaning "Lady's church." Its full name is Dom zu Unserer Lieben Frau, which my online translator insists, somewhat improbably, means "cathedral to our love woman."

Liz explained that sometime back in the 1480s, Beelzebub had seen the half-built cathedral, and it struck him as a dark and gloomy place that would drive people away from God. So he told the architect, Jörg von Halsbach, "If you don't put any more windows in it, I'll send my friends down at night to help, and you'll finish the building in just twenty years." In the thirteenth century that counted as lightning speed, and von Halsbach agreed, harboring dreams of being remembered forever (and it's looking pretty good so far). When the cathedral was finished, the Prince of Darkness returned to gloat, only to discover that he'd overlooked the big window behind the high altar, installed before the bargain was struck. The church was now flooded with light, filled with people, and already consecrated, so that Satan would be forever blocked from passing beyond the entryway.

He did not take it well.

"So when the Devil stamped his foot in rage," Liz said, "the force was so great that it left an actual footprint here in the entrance to the cathedral." She showed us the depression, which looked more like a size nine shoe than the cloven hoofprint I would have expected. Visitors were taking turns fitting their feet into the imprint and giggling.

There's nothing like a little brush with the forces of evil to cheer people up. Apparently we all need, at some level, to let ourselves be terrified occasionally, if only to prove to ourselves that we are strong enough to handle it. That's why American children love spooky Halloween thrills and our teenagers embrace horror movies, ghost stories, and Ouija boards, to say nothing of smoking, fast cars, and other genuinely high-risk behaviors. Europe has never lost touch with its darker heritage, and in Munich, stepping over the Devil's Footprint on your way into church is simply one more reminder that demons have always walked the streets of the city, right into modern times. Just think of the 1972 Olympics massacre, or the Beer Hall Putsch of 1923, in which Hitler's first, unsuccessful bid for serious power began in the city's popular Bürgerbräukeller beer hall.

The Bürgerbräukeller no longer exists, having been damaged beyond repair in an attempt to blow up Hitler during a speech he gave there in 1939. But the city's other beer halls remain a major focal point for the city's social, political, financial, and economic life. When we arrived in Munich that August, they were all concentrating on one thing: the run-up to Oktoberfest.

I had, of course, heard of Oktoberfest, the huge beer party that got its start as the wedding feast of Crown Prince Ludwig and Princess Therese of Saxe-Hildburghausen in October 1810. At the invitation of the royal couple, the good citizens of Munich gathered in a field by the city gates to celebrate the happy occasion with a few barrels of brew and a horse race. Everybody had such a good time that they decided to do it all over again the following year, and it soon became a permanent tradition. Today Oktoberfest has been backed up into September for the better weather, lasts sixteen days, and attracts more than six million people a year. As you can imagine, Oktoberfest has been very, very good for the city's economy.

Toward the end of our tour, Liz took us to the city's most famous beer hall, Hofbräuhaus, founded in 1589 by the Duke of Bavaria as a public service — and a tidy little income generator for the crown. In the oldest section of the hall, Liz pointed out the gutter under the tables, where in earlier times men who were too inebriated to stand or didn't want to face the freezing temperatures in the outdoor privy would simply relieve themselves where they sat. Amazingly enough, this practical custom didn't continue into modern times.

I knew that any visit to Munich would include its famous beer halls and beer gardens, but it never occurred to me that I'd be having breakfast in one. I supposed it made sense. Why wait for happy hour or even lunch? As arranged, we met our new friend Mike and his mother, Betty, for a late breakfast under the trees in the enormously popular Augustiner Bräustuben. The centerpiece of the meal was the classic Münchner weisswurst, a white veal sausage, served with pretzels as large as my head. Various beverages appeared in liter-sized steins that — according to beer hall custom — had to be lifted one-handed. In addition to fruit juices mixed with fizzy soft drinks, we drank weissbier (white beer, known outside of Bavaria as weizenbier, or wheat beer), and russin, a dark wheat beer with a Sprite-like mixer. I turned down offers to try another classic combo, white beer with Coke, because even I have some standards.

"The food here is very good," said Betty.

"Yes, it's delicious," I said.

"No, I mean it's good for you."

I stared at my portion of weisswurst, which (I calculated later) contained twenty-five grams of fat, seventy-three grams of cholesterol, and nearly a full gram of salt. Add in the giant pretzels and liters of sugary soft drinks, to say nothing of the beer . . .

"It's because we don't use preservatives," Betty added comfortably.

That was the moment I realized two things: 1) I was in no position to judge whether this breakfast was any less healthy than the typical American breakfast of chemicals and white sugar masquerading as cereal, and 2) I didn't have to say "yes" to every opportunity to eat local foods.

I am not a timid eater. Give me a chance to sample exotic foreign fare — bulls' tails and baby eels in Spain, pig brains in the Republic of Georgia, snake in Vietnam — and I rarely turn it down. Most are pretty tasty. Fried flies, for instance, are crunchy, oily, salty, and a lot like cocktail peanuts — except, of course, for the wings. They're not a bad snack, but I don't think you need to worry that American fast-food franchises will ever start asking, "Will you be having flies with that?" Eating strange foreign delicacies is part of the fun of travel, but I finally met my limits that August morning in the Augustiner Bräustuben.

I wouldn't have missed that beer garden breakfast for anything; the food, the company, and the cultural experience were absolutely delightful. But I was at the beginning of a three-month journey, and my stomach was already overwhelmed by the prospect of adapting to a rich, new cuisine every time we stepped off a train. The spirit was willing, but the flesh would not be able to keep up with locals who had spent a lifetime tucking into German weisswurst, Czech guláš, or Bulgarian kavarma stew.

Even in my younger years, I had hesitated before consuming serious quantities of rich, heavy, meaty dishes; now both my brain and my tummy were sending me signals that I'd better pass up the kielbasa in favor of simple soups and salads, at least much of the time. I realized that by showing a bit more common sense at most meals, I could indulge in the local fare at others. I promised myself that when something truly special presented itself, I could say "yes!" or "*tak*" or "да" with all the enthusiasm I'd shown for the fried flies and the weisswurst.

Breakfast lasted until three in the afternoon, at which point Rich and I announced we needed our siesta. Arriving back at the apartment, we discovered that Kitty had kicked his litter all over the bathroom floor and trailed it into the rest of the living space on his paws. "Talk about the Devil's Footprint!" I muttered, as I searched for the broom and began cleaning up the mess. Kitty went over and began rubbing up against my suitcase, just to make sure there wasn't a spot without cat hairs on it.

"Just two more nights," Rich said. "I think we can survive Kitty that long."

We had just one more major landmark to see in the area, one we'd put off until the last day: the tour of the Dachau Concentration Camp Memorial Site.

On the morning of our tour, as the guide, Tom, passed around a sign-up clipboard, a French-Canadian woman told me, "I'm here with four other women. But they thought Dachau would be too depressing for their last day of vacation, so they went shopping instead." For a moment I thought, "What a bunch of lightweights!" And then I caught myself. Setting foot in a concentration camp under any circumstances was a terrifying prospect, and no one could ever be blamed for wanting to avoid it.

I still remember the day in eighth grade when the nuns told us about the camps and showed us a film that some Allied soldiers had made the day they liberated one of them, quite probably the one I was about to visit. That film was without a doubt the most shocking thing I'd ever seen. I'd found it hard to breathe as the camera panned across the skeletal figures in rags standing behind the barbed wire. It was, quite literally, inconceivable — yet it had happened, and just a few years before I was born, in the full glare of our own enlightened times. Since then, I've always thought of the camps as the ultimate horror story, the stuff of nightmares, far more terrifying than Hannibal Lecter or Freddy Krueger because they were real. That day in Munich, I couldn't blame the women who had elected not to go to Dachau. You have to choose your moment for facing down a fear that big. And for better or for worse, my day for doing it had come.

Our group rode the Munich metro ten miles to reach the town of Dachau. Tom told us that after the war, the town's residents were reviled by other Germans and the rest of the world for their association with the camp and have been dogged by prejudice to this day. I knew the townspeople had no control over events that placed this horror on their doorstep; Heinrich Himmler didn't exactly conduct focus groups to make sure the community was comfortable with his idea for building the complex there on the site of the abandoned munitions factory. But I found it difficult to work up too much sympathy for the residents' sufferings in light of what happened on the other side of the barbed wire.

Tom led us through the camp gate, and seeing the famous, cruelly ironic words *Arbeit macht frei* (Work will make you free) from the inside sent a shiver down my spine.

Both Tom and whoever designed the memorial made every effort to undercut the horror by maintaining a matter-of-fact tone while presenting a steady stream of essential information. Dachau was the first permanent concentration camp; it opened in 1933 and served as a prototype for all the Nazi camps that followed. Himmler's original plan was to isolate political prisoners there, but it soon became a labor camp for common criminals, Jews, Jehovah's Witnesses, gays, emigrants, Gypsies, and other "undesirables." It became a "school of violence" for the Schutzstaffel or SS men who ran it. During its twelve years of operation, more than two hundred thousand people from all over Europe were incarcerated there. The stories of torture and mass murder were told simply and without emotion. There were thirty-two thousand documented deaths, and it was commonly believed that many others lost their lives there without leaving a trace in the official records.

We saw the grim barracks, the rooms used for medical experiments, and the torture chambers. This was a place where the very worst of human nature was given free rein — even encouraged — for a long time. Toward the end of the tour, Tom took us to see the gas chamber and the ovens of the crematorium. By that time it was hard to absorb the creeping horror of the scene, let alone react to it. I was walking around inside a Devil's Footprint so huge that my mind and heart could simply not take it all in.

Rich and I rode the metro back to the Ludwigsvorstadt neighborhood in dazed silence. We walked past the Middle Eastern restaurants, strip clubs, and concrete apartment blocks to our favorite Persian place and ordered a meal. As we sat over plates of saffron chicken and bowls of yogurt with cucumber and mint, I looked around at the other customers, most of whom were Iranian families. Outside, people of every race, culture, lifestyle, and dress were strolling along the sidewalks; no doubt many of them were on their way to commit all sorts of acts that had once been strictly forbidden under the Nazi code of conduct.

I felt my spirits begin to lift a little. Because seeing so many diverse kinds of people here, with the freedom to be who they were and to live as they chose, was a powerful reminder that yes, every once in a while, you really can beat the Devil. Although even when you do, he certainly leaves his mark.

[CHAPTER 7]

Oh, the Places You Won't Go

When it comes to travel," an American once told me, "I pay top price and expect the best. I want to be certain that someone has gone before me every step of the way to make absolutely sure that I'm seeing the best views, eating the best food, and staying at the best hotels."

To me, that's like paying someone else to take the vacation for you. In fact, it's rather like paying someone to have sex for you. Where's the excitement? The spontaneity? The soaring joy of discovering something utterly unexpected and thrilling? And then there's the expense. When you pay top price and your holiday costs as much as your car, you expect seamless luxury *and* a peak experience, two things that don't naturally go hand in hand. If the benchmark is perfection, every trip is going to fall short somewhere along the line. Even a simple delay at check-in or a substandard steak can leave you feeling cheated and disappointed at the "failure" of the trip.

On the other hand, there are moments when getting off the beaten path can be pretty damned annoying in its own way. Take, for instance, our next stopover after Munich, a place somewhere in the outskirts of Salzburg, where we had booked a room in the bed and breakfast that had once been the home of the von Trapp family. As everyone who's seen *The Sound of Music* knows, the von Trapps left Austria when the Nazis took over in 1938. In the film, Julie Andrews, Christopher Plummer, and the children slipped away while performing at a concert in Salzburg; in real life the family dressed as if for one of their usual mountaineering outings, rode a train into the Alps, and continued on by rail through Italy, Switzerland, and France, arriving eventually in London, where they took a boat to the United States. A trifle less dramatic, but that's real life for you.

One of the things they left behind was a large house on the outer edge of Salzburg, a house that was now a bed and breakfast known as Villa Trapp. Normally it was quite pricey, but they were advertising a special rate to fill a last-minute vacancy. I hoped it wouldn't be too cheesy; I had hideous visions of maids in polyester dirndl skirts and endless loops of Muzak playing sappy renditions of "Do-Re-Mi" and "The Lonely Goatherd." But the house *was* a piece of history, and the discount brought it down to somewhere within shouting range of our budget, so we decided to give it a try.

The management of Villa Trapp confirmed our reservation and instructed us to change trains at the main Salzburg station, then take the commuter line to the smaller station of Bahnhof Aigen; from there, they assured us, the Villa Trapp was just around the corner. If only we could figure out which corner. The GPS wasn't working, and even Rich's superb orienteering skills were stymied by the nonsequential numbering and the street names that appeared and disappeared seemingly at random. Coupled with the fact that our train had been quite late, it was hard to believe we were in Austria, a place I'd always associated with Teutonic efficiency.

We passed the leafy complex now housing some former residents of the von Trapp home, a Catholic religious order known as the Missionaries of the Precious Blood. The missionaries had rented the von Trapp house right after the family left, only to be booted out by Himmler, who took over the house as a summer residence, setting up an SS camp in the garden. After the war, the missionaries purchased the home from the von Trapps and remained there until 2008. They then sold it to the present owners, who renovated the house, opened Villa Trapp, and began promoting it to well-heeled fans of the film.

Today, as the Villa Trapp website informed us, with more schmaltz than strict adherence to grammar, "you can follow the authentic footsteps of the von Trapp Family, the real place, where it all began. While the birds are singing in the old trees of the park, close your eyes and relive it again — the first confession of love between Maria and the Baron, the laughter of a child in the large staircase, the first melodies from the lips of the Family Choir under the branches of the trees . . . to world stardom." Maybe we *could* imagine all of that — if only we could find the house. We stumbled on, growing hotter, more tired, and ever more fed up with dragging our suitcases up and down deserted country lanes.

Eventually we took what I felt certain was a wrong turn and discovered the Villa Trapp at last, a large, yellow house nestled in a quiet park that was now blessedly free of both the SS and the Missionaries of the Precious Blood. In moments we were standing in the lavishly decorated entrance hall, talking to a rumpled man wearing a polo shirt and baggy shorts, who introduced himself as the owner.

"But I'm not a baron, ha ha! Did you get my email? You do know you cannot stay here, yes?"

"What? But we had a confirmed reservation," Rich said. "You reconfirmed it last night."

"Yes, but that has changed. It turns out there is no room for you. We tried to contact you this morning, but . . ." He shrugged. "You left no phone number, and all we had was an email address . . ." He shrugged again.

A bit more discussion ensued, as you can imagine, but clearly there was nothing to be done. Thoroughly disgruntled, we dragged ourselves and our suitcases back to Bahnhof Aigen, returned to Salzburg, and began walking up and down the streets near the train station, seeking a place for the night.

The first few hotels we tried were full, but eventually we found one that was funky, old-fashioned, family-run, and cost only twenty percent more than we'd planned to pay for the discounted Villa Trapp room, which was already well above our usual modest budget. The hotel did have one outstanding feature: a sort of happy hour in the parlor at seven in the evening, where guests could enjoy ice-cold beer for a euro. We promised ourselves we'd take advantage of that later, but now, with several hours of daylight remaining, we wanted to see something of Salzburg.

Speeding through our usual routine — bedbug check, consolidating our valuables in one suitcase and chaining it to the radiator — we headed out of the hotel. As we crossed the river and approached the Altstadt, as the old town center is known, I noticed the crowds were denser and the locals scarcer. By the time I caught my first glimpse of the city's most famous shopping street, Getreidegasse (Grain Lane), I was elbow to elbow with a heaving mass of international visitors. Overhead, dozens of shop signs hung out over the street, cunningly fashioned to look like wrought-iron guild signs from ye olde days — except that they were promoting trendy clothing chains, giant international coffee corporations, and McDonald's.

Still, the overall effect was rather charming, and I automatically swung up my camera to take a shot. As I clicked the shutter, I realized there were at least half a dozen other people standing beside me on the same stretch of pavement, doing precisely the same thing. I wondered how many thousands — millions! — of photos just like mine had been snapped over the years. As someone who works hard to find unique ways to photograph the world, I found it rather demoralizing.

"It's like Disneyland's Main Street, USA," Rich said in disgust. He was right. Even though the buildings around us were quite old, the entire street had the artificial feel of a manufactured environment. Had I really traveled all this way just to drink coffee at Starbucks and shop in Zara, the Spanish clothing chain that has four shops and a discount outlet within five minutes' walk of my Seville apartment? Where was the authentic experience, the delightful surprise of discovering a whole new angle on the business of life?

It wasn't as if we hadn't been warned. Rich's sister Jane had said that Salzburg was crawling with tourists and should be avoided if at all possible. And we'd planned to give it a miss, until perusal of the railroad map had shown us that it was the logical place to break our journey. Of course, it was the special offer from the Villa Trapp that had really tipped the scales in the city's favor . . . not that I was bitter.

"Do you want to try to find Mozart's birthplace?" Rich asked without much enthusiasm. Unbeknownst to us, we were actually standing in front of it at the time, a fact we discovered later when sorting through the photos. The gigantic lettering on the building behind us that read "Mozarts Geburtshaus" should have been a clue. But at the time we were too busy trying to avoid getting trampled in the stampede.

"Not if it means more time jammed in here with the rest of the sardines," I said, taking Rich's arm and leading him, unprotesting, down a side street where it was easier to breathe. "Now, about that happy hour back at our hotel . . ."

After a brief, refreshing siesta in our room, we made our way downstairs to the parlor, where three congenial Americans were comfortably ensconced. Our hostess produced a round of frosty beers, the ice was broken, and before long we were all comparing notes about travel experiences. From there it was but a short step to pouring out our grievances about being turned away from the Villa Trapp.

"Oh, they're known for that," said one of our new friends. "My guidebook says that whenever they have a vacancy they publicize last-minute bargains, but the bargain guests get bumped if someone shows up who's willing to pay full price." I should have known. As usual, it came down to dough-re-mi.

The next morning, Rich and I happily put Salzburg behind us. By noon we'd crossed the border into the Czech Republic and were rolling toward the largest, most powerful city in the South Bohemian Region: České Budějovice. I know, it's not a name that's easy to pronounce at first, second, or third glance, and Wikipedia's efforts at providing a phonetic guide — written in characters so esoteric that my computer refused to recognize them — left me more baffled than ever. I soon gave up the struggle and began referring to it as Seskie Beetlejuice. (I'd eventually learn it was something along the lines of CHESS-kay bood-YO-vit-ska.)

Our visit there would be short, another brief stopover to break our journey, in keeping with our effort to travel no more than three hours by train on any given day. After České Budějovice, we were planning to spend a few days in Český Krumlov, a UNESCO World Heritage Site that we'd heard was one of the loveliest places on the planet.

Which České Budějovice most definitely was not. For the jewel in the economic crown of the South Bohemian Region, České Budějovice was looking far from prosperous. The once-grand train station was dim and dilapidated, and the city streets were lined with shabby nineteenth-century apartments and dingy twentieth-century shops. Lannova Street, the broad pedestrian mall in the center of town, was full of teens hanging about with an air of settled boredom that suggested they spent a great deal of time there, having no place to go, nothing to do, and no money to do it with.

It began to rain as we arrived in the main square, a vast open space called Náměstí Přemysla Otakara II, after the thirteenth King of Bohemia. Before I could even begin to work up a more pronounceable version of the name, I saw an object that made me stop and exclaim, "What is *that?*"

"I think it's meant to be a giant shark fin," said Rich.

I stared up at the slightly curved stone triangle that was easily twice as tall as Rich. Had someone on the České Budějovice city council watched *Saturday Night Live* back in the 1970s, when they were doing running gags about land sharks? Could the civic leaders be fans of the movie *Jaws*? The paving stones the artist had used around the fin's base just failed to match the plaza's paving stones, somewhat spoiling the desired effect of the shark fin bursting up through the surface of the plaza as if it were the surface of the ocean.

A few more steps took us to our lodgings, a pleasant, old-fashioned hotel with lots of dark wood, spacious rooms, and a helpful, English-speaking staff. By the time we'd dried off and rested up a bit, it was nearly time for dinner, and the receptionist, in the manner of receptionists everywhere, recommended the most expensive, formal, and stuffy-looking restaurant in town. Rich and I strolled past it and kept on going, seeking other options. But these were few and far between; apparently the locals didn't eat out much. Eventually we returned to the main square and went into a sort of pub full of wood and shiny brass, but sadly lacking in patrons. As we took seats at the bar, Rich pointed to the tap and held up two fingers. In moments we were in possession of a couple of frosty glasses of the local beer.

And here I am touching on a rather sore subject in České Budějovice. The city had been famous for its beer since the thirteenth century; among its many honors was serving as the imperial brewery for the Holy Roman Emperor. The beer was named after the town, but since everyone down through the ages has shared our difficulties in pronouncing it, they used the simpler, German form of Budějovice, which is Budweis, and called the beer Budweiser.

Sound familiar?

That's because six hundred years later, Adolphus Busch was touring Europe's best breweries to get ideas for a business he was setting up with his new father-in-law, Eberhard Anheuser, and when he came upon this golden lager, he felt it would make a welcome alternative to the dark beers popular in the United States at the time. In 1876 Anheuser-Busch introduced America to its version of golden lager, which it named, as all the world knows, Budweiser.

No doubt České Budějovice remained in happy ignorance of this fact for some time, allowing Anheuser-Busch to spread the Budweiser name throughout the New World. Eventually, of course, came epic legal battles worthy of a John Grisham novel. When the dust settled and the corpses had been carted off the field, Anheuser-Busch possessed the legal rights to the Budweiser name in the United States and much of the world outside of Europe. However, in most European countries the Czech Budweiser still maintains legal rights to the name, and the American beer is sold as "Bud." Just to keep matters interesting, in Sweden, Ireland, and the UK, both the Czech and the U.S. brews are marketed as Budweiser, which no doubt creates all sorts of opportunities for confusion and rancor. Anheuser-Busch has made numerous offers to buy the České Budějovice brewery to complete its global hegemony of the name, but so far the Czechs are holding firm, claiming it's a source of national identity and pride.

They have a right to be proud. Czech Budweiser is a great beer, a crisper, more full-bodied version of its younger American namesake, and it proved the highlight of our visit to the pub in České Budějovice.

Otherwise the evening was not a roaring success. Sitting at the bar, we sipped our Budweiser drafts and, using the menu and our highly successful pointing method, ordered some food — all of which seemed pretty ordinary to us, but earned us some very peculiar looks from the bartender. Was it because we were sitting at the bar when there were twenty empty tables? Did he feel as if we were watching his every move? Or was he simply uncomfortable around foreigners? It was hard to pick up on the social cues, as the only other person in the bar was a very large man sitting some distance away, who spent the entire time we were there sipping from a huge stein of beer and staring at us fixedly. We ate with all due haste and departed with relief into the rainy night.

"Did all that staring strike you as a bit creepy?" I asked Rich.

"Yes. But I suspect the bartender is thinking the very same thing about us right now."

In the morning, we braved the drizzle to take a long walk around České Budějovice, and I began to revise my opinion upward. The town was unlikely to regain the prominence it held during the days of the Holy Roman Empire, and no one was about to designate it a World Heritage Site. But it was making an *effort*. Oddly whimsical public art abounded. In addition to the giant shark fin, there were three big, blue-haired mermaids in the river; a statue composed of hundreds of little metal men arranged to make a colossal figure in the pose of Rodin's *The Thinker* sitting atop the Hotel Budweiser; a bronze creature that was half man, half snail crawling down the side of a commercial building; and a white plaster group of eight life-sized men and women in business suits, carrying briefcases and striding along importantly under the town clock. A swath of trees encircled the downtown area, coalescing into a large park along the river. Charming buildings from the thirteenth through nineteenth centuries had been carefully preserved, some painted in quirky and amusing ways. Like Genoa, this was a town people blew through on their way to more glamorous objectives, such as Český Krumlov and Prague, and it was making heroic, if futile, efforts to convince them to stay.

Český Krumlov, on the other hand, was clearly a destination. When I first saw it, I thought I'd rarely seen a city of more breathtaking loveliness. It was nestled in a bowl-shaped valley along the banks of a winding river, and standing on the upper rim, I had a sweeping view of red peaked roofs, leafy green trees, cobblestone streets, and arched bridges, all jumbled together in a delightful gallimaufry (a word I recently stumbled across while looking up synonyms for hodgepodge). On a hill in the very center rose the medieval castle, its gold and white towers topped with graceful, green, onion-shaped domes that sparkled in the sunlight.

"It's magical," said Rich. "Like something out of a fairy tale."

He obviously wasn't the first to make this observation. Our lodgings, a hostel perched on the upper rim of the city, featured a wooden door carved in the shape of a dragon and a whimsical sign in the window that read, "No Visigoths or spiders." The interior, full of stone, brick, hand-hewn wood, and well-worn furniture, looked like a cross between Frodo's burrow in the Shire and the hippie crash pads of my student days at Berkeley.

This was our first stay in a hostel on this trip, and I was curious to see whether this one lived up to all the articles touting them as the latest cool thing in affordable accommodations for travelers of all ages. In addition to the usual dormitories, today's updated hostels often have private rooms; some, like the one we'd booked in Český Krumlov, even boast private bathrooms. Remembering the convivial atmosphere of the hostels of my student days, I wondered what kinds of people were hanging around them now and whether any of them would be interested in talking with us. So far our efforts to socialize had not always yielded the desired results.

We found the common rooms inhabited only by faded armchairs and sofas that were leaning up against one another for support, quietly disgorging stuffing from their arms and backs. We did an *extremely* thorough bedbug check, secured our valuables, and headed down into the town, prepared to fall in love with Český Krumlov.

A decade earlier, we probably would have. Nothing could have been more picturesque than the lovingly restored medieval, Renaissance, and baroque buildings, the quaint stone bridges, and the winding, cobbled streets leading up to the fairy-tale castle. But garish signs protruded from every possible surface, shouting at us to try the mead! Climb the tower! Enjoy two-for-one drinks at a real medieval alehouse! Have your picture taken here! Buy souvenirs here! And here! And here! The only locals we saw were dressed in cotton-polyester folk costumes, inviting us — in English — to come inside and eat "authentic Czech cuisine" in their restaurants. There wasn't a single establishment that didn't cater exclusively to tourists; hours of walking proved to us that there was nothing in the entire downtown area for locals — except, of course, jobs in the thriving tourism industry.

The city had become a theme park. I felt the same morbid fascination I'd experienced viewing the "miraculously preserved" mummies of medieval saints. Český Krumlov's soul was long gone, and its flesh had shriveled to nearly nothing, but everybody seemed perfectly happy with the corpse. Chattering groups dressed in everything from rugged Australian backpacking gear to smart Parisian leisurewear pressed in on us from all sides, exclaiming delightedly over the thrilling views of the castle, the cute old wooden doors, the quaint cobblestones, the adorable souvenirs . . .

"Is it us?" I asked Rich, as we stopped for free samples of mead given out by a smiling woman in front of a wine shop. "What do all these people like so much about this place?"

"They come here for the fantasy," he said. "They want to walk around in the fairy tales they read as children."

"I guess that makes sense," I said, remembering Juliet's balcony and 221B Baker Street. "And the more artificial it is, the easier it probably is to fall into the fantasy."

"And the more artificial it is, the safer it feels. They don't have to worry about real Visigoths or spiders."

"We're leaving tomorrow, right?"

"Oh, yeah."

We had long since learned the wisdom of walking away from places that weren't right for us. As that venerable sage Dr. Seuss put it, in his seminal work *Oh, the Places You'll Go!*:

You'll look up and down streets. Look 'em over with care.
About some you will say, "I don't choose to go there."
With your head full of brains and your shoes full of feet,
you're too smart to go down any not-so-good street.

And you may not find any
you'll want to go down.
In that case, of course,
you'll head straight out of town.

I knew that Rich and I could have a good time almost anywhere; we had, for instance, thoroughly enjoyed our twenty years in Cleveland, a city not universally viewed as the garden spot of America. I like cities with a funky side, a touch of grittiness, and a we-try-harder attitude. I find it difficult to warm to places that are so self-satisfied that they want to preserve themselves in plastic, as Český Krumlov had done.

Returning to the hostel, I told the young man at the front desk that we were leaving early and (when he asked) why. He seemed astounded that I hadn't fallen in love with the city and, in an act of extraordinary generosity, agreed to refund our prepayment for the second night.

Rich and I spent a cozy evening sitting around the hostel's shabby common room chatting with a family of five. At first I took them for Americans, but I soon learned that the father was Canadian and the mother was a Czech who had grown up in Prague.

"We used to come out here to Český Krumlov every summer for camping and sports," she said, rather wistfully. "I liked the fresh air and the quiet, the feeling of being in the country." I could — just barely — imagine the town with that kind of rustic tranquility.

We exchanged tales of our childhoods, travels, and places we'd lived. I regaled the kids with stories I thought they would find entertaining, such as the time a six-foot snake crawled into our Ohio home and went to sleep on our bed. The youngest child stood up and sang for us, then collapsed in giggles. I thoroughly enjoyed sitting in the familial circle, swapping stories and easygoing banter; it was the homiest evening I'd had yet on the road.

But it didn't change my mind about leaving.

On the train the next morning, I sat next to a lively young Irishwoman who told me her name was Denise and made a slight sweeping gesture over her knees to give me an instant memory aid for her name. Denise had been traveling alone for six months through Central and Eastern Europe, and with a little prompting, described with pleasure her time in Romania and Bulgaria. I asked what she thought of Český Krumlov.

"Sure, it was pretty," she said. "But at this point, for me to say a place is special, it would have to be dipped in gold. As far as I'm concerned, liking a place really comes down to two things: it's the weather and who you meet."

She told me about a young woman she'd traveled with once who liked to go on holiday but hated to make arrangements, so she'd often tag along with others on trips they had organized. "A lot of the time she didn't even know what country she was in. For her, travel was just moving from one pub to another."

In a weird sort of way, it was kind of a relief to hear this. Just that morning, I'd started adding up all the places we'd bypassed, including lots of major points of interest — or POIs, as an old guidebook of mine called them. It's a curious but well-known phenomenon among travelers that once you've been presented with a list of must-sees in the district, you feel almost honor-bound to pay each one of them a visit. Even if you'd never heard of, say, the Erratic Boulder of Česke Budějovice, suddenly you have the uncomfortable sensation that you're letting down not only yourself but all of touristkind if you don't go and pay homage to it.

However, as the trip progressed, Rich and I were becoming increasingly cavalier about neglecting POIs both great and small. In Salzburg alone, we had ignored Mozart's birthplace, the castle, the cathedral, the palace of the Prince-Archbishops, various abbeys and churches, and Schloss Klessheim, a baroque palace (now a casino) where Hitler used to hang out with Mussolini. Česke Budějovice's POIs were rather more modest, but we had managed to skip, among other attractions, its Erratic Boulder, a stone marking the site of the old hangman's scaffold. According to legend, if you pass by it after ten o'clock at night, you'll be wandering the streets until dawn, unable to find your way home. So perhaps it's just as well we gave it a miss.

When I was younger, I found it much harder to skip must-see POIs. But one of the advantages of traveling when you're older is that, at least in your more rational moments, you know that you can't see everything, no matter how quickly or efficiently you travel, and there's no point in trying. Accepting this is a great relief. I often get visitors in Seville who are there for three days and want to squeeze in side trips to Cordoba, Granada, and possibly Morocco and Portugal during their stay. I'm exhausted just trying to talk them out of it.

By this point in our railway adventure, Rich and I were taking pleasure in blowing off must-sees and structuring our days according to our preferences and whims rather than lists compiled by Fodor's, Lonely Planet, or Wikitravel. Our days gradually fell into a pattern. In the morning, I'd spend an hour or two working on my photos and my blog, while Rich researched local tours, places to visit and eat, and potential next destinations. Then we'd have breakfast — generally coffee and a croissant or the local equivalent — and discuss our plans for the day.

Our first morning in any city usually involved a free guided walking tour; otherwise we'd pick out a few POIs, such as the cathedral and largest park, to point us in a direction for our morning walk. Lots of days were spent simply strolling about, enjoying various local curiosities and stopping at sidewalk cafés for a coffee and some people watching. Then it would be time to pick a modest eatery for lunch, our main meal of the day. And here Rich's gift for discovering great places to eat — generally referred to as "the sniffer" — proved invaluable (although not infallible, as you'll see later). After lunch we would, in the Sevillano tradition we've adopted, head to our lodgings for a siesta. Later, we'd go for another walk before dinner, checking out local sights, often ending up at dusk in a café for a bite to eat. I felt extraordinarily rich in that rarest of all commodities: time.

Still, I occasionally felt a slight pang at missing out on so many world-class POIs. Now, hearing Denise talk about her friend, I was comforted by the knowledge that, judged against *that* low bar, I was not doing too badly. I might not visit every must-see in Fodor's, but I always knew what country I was in, and on a good day, I remembered that I had all the time I needed to enjoy it.

CHAPTER 8

Reality Czech

In Franz Kafka's existential novels, Prague always bears an air of brooding menace, but I was pretty sure, from posts and emails describing my friends' riotous pub crawls there, that the city had become a bit more hospitable in recent years. Yet within an hour of my arrival, I'd managed to make two enemies, get ejected from a taxi at a police checkpoint, and stumble across a KGB outpost. I was beginning to come around to Kafka's point of view. This town was going to be tougher to negotiate than I'd expected. It seemed that Rich and I had been right in all those conversations we'd had about the trip: when you hit Prague, you are really starting to get *out there*.

I made my first enemy at the train station espresso bar, where Rich and I stopped for our customary coffee before plunging into the city. It was midafternoon, so I attempted to order a decaf, a commodity that had been readily available all through Spain, Italy, and Austria but was unknown here — and, as it turned out, in all the other countries we would visit on this trip. The barista, who prided himself on his English and his coffee-dispensing skills, simply could not understand my request. This wounded his pride so profoundly that he could only express himself by prolonged hair tossing and cup rattling and stomping about behind the espresso bar. Rich and I hastily shared a (full-caffeine) cappuccino and headed outside to the taxi stand and our next confrontation.

"The house is in the center of town," our landlady, Eva, had written, "and the fare from the station should not be more than 250 or 280 koruna," which is about thirteen dollars. However, the taxi drivers all showed us plasticized price lists that read "Center 660 koruna," the equivalent of thirty-two dollars. Naturally we objected to paying more than twice the standard fare. Finally one of the drivers, a chunky, bald fellow with the air of one grudgingly bestowing an enormous favor against his better judgment, agreed to lower the price to 450. When I shook my head, the cabby threw up his hands in disgust and looked as if he wished he had cups to rattle or hair to toss in order to express the depth of his outrage at my ingratitude. I walked away with his irate mutterings ringing in my ears.

A block later we found a taxi driver willing to transport us to our destination for 300 koruna. Once we were underway, he mentioned that the fare would be "around 300, maybe 330," and we were still arguing about that when he slammed on the brakes and told us to get out of the cab. He couldn't take us any closer to our destination, he said, because of the security checkpoint. A glance out the window revealed stern-faced, uniformed police officers waving down all approaching vehicles and doing exhaustive searches, right down to examining the cars' undercarriages with mirrors on the ends of rods. It turned out our Prague apartment was close to several embassies, and they were taking no chances on letting any suspicious characters or cars into the neighborhood.

Rich paid off the cab, and as I hiked up the street, I couldn't help thinking that if they were looking for suspicious characters, they might want to start in the dingy storefront that proclaimed itself — in large, red letters, with a hammer and sickle — to be the KGB Museum. I'd read about it on the Internet but hadn't realized that it was directly across from our apartment. The museum's website managed to suggest, in a pssst-you-didn't-hear-this-from-me manner, that the establishment wasn't so much a museum as a sort of recruitment outpost. A place to keep the flame alive. The website proudly proclaimed that the exhibits included "things that belonged to the first persons of the Soviet state," plus such must-sees as Lenin's death mask and the ice pick used to assassinate Trotsky. "The bright part of the KGB museum," said the website, "is the photo exposition 'Prague 1968 in the eyes of KGB officer.'" Yes, what could be more heartwarming than that? But such pleasures would have to wait until we'd made our rendezvous with our host. I didn't want to arrive late and offend yet another citizen of this fair city.

Our host was a tall, affable man who ran an art and antiquities shop on the street level of the centuries-old house in which we'd be staying. Using his few words of English and many hand gestures (a sublanguage I came to call "Charades-lish"), he welcomed us and led the way up four flights of stairs.

Our attic apartment turned out to be huge and quirky and marvelously bohemian — which shouldn't have surprised me, as we were now actually in Bohemia. There was a fireplace with a big, comfy, red armchair drawn up to it, a full kitchen, and a large open space with half a dozen beds and couches in richly patterned reds, oranges, yellows, and greens. The massive wooden beams that you might expect to find on the ceiling were on the floor, and being nearly knee height, had to be negotiated with some care. The ceilings, which sloped steeply at the outer edges — for instance, where our bed was located — would contribute to the difficulty of avoiding injury, especially if climbing out of bed half asleep.

Standing on tiptoes and peering out of the skylight, I had a nice view of the KGB Museum, and as we headed out to explore the city, I managed to convince Rich, who somehow failed to appreciate the museum's allure, that we should at least stop in. I wanted to find out when it was open so I could plan a later visit. Poking my head inside, I found a dim entryway, a dusty glass counter, faded KGB posters, and a thick, dark curtain of what might once have been red velvet. Low murmurs from behind the curtain ceased abruptly when I called out, "Hello?"

There was a long pause, during which I pictured weapons being concealed and documents being held over the shredder, and then the curtain stirred and a young man emerged. He wore battle fatigues, a large bandage on one arm, and a deeply annoyed scowl. In answer to my question he barked, in heavily accented English, "Is open every day!"

Turning on his heel, he stomped back behind the curtain.

Rich and I scurried away, vowing never to return. Call me paranoid, but my survival instincts insisted that I steer clear of the KGB man and whomever he was conspiring with behind the curtain. I didn't want to pay for the tour (a very capitalist eighteen dollars per person) by credit card, share my email address with them, or become their Facebook comrade — or in fact leave any trace that could lead them back to me. Throughout our stay in Prague, we would pass by the KGB Museum often, and frankly, it seemed wiser to do so with jacket collars flipped up and hats pulled down over our eyes to evade notice. For those few moments each day, Prague really lived up to its Kafkaesque reputation.

The next morning, I discovered that our neighborhood was home to another iconographic POI: the Infant Jesus of Prague. In the Catholic schools of my childhood, replicas and photos of the statue were everywhere: a standing Baby Jesus wearing magnificent robes and a crown larger than his head. One of the odd things about this figure was that he kept changing his outfits; even in photos of the original statue, he might be shown one day in blue and white satin embroidered with silver, another in red velvet embellished with gold, at times with a big lace collar, at others wrapped in an ermine cloak. Even his crowns would vary. But he was always resplendent in his royal raiment, and had a long track record of performing wondrous miracles, especially for children and pregnant women. When a glance at the city map showed us that this miraculous figure was just a few blocks away from our apartment, we descended from our attic to the street, hurried past the KGB Museum with our heads averted, and walked over to the Carmelite Church of Our Lady of Victory to pay him a visit.

The Infant Jesus of Prague was small, a mere nineteen inches high, and utterly dwarfed by the vast gold and silver baroque shrine that surrounded him. After paying suitable homage, I looked in at the gift shop where, among the cheap medals and glow-in-the-dark plastic replicas, I found a book about the statue's history. Idly thumbing through the pages, I was stunned to discover that the Infant Jesus of Prague was actually from Seville.

The legend (and I am by no means vouching for its authenticity) goes like this: In the mid-sixteenth century, wicked foreign soldiers destroyed a monastery near Seville. As the survivors labored to rebuild, their leader had a vision of the Infant Jesus, who told him to keep up the good work. The monk later fashioned a wax likeness of the baby he'd seen in his vision. Naturally, this Infant Jesus was soon credited with all sorts of miracles, bringing it to the attention of the faithful — and the wealthy. As was so often the case with rare and precious religious objects in that part of the world, this wondrous statue eventually found its way into the possession of a rich aristocratic family from Seville. When one of the daughters married a nobleman from Prague, she brought the statue with her, and in 1668 her daughter, who bore the tongue-twisting name Princess Polyxena von Lobkowicz, gave the statue to an order of nuns known as the Barefoot Carmelites.

The fact that the statue hailed from Seville might explain the constant changes of clothing. For centuries, Spanish nuns had been fashioning elaborate little outfits for statues of the Infant Jesus that would be displayed in their convent's chapel or parlor. Naked, anatomically correct statues of the Baby Jesus are still sold for this purpose and are a common sight in the shop windows of Seville's religious and antique stores. Some believe the nuns' tradition is a charming way of paying homage to one of the most beloved aspects of God known in the Church, while less charitable observers view the custom as a perversion of the maternal instinct and frankly rather worrying.

Did the Infant Jesus arrive in Prague with a wardrobe of outfits from his Seville home? Or did the Barefoot Carmelites of Prague start the practice, which then spread back to Spain? So far I haven't been able to dig up any evidence one way or the other. But having visited the upper room in Our Lady of Victory Church, where his wardrobe is housed, I can tell you that the Infant Jesus of Prague remains a strong candidate for the best-dressed statue in all of Christendom.

Rich didn't accompany me up the stairs to view the statue's wardrobe, as that day his leg was hurting abominably. After several pain-free days in Genoa, his sciatica (or whatever it was) had notably worsened. On good days, he could walk for hours with minimal discomfort; on others, after forty-five minutes' easy stroll, he'd suggest, white-lipped, that we sit down on that upcoming park bench *now*. He never complained and didn't like to talk about it much; I had to pry information out of him and promise that I wouldn't write about it in my weekly blog posts. But even on bad days he did a considerable amount of walking, and if he had to rest more often than usual, neither of us minded sitting down and watching the passing scene.

Park benches and café tables provided a great vantage point for viewing Prague's stunning skyline, with its endless vistas of peaks, spires, towers, arched bridges, castles, palaces, and churches, built in every conceivable tradition from Romanesque to ultramodern. Prague had been a regional powerhouse for more than a thousand years, and it had acquired the wealth and the civic will to hire the best architects of every age and commission them to produce breathtaking monuments in the current style. The real miracle is that each architect somehow managed to blend the new work with the old in a way that was constantly surprising but never jarring.

Arguably the most important structure ever built in Prague is the Karlův Most, or Charles Bridge, which from the fourteenth century until 1841 served as the only link between the city's two halves that stand on opposite banks of the Vltava River. Holy Roman Emperor Charles IV personally laid the first foundation stone at 5:31 a.m. on July 9, 1357 — a date which, when written as 135797531, is palindromic (that is, the same backwards and forwards). The emperor's royal astrologers and numerologists felt the date was highly auspicious, and apparently they knew their stuff; the bridge has survived numerous floods and wars, often sustaining damage but still standing after more than seven hundred years. Local legend says the original builders mixed egg yolks with the mortar to strengthen it; I knew egg yolks gave chocolate chip cookie dough a denser texture, but I had no idea they worked with bridges too.

I know it will come as no surprise to you that the Charles Bridge is haunted. In 1621, after putting down the anti-Hapsburg revolt, town officials saw fit to mount the leaders' heads on spikes along the bridge as a deterrent to others. The ghosts of the executed men haunt the bridge to this day, singing gruesome songs and frightening passersby. Should you hear them, do *not* jump into the river to escape their terrifying crooning, as a water goblin lurks below, just waiting to devour your soul. Or so I was told.

Did the ghosts sing their terrible songs to me as I crossed the Charles Bridge? If they did, their voices were drowned out by the din of thousands of tourists exclaiming over the souvenirs sold by street vendors and shrieking with laughter as they snapped photos of one another in front of the baroque sculpture showing prisoners being tortured in a dungeon. The ghoulish images didn't seem to dampen anyone's spirits, nor did the weather, although it was trying; the sky was low and gray and inclined to sudden fits of drizzling and gusts of wind. It was August but felt like November, and as I struggled to keep my umbrella from turning inside out, I muttered to Rich, "Wouldn't you love to see what this city is like in summer? Oh, that's right, this *is* summer."

When it began to rain in earnest, we checked our map to see what was close to the bridge and decided to take refuge in the nearby Franz Kafka Museum.

To get to the museum, you must first pass by one of Prague's more remarkable works of art, affectionately titled "Piss." It's a sculpture showing two naked bronze men peeing into a fountain shaped like the Czech Republic, spelling out famous Czech literary quotes with their "urine." (No, I am not making this up!) I later read that you can text a number to have them write messages for you in the fountain. If only I'd known! I could have videotaped them writing the title of my book and posted it on YouTube. Another great marketing opportunity missed.

Sadly, the museum experience was all downhill from there. Kafka, as you may recall from high school or college reading assignments, was the author of *The Metamorphosis*, a novella generally referred to as "the one about the guy who turned into a giant cockroach." Like so many works of fiction, it was, at heart, autobiographical; Kafka felt he was different from others and feared that people would find him physically and mentally repugnant. Biographers tend to use words like "isolated," "anguished," and "tortured" to describe his personality.

He would no doubt be astounded to discover that today he is much admired as Prague's favorite literary son. His name appears everywhere, on tote bags, postcards, posters, T-shirts, and ads for his museum. Before heading over there, I perused Lonely Planet's review of the museum, which concluded, "Does it vividly portray the claustrophobic bureaucracy and atmosphere of brooding menace that characterized Kafka's world? Or is it a load of pretentious bollocks? You decide."

It didn't take us long to cast our vote. We suffered through a ridiculously convoluted ticket purchasing procedure (claustrophobic bureaucracy!), viewed the handful of photos and letters surrounded by an excessive amount of black space (brooding menace!), and saw a grainy black-and-white film of old Prague, artfully distorted with a ripple effect (existential angst!). Additional angst was provided by the fact that we spent the equivalent of fifteen dollars for the fifteen minutes it took to tour the exhibits. We could hardly wait to get back outside into the pouring rain.

Coincidentally, a load of pretentious bollocks was precisely what we *didn't* find at Prague's Museum of Communism, an institution that deals soberly with an important subject without ever taking itself too seriously. One of its early promotional activities was to send out two large, sinister-looking men to follow tourists through the city streets, lurking, spying, and acting like secret service agents. When the tourists noticed them, usually with a start of surprise bordering on terror, the two men would then present a flier that read, "Experience How Life Was Under Communism." Everyone would laugh, and they'd all stand around talking about the museum's theme: "Communism: the Dream, the Reality, the Nightmare." It was a great, tongue-in-cheek marketing concept handled with originality and flair.

"Lenin," as the museum's website remarks, "must be turning in his grave."

The Museum of Communism isn't sleek or glossy or upmarket; it doesn't strive for extravagant artistry or use special effects to make sure you understand that this is deep stuff. The story is told simply, in a rabbit warren of rooms crammed with artifacts and photos, and the overall effect was, at least for me, stunning. Until that day, I had never fully appreciated the one-two punch that the twentieth century had delivered to the Czech people (and others in the region). As a prelude, there was the Great Depression and the rise of communism, whose theory — a more egalitarian approach to distributing the world's wealth — must have seemed like a good idea to many at the time. Then came the first big hit: occupation by the Nazis. Their goal here was "Germanization" of the population, and those who didn't fit the Aryan mold — Jews, intellectuals, people with college educations and a conscience — were carted off to concentration camps or killed. Then at the end of the war, when all over Europe people were celebrating their newfound freedom, Czechoslovakia got the short end of the stick *again*.

"The Americans were just two hours away," a man from Prague told me. He shook his head. He was too young to remember the day himself, but it was clear the memory had been passed down through the generations. "*Two hours*. We wanted to surrender to them. But we were told no, it had been agreed that the Russians would liberate us. It took days more for them to reach us. And after that . . ." He shrugged. Liberation soon turned to occupation and led to forty-four years of repression, indoctrination, and starvation.

Then came the Velvet Revolution. I had only the haziest memories of reading some headlines about it at the time; I was busy with my career as a journalist in Cleveland, and my thoughts were fully occupied with my own headlines and deadlines. But now I began to appreciate how sudden and almost miraculously swift and sweeping the changes were, ignited by a student demonstration just a few blocks from the Museum of Communism, in Prague's Wenceslas Square.

It happened on November 17, 1989, International Students' Day, when fifteen thousand kids showed up for a peaceful demonstration and the government troops got nervous. The authorities decided things were going to get out of hand unless they did something, so naturally they instructed the police to do the one thing guaranteed to really inflame the situation: raise their clubs and began advancing toward the crowd. And the kids stood their ground. The museum showed a short video that was taken that day, and I found it harrowing to watch those young Czechs face down the club-swinging riot troops advancing toward them. I was awed by the sheer courage it must have taken for those students to risk everything — their bodies, their freedom, their lives — to hold their ground.

My mind went to that famous line of Ralph Waldo Emerson's about America's own fight for freedom: "Here once the embattled farmers stood, and fired the shot heard round the world." Of course, the Czech students weren't firing any shots; they had assembled peacefully, armed with nothing but the sheer mass of their bodies. Eventually they were forced to break ranks and run, but they kept reforming that day and over the next several days, their ranks swelling to two hundred thousand, then half a million as protesters of all ages joined in. The tipping point was reached, and change happened with shocking speed; within days the government leaders had resigned, within weeks communist rule ended, and within a month a new, freely elected president was in office.

Thinking about the demonstrators in Wenceslas Square, it occurred to me that while I've spoken out for various causes over the years, I've rarely risked very much to do it. As a student at the University of California at Berkeley, I joined in the antiwar protests, which did turn ugly; one man was killed and an artist blinded. But the worst I ever suffered was the temporary discomfort of being tear gassed. Since then, in speaking up for my beliefs, I've never again risked even that much — a little social ridicule maybe; once, the loss of a client. I wondered what choices I would have made if I'd been in Wenceslas Square on November 17, 1989, as a young student — or as a sexagenarian, for that matter. In your twenties, it's easier to believe yourself invulnerable; in your sixties, you have a much keener appreciation of what happens, especially to older bones, if a police club lands on your hip, shoulder, or head. I felt a deep, abiding respect for the older women I saw in the museum's film, who came out to stand beside the students and stepped forward instead of back.

When we left the museum, Rich and I decided to walk the few blocks to the place where the Velvet Revolution started. It turned out that Wenceslas Square wasn't really a square at all, but a wide, tree-lined boulevard nearly half a mile long. A single glance was enough to show me that this was one public space that had moved with the times, embracing capitalism with tremendous enthusiasm, if not always high standards of good taste. By day it was home to department stores, hotels, apartment buildings, fast-food eateries, and strip clubs; at night it was a favorite haunt of prostitutes and stag parties.

At the moment, in the first bright sunlight we'd seen in days, a mediocre Christian rock band was playing, largely ignored by the hundreds of young people hanging about, most of them sporting shock-your-parents tattoos, outlandish hair styles, and grunge clothing. Mothers pushed prams, businesspeople hurried by with briefcases, old people sat enjoying the sun (and possibly the music, although I strongly doubt it). I wondered whether any of the older Czechs I saw had been here in 1989 and how they viewed the new world that so many had risked so much to bring about.

I have read that some Czechs are disappointed that the revolution failed to transform their lives as completely as they had hoped; occasionally they even wax nostalgic for the communist era. Vaclav Havel, who led the Velvet Revolution, compares that viewpoint to the attitude of those recently released from prison. "In prison everything is laid out for you; you don't have to decide on anything. They tell you when to get up, what to wear, everything is decided for you by others. If you live in this for years and are then suddenly released, freedom becomes a burden." Of course, many Czechs had no such regrets and were only too eager to embrace their newfound liberty. Mirek Kodym, a dissident poet who marched on that fateful day in 1989, recently told the *New York Times*, "Today you can be what you want to be and do what you want to do, and no one will interfere. The nostalgia for the past is a stupid thing."

In the Czech Republic, the past, in one form or another, is always with you. Nearby, at the southeast end of the square, stood a life-sized bronze statue of the man for whom the place is named: Wenceslas I, Duke of Bohemia, shown astride a horse, a war banner fluttering in his hand. As ruler of Bohemia in the tenth century, he was immensely popular with just about everyone except his brother, Boleslav the Cruel, who engineered the duke's assassination when Wenceslas was just twenty-eight years old. After his death, Wenceslas's popularity continued to grow, and he was declared a king, canonized as a martyr, and eventually immortalized as the subject of the famous nineteenth-century Christmas carol.

But his work isn't over yet. According to local legend, at the hour of the nation's greatest peril, the statue of Wenceslas will come to life and raise the army of knights that has been sleeping for centuries inside nearby Blaník Mountain. Wenceslas will then lead the knights across the Charles Bridge, and when his horse stumbles on a stone, underneath that stone he'll find the legendary sword of Bruncvík. With the sword and the army of knights, Wenceslas will slay all enemies and bring peace and prosperity to the land.

Now I know what you're thinking: if the one-two punch of the Nazi and communist occupations wasn't peril enough to reanimate the good king, what fresh hell *would* trigger his return? Space invaders? The zombie apocalypse? Land sharks? Whatever it is, I'm pretty sure I don't want to be around when it happens.

After paying our respects to King Wenceslas, Rich and I started walking back to our bohemian attic apartment, discussing our departure on the morrow. "You know what we need?" Rich said suddenly, ducking into a small liquor store we were passing. "A little vitamin G."

Rich has long considered a small flask of vitamin G — or, as the rest of the civilized world calls it, gin — essential for warding off foreign germs and boosting our spirits in trying times. Not that we were facing perils of a wake-King-Wenceslas level, but we'd booked tickets for the following night's sleeper train to Kraków, which had a pretty dubious reputation.

"My friend and I got robbed on the Prague-Kraków overnight train some 5 years ago," someone identified as Gwan had posted on a travel website, "and I've since heard it's quite notorious for theft." It seems a strange woman showed up at their compartment, unable to speak English, French, Czech, or Russian, but somehow managing to convey that she'd like to sleep in there with them. The woman "waited for us to fall asleep and then went through our stuff before disappearing. Luckily enough, she only got the equivalent of £20 and no cards or electronics or whatever, but it was really creepy to think that she managed to get my wallet out of my bag which I was sleeping on without waking either of us . . . Anyway, 'civilized and safe' wouldn't be my way of describing this particular experience, but if you do have a first-class lockable compartment to yourself I don't see why it shouldn't be fine."

We *had* booked a first-class, lockable compartment, paying a ninety-dollar supplement to our Eurail pass for the privilege. We would leave Prague around half past ten that night and — barring any fatal encounters with cutthroats or other uncivilized elements — roll into Kraków, Poland, the next morning shortly before six thirty.

On the afternoon of our departure, Rich and I spent several pleasant hours in the flat just below ours, chatting with our landlady, Eva. She spoke much better English than her husband, and after handing around small, exquisite glasses filled with vermouth, she began talking about her life. It had recently undergone a radical change when she had given birth to a pair of beloved but, I gathered, unplanned twins.

"My life, my old life, is becoming impossible to continue. This house has been in my family for a long time; it has been home to many generations, but now, with the twins, it is becoming too much for me. It takes too much time. My husband helps as he can, but . . ." She shrugged philosophically.

"What would you like to do?" I asked.

Her face lit up. "I would like to write. Poetry, yes, but I am thinking perhaps a blog like you. How do you do it?"

We talked for a while about the technical side and about some of the free, reasonably simple, and intuitive software that's available for writers these days.

"What would you like to blog about?" I asked.

"Myself, I suppose," she said. "What I am thinking and feeling."

The honesty! Most Americans would shy away from stating it so plainly. I'd never describe my own blog that way, but if it came right down to it . . . wasn't that pretty much what I was writing about too?

Some months later, Eva sent me her first blog post, "A Base Camp of Writing." In it she likened the process of launching a blog to climbing Mount Everest. Having read several books on procrastination in order to put off the actual writing, she said, now she had finally come to the point where she was *almost* ready to begin.

"It felt," she wrote, "like sitting in Mt. Everest base camp, preferably in a comfortable armchair, with a soft light of an antique standing lamp, legs stretched out on another small armchair, something nice to drink and eat (and plenty of it) at hand, a new notebook and a pencil (a pen might freeze out there) ready, with an apt motto on the page No. 3 (I never start a new notebook on page 1, because it would have to be perfect to aim at being on the page 1, and perfect is just a step distant, ahead or just round the corner or waiting at one of tomorrow's moments), reading a guide on climbing Mt. Everest (Easy and Fast)."

It was the only article she ever posted on her blog. But it was, in its own way, quite perfect, capturing that sense of anticipation we all feel on the brink of a new endeavor, sitting in a safe and cozy place, gathering strength before lacing our boots and taking the first step on a climb of 29,000 feet.

The afternoon with our hostess ended on a more down-to-earth note as we discussed when and how we should leave for the station, and Eva called for a cab to come pick us up in a few hours.

The taxi pulled up right to the door — none of this nonsense about refusing to pass the police checkpoint — and dropped us at the station, all for just 180 kroner, about nine dollars. And to think that when we'd arrived in Prague we'd paid 300 kroner to take a taxi from the station to the police checkpoint and had counted ourselves lucky not to be gouged for the full 660! From that point on, Rich routinely asked our hosts about the appropriate fare from the main train station, thereby saving us a not inconsiderable sum and avoiding the annoying sensation of being ripped off.

Arriving at the Prague train station in the late evening, I discovered that it had taken on the atmosphere of Edward Hopper's painting *Nighthawks*; everyone looked isolated, surreal, and not quite like themselves. The last of the station shops and cafés were closing, and passengers were killing time in a dimly lit central area with a cluster of metal benches. Most were students or backpackers, although there were a few businessmen with shabby coats and briefcases, and one tall, slender, blonde woman in her twenties wearing a floor-length, flaming-red evening gown. She looked Russian or Ukrainian and paced back and forth in heels so high it made my feet hurt just to look at them.

I idled away the time trying to imagine the scenario that had brought her to the station at that hour of the night. Was she on her way to a late tryst, possibly in a professional capacity? Heading home alone after a lover's quarrel? Just released from some sinister police stronghold, where she'd been enmeshed in claustrophobic bureaucracy and questioned by large, trench-coated men with an air of brooding menace?

As the hour of ten thirty approached, Rich and I made our way to the appropriate platform and found our train car. We passed a large, boisterous Chinese family settling into their compartment and then located our own. It was smaller than the powder room in our California cottage, containing two modest bunks and a sliver of floor space that was barely large enough for our small bags. I was pleasantly surprised to discover that the bunks were made up with crisp, white, reasonably clean linens, with a pillow and folded blanket placed on top.

I went down the hall to check out the bathroom, always the Achilles' heel of train travel. A middle-aged American man was just emerging, looking pale and shaken. "It's not . . . It's a bit . . . I guess you can't expect . . ." He stumbled off, dabbing at the sweat on his brow. Fearing the worst, I opened the bathroom door.

Actually, by railway standards, it wasn't all *that* bad. There was nothing too grisly to see — beyond, of course, the usual peeling paint and grubby fixtures. And unlike some bathrooms I shudder to recall, it didn't give the impression that deadly diseases were lurking on every surface, waiting to jump into my bloodstream and give me cholera, typhoid, and worse. No, the only really revolting thing about this particular bathroom was the smell. It emanated from the simple, mechanical, water-free toilet, which featured a foot pedal that released the bowl's stopper to deposit the contents efficiently onto the tracks below. Unfortunately, some genius had fashioned the stopper from some sort of rubberized plastic that did a masterful job of retaining all possible odors for the longest possible time. The trip hadn't even started yet, and the effluvium was already at epic proportions.

It was going to be a long night's journey to Kraków. I went back to our compartment and said to Rich, "So about that vitamin G . . ."

CHAPTER 9

Here There Be Dragons

"And after dinner, of course," said one of our new Kraków friends, "vodka and pickles."

At that point in the evening, I felt nothing could shock me. Earlier I'd been staggered to observe people casually drinking liters of beer through large plastic straws. When I asked a local woman about it, she laughed and said, "Oh, that's not beer." I was so relieved; call me old-fashioned, but somehow sipping beer through a straw seemed to be flying in the face of nature. "No," she continued, "That's beer with ginger flavor added to it."

I was still reeling from that appalling revelation when a round of tiny vodka glasses appeared on the table along with enormous green pickles. "You eat them after drinking the vodka," someone explained. "It helps keep you hydrated." Oh, well, if it's good for my health . . . *Na zdrowie!*

By now Rich and I had been on our nomadic railway adventure for nearly a month, and I was still constantly gobsmacked by how much I had yet to learn about the world. So far we'd traveled through Spain, Italy, Germany, Austria, and the Czech Republic, and we were now in Poland. Arriving at the Kraków railway station, Rich marked the city as a waystation on his Track My Tour app and wrote to the friends monitoring our progress, "Now we are heading *out there*."

I had long nurtured hopes of arriving at places that were the cultural equivalent of the spaces on the old maps marked, "Here there be dragons." But it had never occurred to me that there might *literally* be dragons. Which just shows you how much I didn't know.

Kraków's dragon was called Smok Wawelski, and he lived a long time ago in a cave under Wawel Hill (now the site of Wawel Castle) at the edge of the Vistula River. Like all dragons, Smok lived for the pleasure of ravaging crops, livestock, and maidens. When all the local knights had died attempting to slay the beast, a poor but crafty cobbler's apprentice named Skuba came up with a clever plan. He filled a lamb's carcass with sulfur and laid it temptingly in front of the dragon's cave. Smok gobbled it up and was seized with such a monstrous thirst that he ran down to the Vistula River and drank without ceasing until he exploded. Problem solved!

And I know every word of this is true because I have seen Smok's bones, mounted at the entrance to Wawel Cathedral in the castle complex. Naturally, there aren't many bones left after the big explosion, and as Tomak, our guide on the free walking tour, was telling us about them, Rich stood in the back of the crowd, craning his neck in an effort to see them high overhead in the shadows. Finally he leaned over and whispered, "Where are the bones?" Unfortunately, he whispered this into the ear of a strange woman with my hair color who happened to be standing next to him at the time. A few awkward moments of confusion and consternation ensued until the woman's male companion, evidently deciding Rich was a harmless lunatic, pointed to the rafters and said, "Up there."

Chained high on the wall just below the roof beams were three bones of gargantuan size, one long and curved like a rib and two that looked like massive joints. Now, I know you'll find this hard to credit, but some naysayers have seen fit to question the authenticity of these bones, suggesting they might be from a blue whale, a rhinoceros, and/or a wooly mammoth rather than an actual dragon. However, the chances of those bones being taken down and subjected to scientific scrutiny are precisely zilch because according to legend, so long as they remain in place, Kraków is safe from destruction. Are they working? You bet.

Otherwise, how would you account for the fact that during World War II, when just about every other major city in Poland was bombed to rubble, Kraków survived more or less intact?

Well, there *was* one other possible explanation for the city's survival: the Wawel Chakra Stone. If you're a little hazy on the whole chakra thing, they're sites of highly concentrated physical and spiritual energy as defined by ancient Hindu tradition and popularized today by yoga teachers and New Age gurus. The human body has seven, from the first or root chakra at the base of the spine to the thousand-petaled lotus of enlightenment at the seventh chakra atop the head.

The earth is said to have seven chakras as well, marked by stones that radiate enormous energy and transformative power. One of these stones was (I was informed by our guide) set inside a wall in Wawel Castle, where it's believed to be busy absorbing negative energy, cleansing the aura of the earth, and reanimating the seventh chakra of those who come into contact with that wall. Ever since word began to circulate about the Wawel Chakra Stone in the thirties, foreigners have been coming to lean against that particular piece of wall to recharge their spiritual batteries and give their seventh chakra a bit more zing.

"Want to try it?" asked Tomak.

He had to ask? I placed my palms against the place he indicated and leaned in. Nothing whatsoever happened.

Or did it?

For all I know, my spiritual batteries are fully topped up, all thousand petals of my lotus are open, and my seventh chakra is doing a happy dance — but all in ways too subtle for me to notice. Or maybe, as some say, the stone's real power is protective, and that accounts for the fact that — spoiler alert! — Rich and I both made it through the trip alive. There are those who believe that Kraków has been protected by the Chakra Stone since time immemorial. As for who protects the Chakra Stone, the most ancient guardians of places of power were dragons, and we all know that Kraków had one of those.

Tomak managed to impart all this and volumes more, in a rapid-fire delivery that suggested he'd recently ingested so much Red Bull that he was in danger of exploding like Smok the dragon. He zipped us around the city at a brisk trot, pointing out, POIs great and small.

"This used to be called Boner Palace," he said, stopping in front of a luxury hotel on Kraków's Main Market Square. "But then, after communism, when English-speaking tourists started arriving, they made fun of the name." Go figure! "The bachelor parties were the worst; they'd go out and get drunk, then show up in the middle of the night, howling with laughter and making jokes at the hotel's expense. Bachelorette parties, too. Finally the management changed the name to the Bonerowski Palace." A step in the right direction, but I gather that some youthful tourists still find cause for merriment in the new moniker. The little scamps.

Tomak continued moving our group onward at lightning speed. "This was the first McDonald's in Kraków," he said, stopping in front of a venerable old building with the all-too-familiar golden arches emblazoned on its windows. "When it opened in 1992, forty-five thousand people came to look on the first day, and more than thirteen thousand people, all dressed in their best clothes, lined up for hours to get in."

We all gazed at the McDonald's, which now held a scattering of locals and tourists placidly sipping Cokes and eating french fries. "They're a little more used to it now," he added, rather unnecessarily.

At the end of the tour, Tomak handed us all maps of the city that contained suggestions for further exploration plus a few Polish phrases he and his colleagues thought we might find useful during our stay. Along with the usual greetings and thanks, they had seen fit to include *Dwa szoty czystej wódki, proszę* (Two shots of pure vodka please), *Masz zgrabne pośladki* (You have shapely buttocks), *Proszę daj mi PIN kod do Twojego serca* (Please give me the PIN code to your heart), and the local toast, *Na zdrowie*. It was pretty clear how they thought we'd be spending our time.

While our social life didn't call for any of those particular phrases, Rich and I did make friends in Kraków and went out with them to enjoy some of the city's nightlife. I'm often asked how I meet people when traveling, and I'm going to let you in on my trade secrets. First, of course, is being open to chance encounters and friendly overtures. And here, naturally, you'll want to use your common sense; I wouldn't recommend going to a stranger's apartment to look at his collection of KGB memorabilia or her tattoos of Hitler's greatest moments. I contacted some people in advance; as I mentioned earlier, I correspond with people all over the world, and several kindly put me in touch with friends, relatives, or colleagues who were open to meeting us for coffee or a meal. You'll be hearing more about some of them later. And finally, there's InterNations.

InterNations is a global social network whose simple yet noble aim is to arrange opportunities for expats to gather at a local café to make new friends and pass an agreeable evening chatting over drinks. While some members have been known to pursue romantic or business interests at such gatherings, for most of us it's just about getting to know our fellow expats and such locals who have joined to practice their English, which is nearly always the common language on these occasions. Rich and I had often talked about attending an InterNations gathering in other cities, but this was the first time one of the get-togethers had coincided with our itinerary. We were very curious to discover how the Kraków group compared to Seville's chapter.

As is so often the case with InterNations, all we had to do was walk up to the first cluster of people we saw and say, "Hi, we're new in town, visiting from the Seville chapter . . ." And everyone jumped in to offer advice on where to go and what to do during our stay.

Rich and I spent a convivial evening talking to fellow Americans and local Krakówians, who confirmed that we were staying in the coolest part of town, recommended several bars in our neighborhood, nodded soberly when we mentioned that we would be visiting the concentration camp at Auschwitz, and suggested we also consider several more agreeable points of interest, such as the Wieliczka Salt Mine just fifteen minutes outside of town.

When I asked a young American psychologist named Christopher how he came to live in Poland, he explained that he was married to a Polish woman, and after the couple had lived for a year in the United States, she missed her native land and had persuaded him to return with her to make their home in Kraków.

"I'm setting up a practice here now," he said.

"How's that working out?" I asked, my mind a trifle boggled at the prospect of launching such a language-based business in a foreign culture.

He shrugged and smiled. "There are a lot of challenges. I'm taking classes in Polish and getting to know the community. But I think it will be great. I really love living here. Right now, Kraków is a city with a *lot* of opportunity."

And then the conversation flowed on to something else, and soon somebody was teaching me how to pronounce the local toast, *na zdrowie*. (It's nah STROvia. Who could have guessed?) Rich and I left the gathering late that evening, having exchanged Internet addresses and promises to meet up two days later for dinner with Christopher, his wife, and a few of the others.

Walking home that night to our rental apartment though the dark, quiet streets, I was struck by the fact that here we were in a strange city, pretty far *out there* by most standards, yet passing what was, for us, a pretty typical evening and feeling quite comfortable and safe.

"I could live in this city," Rich remarked.

"Me too," I said. And then, after a short pause for reflection, I amended, "Except, of course, for the winter."

I freely admit that I am no fan of abominable weather. Having braved thirty bone-chilling winters in Ohio and Massachusetts, I now spend the colder months in the more civilized climates of southern Spain and northern California. I no longer own a down parka, a fleece-lined red plaid hat with earflaps, or an ice scraper. But even the hardiest soul might hesitate before wintering in Kraków.

As Holiday-Weather.com put it, "Winters in Kraków are long, harsh and dark. The city averages a dreary 90 minutes of sunlight per day in the height of winter, and the temperature stays at or below freezing for much of November to February." Egad! That's worse than our old neighborhood in Cleveland's snow belt! After providing further unnerving details, such as October's average of thirteen inches of snow, the site attempted to end on a cheerier note. "You may feel that the snowfall and cold simply heightens the medieval, Gothic and mysterious experience of the city." Then again, you may just find it wretched and depressing, as the author of this article clearly did.

During our visit, as August gave way to September, we were lucky enough to have mild temperatures and unlucky enough to catch the tail end of the summer's rainy season. As the ever-upbeat Holiday-Weather. com noted, "The summer months are Kraków's wettest months . . . It is difficult to imagine but a Kraków summer can sometimes be wetter than a London winter!"

Even on the soggiest days, I loved Kraków and especially our neighborhood, the old Jewish quarter known as Kazimierz, where Polish Jews had lived and worked since the thirteenth century. Of course, all that ended in September of 1939 when the Nazis marched into town. If you remember your high school history or *Schindler's List*, which is set in Kraków and mostly shot in Kazimierz, you have a pretty good idea of what happened next. After the war, the few Jews remaining in the city when it was "liberated" by the Russians soon discovered that life wasn't much better under communism, and most of them sensibly took off for Israel or the United States. Kazimierz became a ghost town.

Then communism fell, Steven Spielberg showed up to film *Schindler's List*, and Kazimierz was once more on the map, attracting tourists, and then hip, young Krakówians seeking affordable housing with character; eventually Jews who'd moved abroad began returning to the old neighborhood. We found it to be a thriving, bohemian scene filled with wonderfully atmospheric bars: dark, candlelit dens with tables made from antique sewing machines and old cobbler's benches, where the current crop of ubercool young people lounged about in carefully casual postures, all dressed in black, sporting tattoos, and smoking cigarettes to show what nonconformists they were. Jewish-themed tours were very popular, and open-sided trams trundled by at frequent intervals, heading to the Jewish cemetery and Schindler's Factory Museum.

Rich and I were staying in a roomy, two-story apartment above a shop serving late-night pierogi, delicious little dumplings you could order stuffed with an impressive range of fillings such as sauerkraut, cheese, or cherries. Around the corner was Plac Nowy, the plaza where all of Kraków came to buy the city's trademark street food, *zapiekanka*, huge, open-faced, toasted baguettes smothered with mushrooms, cheese, sliced sausage, mustard, and whatever else you desired. Eager customers lined up day and night to down these massive foot-long, eight-inch-wide treats; once we saw a bride in full regalia and her new husband, each chowing down on one, huge grins on their faces.

Rich and I managed to resist the lure of the *zapiekanka* stands, since we were following our plan to eat fairly modestly. In our month on the road, we'd developed two key strategies for keeping our mental and physical equilibrium: eating as sensibly as possible (while sampling local fare on occasion) and spending many evenings quietly "at home" wherever we were staying, usually with our feet up watching movies on the computer. You'd be amazed by what's available on YouTube, including films and entire TV series. After a long day of looking at dragon bones, rebooting our seventh chakras, and keeping up with the frantic pace set by Tomak, our tour guide, we were ready for an evening spent matching wits with a bumbling yet brilliant detective and nibbling on a picnic of cheese, smoked salmon, bread, and fresh fruit purchased from the stalls in Plac Nowy.

The next day I had one of those moments which occur during any long journey; I looked in the mirror and faced the fact that my hair was overdue for professional attention. We've all been there. Perhaps a *soupçon* of gray is showing where it shouldn't, your faux hawk is beginning to flop, your bob is becoming a blob, or your undercut is growing out over your ears. Finding a decent hair stylist to remedy matters is never easy, and it's even more complicated when you don't speak a word of the language and can't read any of the signs.

Over the years I've taken leaps of faith in many foreign hairdressing establishments, nearly always with acceptable to excellent results. Of course, I begin by lowering my expectations; if both sides of my simple bob are more or less even and my bangs are out of my eyes, I rejoice. I usually seek out a small neighborhood place where the departing clients look decently groomed and the stylists don't exhibit terrifying extremes of trendiness. And I've learned the hard way to insist that the stylist be sober.

A friend in the Republic of Georgia once took me to her hairdresser, said to be the best in Tbilisi, the capital city. When we arrived to find him drunk, she explained that he was never sober, but that didn't affect his ability to cut hair. True, but his judgment and ability to listen were impaired, and in the blink of an eye I had something akin to a military buzz cut in a country where shoulder-length hair was in vogue. I hated that cut, although I have to admit it was easy to maintain.

When the time came for me to seek a hair salon in Kraków, I happened to pass a likely looking neighborhood *fryzjerski* and stopped in. When it became clear that no one spoke a word of English, I switched to pantomime. In these situations, you don't need to be Marcel Marceau to convey what you want; they already know you're there to talk about hair, not the future of the euro or how they created the special effects in *World War Z*. I made little snipping motions indicating that I wanted to trim half an inch off the length and then pointed to my gray roots. The *fryzjer* nodded, got right to work, and did a lovely job. Okay, the brown was a half-shade darker than ideal and the bangs a trifle shorter, but the look was smart and stylish, the price was definitely right, and we parted with mutual smiles and nods of gratitude and appreciation.

The next day, feeling rested, refreshed, and distinctly better groomed, I set out with Rich to visit the new Schindler's Factory Museum. Somehow we had failed to do much research on this POI and walked over there expecting to see a big, half-derelict factory with a little shrine to Oskar Schindler. I thought there might be a brief description of how he saved twelve hundred Jews from the death camps by employing them in his factory, a display including a few pieces of the enamelware produced there, and some movie memorabilia, such as photos of Liam Neeson. We'd have a feel-good moment celebrating one man's famous good deeds — fifteen minutes in and out, tops — and then we'd find some-place fun for lunch.

Instead, the museum turned out to be one of the most heartbreaking places I have ever visited, and we were there for hours. Like Prague's Communist Museum, it didn't use a lot of fancy exhibition techniques; there were no holograms, computer simulations, or docents dressed in period costumes. There was just a warren of rooms now filled with photos, artifacts, and film clips. And the story I thought I already knew sprang into a new, sharp, and hideous focus.

You probably know, at least in general, what happened in Poland's ghettoes during World War II. It wasn't pretty, and if you want to skip the next few paragraphs and go on to lighter commentary, I won't blame you a bit.

Still with me? Okay.

The first exhibits I saw in Schindler's Factory Museum were rather charming black-and-white photos of the old Jewish quarter, Kazimi-erz. People in clothing from the thirties walked along the now-familiar streets, buying fruit in the open air market in Plac Nowy, passing by cafés where we'd recently stopped for coffee or beer.

Then came photos of the Nazis, sitting at folding tables, giving or-ders for people to report to work at labor camps and factories, including Oskar Schindler's. As moviegoers around the world now know, Schin-dler was a German soldier and spy, a member of the Nazi party, and a war profiteer. What made him different from the other factory owners is that, from the very beginning, he saw the practical value in treating his laborers as employees rather than slaves.

The museum showed a black-and-white film of one of Schindler's workers, now an old man, talking about the food. "Most people, they gave coffee and a piece of bread, that's all you had to work all day. But at the factory, we had *soup*." And just the way his mouth formed that word, you could almost taste it: the thin broth, the beans and vegetables, maybe a tiny bit of sausage. The taste of survival.

Most of the city's Jews, some fifty-five thousand of them, were sent to live in scattered rural areas, and those who remained were corralled in an old, run-down neighborhood across the river. There were fifteen thousand people crowded into housing meant for thirty-five hundred; the lucky ones were sleeping four families to an apartment, while others overflowed into the streets. They were sealed in, with windows overlooking the "Aryan" side bricked up, and high walls enclosing the entire ghetto.

"They built the walls to look like *tombstones*," one woman recalled in a film clip. "They knew how *that* would make us feel."

Each stage was so stunningly awful that it was hard to imagine things getting worse. But of course they did.

The Nazis, figuring that smart people tend to be troublemakers and strategists, rounded up the intellectuals early on. I watched a clip from an old movie that recreated the scene: a bunch of fussy, bespectacled old university dons, arguing and bickering about fine points of scholarship as they headed to what they had been told was a special meeting on campus, only to find themselves surrounded by the SS and informed that the honor of their presence was requested at Auschwitz.

Then Himmler gave the order to exterminate all of the Jews in occupied Poland. At first, to avoid sparking an outright rebellion, the Nazis announced a "resettlement program," and eleven thousand people were herded from the Kraków ghetto into boxcars and sent to extermination camps; those who worked at German-owned factories such as Schindler's were exempt.

Later came the final "liquidation," with orders that no one be spared. On the first day, all the able-bodied laborers were rounded up, ostensibly for a work project, and transported to the Kraków-Plaszów concentration camp. They didn't go quietly; two thousand people were killed in the streets. Schindler's workers were allowed to stay at the factory during the two-day roundup, and so they were spared; later, when the factory moved, Schindler made his famous list of the twelve hundred "skilled" workers he needed, saving their lives again. On the second day of the liquidation, all those who remained in the ghetto — women and children, those too old or infirm to work — were sent to Auschwitz and its satellite concentration camps, the largest of which was Birkenau.

The next day, Rich and I went there too.

I just can't bring myself to write a detailed description of our tour of Auschwitz and Birkenau. In some ways it was much like our visit to Dachau, although the tone was very different. In Dachau, built by Germans to imprison Germans, the rhetoric was sober, respectful, and restrained. "Forty-one thousand five hundred people lost their lives here." In Poland, the sense of outrage flickered under every statement. "More than one million people were *murdered* here."

You can probably picture Auschwitz for yourself. The tidy rows of two-story wooden houses, where the Germans ate, slept, worked, and conducted their administrative tasks, interrogations, and medical experiments. The low, grim barracks where the prisoners were housed. The barbed wire fences, where those who couldn't go on flung themselves in the sure hope of being shot. The photos Dr. Mengele took of his unspeakable experiments on women and twins. The huge piles of hair, "harvested" from corpses to use as pillow stuffing. The vast room full of shoes taken from new arrivals, some so small they had to be from toddlers.

I stood for a while looking at the thin, striped pajamas issued to inmates and thought about the long, harsh, dark winters with ninety minutes of sunlight and temperatures that stayed below freezing for months. The thirteen inches of snow in October. I didn't think I could get through a Kraków winter with a down parka, snow boots, and a well-heated apartment. How anyone in the camps survived, let alone remained sane, was a mystery to me.

But for me, the most devastating moment was standing in Birkenau, looking at the foundations that were all that was left of the barracks that had once held people awaiting execution in the gas chambers. The foundations went on and on and on, as far as the eye could see. The scale of it was absolutely staggering. This was true genocide, the systematic effort to exterminate part of the human race.

Months earlier, at an InterNations gathering in Seville, I had talked about Auschwitz with a young woman from Kraków. "You know," Aleksandra had said, "people always talk about these things being done to the Jews. Those people were *Poles*." And she managed to pack a lot of outrage into that last word. These were her people. Standing at Birkenau, I felt the same way. People talk about these things being done to Jews, or Poles, or Gypsies, or gays, but the point is, they were done to human beings. *My* people. *Our* people.

On our last night in Kraków, we dined with Christopher, his wife, and others we'd met at InterNations. We chose a Kazimierz café filled with antique carpenters' benches, dressmakers' dummies, and other tools of the old trades that once flourished in the Jewish quarter. Christopher asked about our visit to Auschwitz, and I explained that I was now going to be permanently depressed for the rest of my life, but I was very glad that I'd gone. His wife nodded.

"You need to see it," she said. "I first went to the camp as a child; everyone has to go with their class at school. I've been several times. But now . . ." She shrugged. "I can't keep going back."

I was glad I'd gone, because it's one thing to hear about it and quite another to see it for yourself. I gained a deeper understanding of the dark side of human nature, which I'm hoping will make me wiser, or a little more compassionate, or at least a bit less naive about what people are capable of doing to one another. But as my new friend said, I can't keep going back, even in my own mind. I rarely talk about it, because when I do, I find I'm still so filled with outrage and sorrow that I can't keep my voice from shaking. And friends look at me as if wondering whether they should have the bartender cut me off . . . or bring me something stronger.

After our dinner at the Kazimierz café, someone suggested a night-cap at a bigger, trendier bar nearby, and there our new friends introduced me to the custom of taking pickles with your vodka. When they heard Rich and I would be leaving the next day, someone asked if I thought I'd ever come back to Kraków.

"I'd love to," I said. And I would. But all the same, it hadn't been an easy visit. Here there be dragons indeed.

CHAPTER 10

A Nice Place to Spend Eternity

"Katowice is the butt of jokes throughout Poland," a tourist brochure informed us. That's right, a tourist brochure. Written by public relations professionals hired to attract visitors. Makes you wonder what the city's *detractors* might find to say, doesn't it? However, having lived in rust-belt Cleveland at a time when the city's name was considered a punch line, I felt sympathetic toward the good citizens of Katowice and was fully prepared to cut them some slack.

We had chosen Katowice somewhat arbitrarily, as it stood a convenient train ride away from Kraków along a route that would eventually take us through Slovakia and Hungary to Romania. When we'd mentioned this plan to our new friends during our last night in Kraków, one of them exclaimed incredulously, "Katowice? I'm from Katowice. Why in the world are you going *there*?"

"We wanted to see something off the tourist track," I explained.

"Well, it is that." She shook her head in disbelief. These crazy Americans! "You *do* know that it's all under construction." I vaguely recalled some mention of a construction project on the Internet. But surely they didn't mean the *entire town*. "But that doesn't really matter," she added, "because there's nothing to see there anyway."

"Then I guess it's lucky we're just staying one night," I said. But I was already wondering if we'd made a foolish mistake. As soon as we were alone I asked Rich if we should reconsider. Was it too late to get our money back?

Yes, it was, he informed me, adding soothingly, "I wouldn't worry about it. How bad can it be?"

On first impression, it was very grim indeed. Katowice was a gritty, post-industrial city whose coal and mineral mines, having been exhaustively exploited by the Nazis and the Soviets, had finally been abandoned years earlier. The landscape visible from the train windows was dotted with the monstrous, rusting hulks of derelict factories, looking like film sets for end-of-the-world action movies.

At the big, modern, nearly deserted railway station, I found an information booth and asked the two young men on duty for directions to our hotel, which according to the online booking service was a mere three hundred yards from the station. The tall, skinny one with braces on his teeth started to answer, pointing one way, but the short, stocky one disagreed, gesturing in the opposite direction, and they bickered back and forth, sounding so much like the two wild and crazy guys from the old *Saturday Night Live* routines that Rich and I went into whoops and had to hurry away.

We soon found our hotel, which was so close to the station that I could hear them announcing arrivals and departures from our room. A stroll through downtown Katowice revealed that our Kraków friend had, if anything, understated the case. Nearly every inch of every street had been jackhammered up and removed, right down to the soil. I had to pick my way across gravel, dirt, and the broken remnants of sidewalks to move around the city, which had a few lovely old buildings, some rotting piles of lumber where old wrecks had recently been pulled down, lots of drab, modern architecture, and some modest shops, all closed. There were no open restaurants or bars either, which was rather worrying. Our hotel — as the receptionist had regretfully informed us — no longer served food or beverages of any kind. I need hardly add that there was no minibar in the room.

Rich and I walked around for nearly an hour and were just contemplating the dismal prospect of returning to the train station to see what the fast food snack bar had to offer when we ran across an eatery called, improbable as it seemed, Hurry Curry. With the joy of Stanley beholding Livingston, I took in the cleverly worded menu in Polish and English, the downscale-chic décor, and the lively crowd tucking into large, steaming bowls of curry and rice.

"Someone in this town has visited the larger world," I remarked to Rich, with a sigh of satisfaction.

After our surprisingly delicious meal, we wound up the evening at the only other place that was open, an upstairs café-bar near our hotel. There was a small, convivial crowd sipping tea and flavored beer while gathered around café tables playing board games. The bartender was delighted to pass the time practicing her English by giving us an impromptu lecture on Polish beer.

There were nearly a hundred breweries in Poland, she explained, the most popular being Żywiec, Okocim, and Tyskie. The biggest was Żywiec, founded in the nineteenth century by the Hapsburgs, nationalized by the communists, and recently purchased by Heineken.

"You see the label," the bartender said, gesturing toward a shelf behind her. In the dark bar, I squinted uncertainly at the bottle, which bore a label displaying figures of a man and a woman dressed in colorful folk costumes and capering energetically arm in arm, knee to knee. "The couple is dancing the Krakowiak."

Looking it up later, I learned that the steps of Krakowiak, a folk dance originating (you guessed it) in Kraków, was meant to imitate the prancing of horses; I guess you have to know the actual dance — or drink a substantial amount of Żywiec — to see the resemblance.

The evening reached its zenith when someone set off the fire alarm at the abandoned building across the street, formerly a part of the train station. The Katowice Fire Department showed up in force and ran around the building for ages trying to get in, and their antics kept us all entertained for more than an hour. It was the most exciting thing happening in town that night, and we felt lucky to have a front-row seat for it.

Katowice's gritty streets and lack of commercialism gave the impression of stepping back into the old Soviet days, only with better food and less likelihood of being sent to the Gulag. We were grateful to its citizens for the hospitality they showed us — and more than ready to leave on the first train out in the morning.

Our next stop was Žilina, a small city in Slovakia that was first settled back in the Stone Age, probably around 20,000 BC. Coming from America, where anything dating back to the eighteenth century is considered positively antediluvian, I found this rather impressive.

Back in the day, our fledgling nation was founded by people who arrived from elsewhere, ready to abandon the past and embrace the future. And even now we can't seem to stop moving. Not everyone has lived in nineteen different homes like I have, but I'm hard pressed to think of an American family that isn't scattered across half the continent, if not half the globe. Home is anywhere we hang our hats and set down our passports. The Spanish refer to this as having a *culoinquieto*, literally a restless backside, conjuring images of schoolboys squirming in their chairs, itching to be elsewhere on a fine day. I could scarcely imagine living in a town in which I'd grown up, let alone one my ancestors' ancestors had settled back in the Stone Age.

Disembarking at Žilina, we found a vaulting, nineteenth-century train station whose interior had been renovated into a boxy, utilitarian hall. Stained glass windows executed in the socialist-realist style showed the proletariat gloriously gathering the harvest, herding sheep, and leaping over a fire while holding an axe. This last image, I could only assume, was some ancient local ritual, and I was sorry we wouldn't get a chance to see it enacted during our brief stay.

Apparently the café had been eliminated during the Soviet makeover, so in lieu of our customary arrival coffee, we had to make do with a Coke purchased from a newsstand and drunk while sitting on a bench in the waiting room. Perhaps fortunately, we remained in happy ignorance of the warning which I later read in the "Stay Safe" section of Žilina's Wikitravel page: "The railway station is not the greatest place to 'have' to stop over in for any length of time based on experience. Suggest avoid waiting room, and stay near kiosks. Otherwise, Žilina is fine. Enjoy!"

Apparently the town's criminal element was devoting its talents to some other part of the city that day, because we made it out of the waiting room unharmed and still in possession of all our possessions.

The iPad showed that our bed and breakfast was on the main square, just a short walk away. The drably muscular Soviet architecture near the railway station soon gave way to three-story townhouses from the seventeenth and eighteenth centuries, their simple lines and peaked roofs creating a considerably more inviting atmosphere, especially in the main square.

Finding the square was easy; locating our bed and breakfast, however, proved something of a challenge. There were no street numbers on any of the buildings, and although we circumambulated the square two or three times, we couldn't find a sign bearing the name of our lodgings — or of any hotel, bed and breakfast, or guest house, for that matter.

The complete lack of markings is not an uncommon phenomenon in Central and Eastern Europe. Often house numbers, street names, and signs for public establishments are conspicuous by their absence, as if they were all speakeasies, and you couldn't expect to go there without an insider's invitation and possibly a whispered password. I've developed a theory that during turbulent political times, the citizens of Soviet countries found it prudent to fly as far under the radar as possible to make it more difficult for the secret police to find them. I don't know how well that worked for evading the undercover agents of the Ministry of Public Security, but it did a bang up job of concealing from us the whereabouts of our Žilina bed and breakfast.

Finally, in desperation, we walked into the nearest place that was open, which happened to be a bakery, and Rich showed the young man behind the counter the address we were looking for.

"Yes, is here," he said. Here? Here where? "One moment." He finished putting the decorative foam on a cappuccino, placed it before a waiting customer with the meticulous reverence of a true barista, and disappeared up a back staircase.

A few minutes later our host arrived, a tall, easygoing man who welcomed us in English and by name, inviting us to follow him up two flights of stairs to our room. As I hoisted my bag up the steps (once again grateful that I had packed light) I passed the open door to his apartment, where I saw a floor littered with plastic toys and heard a toddler's wail followed by a woman's soothing murmur.

"My family," our host said with a proud smile.

He ushered us into a suite that would easily sleep twelve; there were half a dozen double beds in two rows, separated down the length of the room by cloth curtains. We also had a large dining area and a lounge with a TV and several big brown sofas. I felt as if we should be sharing the suite with at least two or three other families. I think we were paying about forty-nine dollars for the night.

Assuring him that the apartment would suit us admirably, I asked our host about the town, which he told us was lovely and quite safe. (Evidently he considered the dangers lurking in the train station waiting room too trifling to mention.)

"Are you from Žilina?" I asked. "Were you born here?"

He nodded. "I was born here, raised here, married here, had my children here." He smiled, and added comfortably, "And I will die here."

To me, this was an astonishing statement. The certainty of it! The sense of belonging! I'd never expect to hear a comment like that from an American. In my country, friends who still live in their hometown usually confess that fact with a little shamefaced grin, as if to say, "I know, I'm *so* dull." In Europe it's a mark of success. Kudos to your family if successive generations have been wise, lucky, and stable enough to stay put rather than being forced to decamp by war, financial disaster, or an irate husband. An Egyptian friend once told me (in slightly more tactful terms) that Americans are restless neurotics because we all originated elsewhere and have no deep roots in the land.

For a moment I imagined what my life would have been like if I'd remained in the town where I was born: Palo Alto, California. Back then the town was home to Stanford University and thousands of veterans who had returned a few years earlier from World War II and were busy raising young families and re-starting careers. Today, of course, it's the heart of Silicon Valley, where my older brother has spent most of the last thirty-five years happily living in the same house and helping the high-tech revolution advance a bit more quickly on several key fronts. Would my life have been more satisfying if I'd found a single place that suited me so perfectly that I never wanted to leave it? I doubt it. As important as it is for me to have a home base or two, I have a deep-seated need to explore the larger world. I have too much *culoinquieto* in me to let a single place define my life.

Let alone my afterlife. Talk about planning ahead! Our host in Žilina seemed perfectly comfortable outlining his post-demise plans, some-thing few Americans would mention so directly in casual conversation. We downplay the subject with euphemisms such as the genteel "passing away," or irreverent slang such as "give up the ghost," "bite the dust," or "take a dirt nap." And we *really* dance around any direct reference to our own death. We like to think "departing this world" happens to other people, not us, and we wouldn't want to jinx ourselves by talking about it. I think Groucho Marx spoke for most Americans when he said, "I intend to live forever, or die trying."

Žilina was a nice place to live, and perhaps to spend eternity, but you wouldn't want to visit there, at least not for very long. Rich and I managed to amuse ourselves for what remained of the afternoon by checking out the old buildings and new construction projects around town, and then we turned in early. In the morning, after croissants and cups of excellent cappuccino, we again survived the perils of the railway waiting room and boarded an outbound train to Košice, Slovakia, where we planned a stay of several days.

Košice is known as the cultural and economic epicenter of eastern Slovakia. Some years earlier the region's largest employer, a steel com-pany, had been purchased by an American firm, thus bringing a much-needed infusion of cash into the community. Apparently some of this cash was finding its way into a series of public works designed to attract tourists. Like Genoa, Košice was discovering this to be uphill work. The city was still, as the Wikitravel page summed up so neatly, "a place not often visited from elsewhere."

One of Košice's most ambitious civic projects was the Singing Fountain in the middle of *Hlavná ulica* (Main Street), right in front of the cathedral. It consisted of a large, flat network of pipes, from which water alternately trickled, gushed, or shot thirty feet into the air, in rhythms that were roughly synchronized with piped-in music that ranged from *Ave Maria* to *Feelings*. As if that wasn't enough excitement, after dark it was flooded with pulsing, jewel-toned lights, which changed color in time with the water and the music — a sort of Trevi Fountain meets *Saturday Night Fever*.

At first the Singing Fountain struck me as garish, tasteless, and a total waste of public funds; in fact, I laughed outright when I saw it. But I have to admit that after a while it grew on me. It was kind of soothing to sit on a park bench, watching the water dance and listening to *Yesterday* and *Don't Go Changin'*. Pretty soon Rich and I were making a point of dropping by in the warm evenings after dinner to sit on the park benches beside ice-cream-eating locals, all of us staring, mesmerized, at the flashing spurts of water changing from yellow to orange to red to blue to green, more or less in time with Beethoven's *Fifth Symphony* or the Bee Gees's *More Than a Woman*.

Apparently some outsiders had been won over by Košice's efforts to reinvent itself, as the city had just been named that year's European Co-Capital of Culture, along with Marseille, France. New maps of Košice had been printed, showing such POIs as the late fourteenth-century Tower of St. Urban (honoring the patron saint of wine growers), the Plague Column (commemorating victims of the plague that lasted from 1710 to 1711), and the newly minted bronze sculpture of a shield with six stylized lilies and half an eagle (celebrating the fact that in 1369 Košice became the first European city to be granted its own coat of arms). The long, wide Main Street had been entirely repaved in stone, with the location of the old city walls cunningly picked out in contrasting paving stones so that history buffs could find them. There were plenty of good cafés, a few fairly decent restaurants, and a rambling, quirky museum of local history, culture, and science.

In spite of all this, Košice remained firmly in the tourist industry's no-fly zone. When Rich and I ventured into the downtown tourist information center, the woman at the main desk sadly informed us that there were no free walking tours (due to lack of demand), and there were no paid tours either (due to all of the tour guides being out on strike). Then she brightened and added that her co-worker, Veronica, was apprenticing as an English-speaking guide and would be happy to offer her services at a heavily discounted rate just for the experience. We signed up for a two-and-a-half hour tour the next morning.

Veronica was young, eager, and terrifically well informed; I suspected she'd been up all night memorizing historical tidbits for our entertainment and edification. I learned that Košice wasn't as old as Žilina, dating back a mere twelve thousand years to the end of the Paleolithic era, but it had been a major player on the regional stage since the thirteenth century. Situated at the crossroads between central Hungary's fertile agricultural lands and central Poland's links to far-reaching trade routes, Košice grew rich and became embroiled in an astonishing list of dynastic disputes, insurrections, invasions, and of course both World Wars and Soviet hegemony in the region. City leaders had made the most of prosperous times by investing in architectural projects, and today's Main Street was a charming collection of Gothic, Renaissance, baroque, and Art Nouveau buildings with a bare minimum of modern Soviet monstrosities.

One of my favorite buildings was the vast Gothic cathedral, which happened to be dedicated to my own patron saint, St. Elizabeth of Hungary. At fourteen she was married to Louis IV, Landgrave of Thuringia, and as his queen she devoted herself to feeding the poor and tending to the sick. This naturally brought her under censure from members of the court, who were afraid she'd drain the nation's treasury in order to keep its humblest citizens alive. One day, while taking bread to the destitute, Elizabeth was confronted by suspicious nobles, who demanded to see what she had wrapped up in her cloak. When she opened the folds of her cloak, a shower of roses fell out.

That's her most famous miracle, the one depicted on the little plaque that hung on the wall of my bedroom throughout my childhood. But my favorite of all her miracles was the one where she brought a leper to lie in the bed she shared with her husband. At this, the ladies of the court set up such an outcry that the king came running to investigate. When he flung back the bedclothes, King Louis supposedly saw not a leper but Christ himself lying in the bed. And meaning no disrespect, I have to say that any wife who can convince her husband that the strange man lying in their bed is actually Jesus . . . *that* is a true miracle.

Widowed at twenty and dead by twenty-four, Elizabeth was credited with many miracles of healing and is revered as the patron saint of the sick, the poor, and all those who care for them. I was a bit taken aback to learn that in Košice she is also honored as the patron saint of armed mercenaries — although upon reflection, I imagined they would find her healing powers rather useful in their line of work.

The cathedral was enormous and built in the high Gothic style, with innumerable towers, pointed windows, and fancy embellishments. There was the usual abundance of gargoyles, most of which are beasts that appear to be a cross between dogs and devils, but Veronica pointed out one that was distinctly human and was said to be a caricature of the builder's own wife. Apparently the builder, Štefana, went home each night after working on this glorious edifice to be harangued mercilessly by his nagging, drunken, foul-mouthed wife. Goaded beyond endurance, he created a gargoyle in her likeness, so she would spend the rest of eternity having her mouth washed out every time it rained. And wouldn't you just love to know what Mrs. Štefana had to say about *that*?

The cathedral interior was richly ornamented with colorful stained glass windows, paintings of St. Elizabeth tending to the sick, and golden statues and ornaments that I feel sure the saint herself would have instantly melted down to buy more bread for the poor. Veronica was very excited that she'd managed to obtain special permission for Rich and me to ascend the cathedral's rare double-spiral staircase, normally off limits to visitors.

Sometimes called the Lovers' Staircase, the design is thought to be terribly romantic, as a couple can separate at the bottom step and ascend, each on a different staircase, crossing over at each tiny landing, creating brief but thrilling opportunities for flirtatious dalliance. Unfortunately, flirtatious dalliance was not on Rich's agenda at the moment, as our two-and-a-half hour tour was already well into its third hour, and he really needed to get off his feet and rest his aching leg. But he couldn't bear to disappoint Veronica, who had gone to the trouble of arranging this special treat for us, so he grit his teeth and trudged up the steps.

At the top, Veronica had informed us, was a chamber that once housed a drop of the actual blood of Christ. Sadly, that chamber was now closed up, and even Veronica's powers of persuasion couldn't get us in. After spending some time catching our breath and enjoying the dramatic view of the cathedral's nave from above, we climbed back down to ground level and rejoined Veronica.

"What ever happened to the drop of Christ's blood?" I asked her.

"Some men came and took it away," she said vaguely. "I don't know where it is now."

Having seen *Raiders of the Lost Ark*, I felt fairly certain it was locked up in a warehouse next to the crate holding the Ark of the Covenant. This seemed a pity, as a sacred artifact of that magnitude — real or fake — would certainly have helped with the city's efforts to lure tourists, especially if the PR department leaked a few rumors about miraculous cures. Another great marketing opportunity lost.

Hungry from the exertions of the morning, we finally detached our-selves from Veronica and set off in search of a late lunch. A few blocks away from St. Elizabeth's, I spotted an unexpected icon of American culture: a café based on the old TV series *Friends*. It was called Smelly Cat, after Phoebe's trademark song, and was decorated with New York memorabilia, sofas vaguely like the one the cast hung out on at Central Perk, and a wall-mounted TV running continuous episodes of the show.

We sat for an hour eating our sandwiches and looking at the Statue of Liberty, the Brooklyn Bridge, and the six famous faces that had filled American TV screens from 1994 to 2004 and will, with syndication, probably appear on our entertainment media until the end of time itself.

Košice had proved to be far more interesting and amusing than we'd expected, and we stayed on a few extra days to explore it further. I bought a small, inexpensive daypack to hold our train snacks and my straw hat, and we sent our clothes out to be laundered at our hotel, a lackluster modern establishment where no one spoke any English. As usual, I wrote out a detailed laundry list, and given the lack of a common language, I added little drawings of T-shirts, socks, and so on, providing considerable amusement to the staff and ensuring that we got back every item.

Refreshed by our pleasant visit in Košice, we began making plans for our last stop en route to Romania — a Hungarian town with a convenient location and an unpronounceable name.

As Rich consulted the iRail app, I asked, "Tell me again the name of the next town we're going to?"

"Nyiregyhaza," he said, pronouncing it "Neer-ya-ga-HA-za."

"Gesundheit."

"Very funny."

I soon gave up and began referring to it as "Neerya-whatever" or simply "That Town in Hungary."

As soon as our train crossed the border from Slovakia into Hungary, the engineer began blowing the train whistle with much greater frequency and gusto, and people arriving in our carriage seemed more eager to make eye contact and attempt to make conversation despite our utter ignorance of each other's languages. If nothing else, we were clearly providing the Hungarians with a bit of entertainment to while away the hours on the train.

Nyiregyhaza's train station was done up in a sterile, modernist style and our hotel in basic bordello. The walls of our modest attic room sported flaming red-orange wallpaper and a huge painting depicting a convoluted sex act involving three naked people of indeterminate gender but impressive muscularity and flexibility. Not a décor I'd want to live with for long, but hey, the sheets were clean and the mattress was free of bedbugs, so we chained our bags to the radiator and went exploring.

The really odd thing about Nyiregyhaza was that it looked exactly like a small American city; we might as well have been in Hoboken or Cincinnati. There was a wide main street full of bland office buildings, a McDonald's, a phone store, and several restaurants that appeared to be corporate chains. Surely there was more to see here in Hungary's seventh largest city?

Wikitravel wasn't much help, commenting in a rather dampening manner, "The city itself is mostly devoid of must-see attractions, though you can take many pleasant walks with the squares and parks . . ." Undaunted, I suggested that what we needed was a detailed local map, something our hotel had been unable to provide.

Rich took out the iPad and Googled the location of the tourist information office, which fortunately was just two blocks away inside a travel agency. We found it in minutes, but at that point our luck ran out. The two women at the desk spoke no English, yet somehow managed to convey that they considered it highly unreasonable of us to expect them to provide information to a couple of strangers who just walked in off the street.

I spent some time pantomiming "map" (elaborate unfolding and poring over a large, invisible piece of paper) and "city" (pointing out the window and circling my finger to indicate that I meant the entire town, not just their street). Finally, light dawned.

"City map!" said one in triumph.

"Yes, yes," I cried. "City map!"

"No city map," she said, shaking her head.

"Well, that's a first," I said, when we were back out on the street. "What kind of tourist information office doesn't even have a city map?"

"I'm guessing they don't get many actual tourists through here."

"I can't imagine why."

Passing a tall clock fitted with large silver wings — it didn't take me too long to work out the subtle symbolism there! — we wandered aimlessly up the main street, passing modern apartment blocks, a few gracious nineteenth-century buildings, and a fountain showing three naked women cavorting in much the same manner as the figures in our hotel room's painting. It was becoming clear what people did for excitement in this town and that you'd have to be pretty athletic to keep up.

Eventually we found ourselves in a residential area with a park containing a small lake, a bridge, and a leafy, well-tended cemetery. Most of the graves had fresh flowers on them. Some tombstones were so overgrown with ivy that the names were barely visible, and several larger plots had been made into pretty little gardens, landscaped with small shrubs, flowering plants, and rock-lined paths. Our favorite was a big, rectangular, raised bed occupied by seven family members, its surface overrun with pink and white flowers and winding tendrils of ivy. In front of it stood a shade tree and a well-worn blue, wooden bench. We decided to sit there for a spell.

"A nice place to call home for all eternity," commented my husband, ever the real estate buff. "And I bet the price is right."

"You wouldn't have to worry about being overrun with visitors."

We listened to the chirping birds for a while, and then he said, "So what do you think happens when we die?"

During our nearly thirty years together, we'd naturally had many discussions about this topic. In long-ago catechism classes, we'd been taught that we would — with luck, and most likely a stint in Purgatory first — go to heaven and be happy forever in the presence of God and loved ones who had died before us. But since then we'd been introduced to a lot of other belief systems and concepts of post-life reality.

"I've always liked the way the Buddhists describe it," I said. "Each individual is like a wave in the ocean, coalescing into a particular form for a while, then subsiding back into the wholeness of the sea."

"Yeah, I like that one too," he said. "Physicists talk about the entire universe being made of energy. And they say we're just the latest formation, a little eddy in the vast field of energy that makes up everything, from us to this bench to the stars."

"Exactly," I said. "And what's the first law of thermodynamics? Energy cannot be created or destroyed. It lasts forever. But it can be rearranged for a while — into you or me or the Singing Fountain of Košice. And then afterwards, it's released back into the universe. Which is just what the Buddhists are saying." Later I would discover writer Aaron Freeman's lovely line about this: "According to the law of the conservation of energy, not a bit of you is gone; you're just less orderly."

Rich was looking around the cemetery with the appraising air of someone checking out a neighborhood with a promising apartment for rent, and I felt a small chill in my heart. He would be turning seventy the following summer, and even my optimistic nature couldn't ignore the fact that questions about the afterlife were no longer purely academic or something that would arise in the far distant future. We had reached the age where you seriously begin to wonder: how much longer do we have together? I felt the stirrings of anxiety and melancholy. As interesting as this conversation had been, I decided I didn't want to repeat it on a regular basis. I made a firm resolve to avoid cemeteries for the rest of the trip.

"Come on," I said briskly, rising to my feet. "It's getting late. Let's get back to the hotel and see if our fellow guests look like they're all there for kinky hijinks."

We never did see any of the other guests at the hotel, nor, as I'd half expected, did we hear sounds of wild, contortionist coupling bouncing off the walls in the adjacent rooms. Rich and I spent a quiet evening watching the ancient actress playing Miss Marple outwit several fiendishly clever criminal masterminds.

As I turned out the light, I reflected that Nyiregyhaza wasn't a bad place to spend an afternoon and evening, but I wouldn't want to extend my sentence — I mean, my visit — much beyond that. It had already been shortlisted for my "Most Lackluster City on Earth" award. Top contender for the title was Tuzla in Bosnia-Herzegovina, where Rich and I did a week-long volunteer work assignment back in the late nineties. In those primitive times before wifi and Kindles, the highlight of every evening's agenda was watching Bosnian TV, mostly locally produced sitcoms (in Bosnian, of course, without subtitles) and ads reminding people to watch out for unexploded land mines.

When that palled, I would read aloud to Rich from the book I'd brought along, which was Bill Bryson's *Down Under*. The Australian capital, Bryson explained, was so dull that the license plate slogan actually read "Canberra: It's not that bad." Pitching in to compose an alternative, he came up with "Canberra: Why wait for death?"

"Oh my God," I had said to Rich upon reading this line aloud one night in Tuzla. "We're in Canberra!"

And I felt much the same way about Nyiregyhaza. There was nothing really wrong with anything we saw there. But when a city's most appealing real estate is in the cemetery — if the best part of living there is the afterlife — you don't want to linger. Already, having spent just one evening in Nyiregyhaza, I had a new appreciation for the concept of eternity.

"Nyiregyhaza: Why wait for death?" Hmmm, it could catch on.

CHAPTER 11

Do You Need a Passport
for Time Travel?

"Wait!" I shrieked, leaning as far as I could out the train window. "Stop the train!"

Next to me, Rich was yelling, "Our passports! Our *passports*!"

The Hungarian-Romanian border is no place to lose your passport, and it had been with some reluctance that we'd turned ours over to a couple of burly, uniformed men who had come on board, headed directly for our compartment, taken our passports (and *only* ours), disembarked, and disappeared into the station. We weren't even sure which country we were in. I was guessing they were border officials, but not having looked too closely at their badges, I hadn't a clue whether they were Hungarian *bevándorlási tiszt* or Romanian *oficial de imigrare*.

Whoever they were, they took their time inspecting our passports in the comfort of the train station. Rich and I spent the next quarter of an hour watching the station attendant bustle about importantly, checking the brakes and peering under the railway carriages. Then, moving more purposefully, he began slamming doors, and finally he blew on his whistle and waved his paddle to indicate that the train was ready to move on. Rich and I heard the engine start and felt a jolt, and that's when we leaned out the window and began shouting to the station attendant, "Wait! Our passports! Stop the train!"

Only then did I realize that our railroad car wasn't, in fact, going anywhere. The okay-to-go signal was for the back half of the train, which was separating from our car and returning to Hungary. The fact that everyone on the station platform knew this, and had no doubt witnessed this little drama many times, didn't seem to diminish their innocent delight in watching us make fools of ourselves. Luckily, after all the linguistic and cultural pratfalls I'd taken while living and traveling abroad, I had precious little dignity left to lose and didn't mind the locals enjoying themselves at our expense.

By that point in our career as railway nomads, Rich and I had logged a total of 2,416 train miles, and you'd think that we'd be a bit more savvy. Problem was, as soon as we'd found a way to overcome one hurdle — for instance, convincing suspicious conductors that one Eurail pass applied to two travelers by repeatedly pointing to ourselves and the two names on the paper — we'd trip over some fresh stumbling block. We would know better about the passport game in the future, but I could only assume the various European railroad systems would find ways to ambush us with something even more unexpected the next time. As Evelyn Waugh put it in *Black Mischief,* "One learnt to expect anything, but was always surprised."

Rich and I were still chuckling over our near panic, and everyone on the station platform was suppressing grins when the two burly men returned our passports and wished us, in passable English, a safe journey into Romania.

I was very excited to be entering Romania at last. I'd long harbored intensely romantic images of the country, especially Transylvania, where I expected rustic villages full of hay wagons, Gypsies in colorful skirts, and of course vampires. Yes, I realized it was unlikely I'd run into any of the undead, but then, I hadn't expected to see the remains of Smok, an actual dragon, either. If I'd learned anything during our journey to this border crossing, it was that you could never be certain about what you might find around the next corner.

Following the little contretemps over our passports at the border, the train sped southwards into Transylvania, and somewhere around midday we pulled into the city of Oradea, Romania. One glance out the window showed me a station platform liberally sprinkled with Gypsy women darting about in colorful skirts. I could check off one Transylvania must-see already.

"Roumania without its Gypsies," wrote Romanian émigré Konrad Bercovici, an author who favored the old spelling, "is as inconceivable as the rainbow without its colours or a forest without birds." Clearly Romania needn't worry about running out of Gypsies anytime soon. There were dozens of them enlivening the landscape around Oradea's train station; the bold colors of the women's headscarves and long skirts provided a flashing contrast to the sober hues worn by most of the disembarking passengers.

A handful of Gypsy children followed the exotic American couple, circling ever closer and eyeing us with interest as we made an abortive attempt to withdraw some Romanian lei from the ATM at the Banka Transylvania. For some reason the ATM machine seemed suspicious of our card — the first difficulty we'd had with a cash withdrawal on the trip — and we soon gave up and strode off in the direction of our lodgings. The kids, I was relieved to see, chose not to follow us. They were small and cute, but they looked much like the professional bands of pickpockets I'd seen in Spain and the Republic of Georgia, and I was just as glad not to have to fend off a concerted effort to relieve us of our belongings.

Arriving at our small, modern hotel, we discovered a wedding reception was in full swing out back in a large, open-fronted bamboo hut. Music and voices boomed merrily in through the windows as we followed the desk clerk up a set of winding stairs, carefully ducking at the battered spot where the ceiling was precisely engineered to decapitate taller guests. Our suite consisted of a small, dark bedroom; a large, sunny sitting room fitted with eight oversized, red plush chairs; and a small balcony overlooking — and overhearing — the bamboo hut. We checked for bedbugs, secured our luggage, obtained a map at the desk, and headed downtown.

I felt a shiver of anticipation, and possibly just a teeny, tiny bit of apprehension at the strangeness of it all. The very name Transylvania conjured up all manner of exotic dangers to body and soul. Of course, this was the twenty-first century, and no one believed in vampires anymore. If only I could be sure the local undead had gotten the memo on that topic.

When we happened to pass a news kiosk selling everything from candy bars to videos, I glanced with idle curiosity at its offerings, and my eye zeroed in on the plastic casing of an audio book entitled *Doamna și Vagabondul*, Disney's *Lady and the Tramp*. On the cover was the famous spaghetti scene where Tramp pushes the last meatball over to Lady with his nose. For a moment I was catapulted back to a steamy night dining under the stars in Genoa and then further back to my childhood, when I first fell in love with the story. Maybe I had more in common with Romania and its people than I'd realized. Cheered by the thought, I shook off my momentary anxiety and began looking forward to exploring our first Romanian city.

Oradea had been home to humans since the New Stone Age, when we were fooling around with such hot new technologies as tool use, agriculture, and the domestication of animals. And it's been making pretty good use of its time ever since. The city really began to hit its stride in the eleventh century under Hungarian rule, tanked a bit with invasion by the Turks in the fifteenth century and occupation by the Ottoman Empire in the sixteenth, but entered a golden era when the Hapsburgs took over in 1692. A Viennese engineer, brought in to remake the city as a baroque masterpiece, filled the downtown area with exuberant palaces, churches, and theaters. And then, just a hundred years before we got there, the city underwent a sudden craze for the undulating lines of Art Nouveau, giving the city a dash of *belle-époque* character and a new nickname: Little Paris.

I was dazzled by the broad boulevards and the grand and glorious old buildings. Little Paris had so much charm that even the Soviets couldn't delude themselves that they could improve upon it, and they'd refrained from blighting it with any of their usual concrete eyesores.

Noticing an especially magnificent building with a clock tower, I suggested strolling over for a closer look. Three young musicians were lounging about on the front steps and seemed delighted to chat with a couple of strangers. The one wearing a striped purple shirt spoke the best English, and he explained that this was City Hall and that they were taking a break from playing at a wedding. I noticed his curious instrument, a very skinny violin on which was mounted the head of a trumpet, and he told us it was a *vioara cu goarnă*, a horn-violin, a four-stringed instrument that amplified the sound via the trumpet rather than the conventional wooden sound box. It was common here in Romania, he said, and it didn't take much to persuade him to entertain us with a little lively fiddling. When I told them we were here to tour Romania, they seemed thrilled that we had chosen to visit their country, asking eagerly where we would be going.

"A village called Botiza," Rich replied. We'd heard about this small, rural community from our friend Cat, who writes the travel blog *Sunshine and Siestas*; she'd visited the village the year before and suggested we stop by if we were ever in the neighborhood. In global terms, being a mere 175 miles away seemed to count as a neighborly distance.

Instantly, the faces of all three musicians softened, as if at a cherished memory. "Ah, Maramureș," they murmured. "Maramureș, yes . . ."

I had no idea who or what Maramureș was — were? — but at least the musicians hadn't recoiled in horror or burst into derisive laughter. Later I learned that Maramureș was the name of the county in which Botiza was situated, a region known for its small, old-fashioned farms, picturesque villages, seventeenth-century wooden churches, and something called "The Happy Cemetery." Infrastructure was apparently not its strong suit; paved roads, electricity, and running water were known but had not completely caught on yet.

"And here in Oradea?" asked the one in the striped shirt. "What do you see?"

I didn't have the heart to admit that I had done virtually no research on his city, which we regarded as a brief stopover en route to more significant destinations. So I asked tactfully, "What do you recommend?"

"You must go to the Moon Church," he said promptly. His companions nodded eagerly.

The Moon Church? For one dizzying moment I wondered if we'd stumbled across a Romanian outpost of the Moonies, one of the world's more offbeat (some might say lunatic fringe) religions. It was founded in 1954 by Korean teenager Sun Myung Moon, who claimed to be able to talk with the dead, to be the second coming of Jesus Christ, and to think that Richard Nixon was a pretty good guy, to name but a few of the highlights. His message spread throughout the world, thanks to compelling evangelical techniques that journalists and lawyers often describe using such terms as cult, brainwashing, and mind control. Had the Moonies established a base here? But before I could probe delicately into the religious profile of the Moon Church, Rich was asking, "Where is it?"

Our new friend pointed across the wide boulevard at what I noted with relief appeared to be a pretty ordinary church with a large, square central steeple. "Very beautiful," he said. "It has the moon clock."

"We will go now and see it," I said. Conversing with non-native English speakers, I have a tendency to lapse into formal language worthy of characters in a badly written nineteenth-century play. "It has been a pleasure to meet you. Thank you for your kindness." I'm not sure, but I believe I may have even added a small bow.

The Moon Church was not, thank heavens, a Moonie outpost but rather the Romanian Orthodox church of the Assumption, which served as the city's cathedral. The interior was fabulously ornate, with every inch of the vast vaulted and domed space covered with murals and embellished with gold trim and thick, red velvet hangings. The layout and lavishness reminded me of Seville's crumbling baroque basilicas, except that Oradea's cathedral was in infinitely better repair.

The air was thick with the heavy, muffled silence that inhabits old churches, and Rich and I crept in as quietly as we could and sat down on smooth, wooden benches that stood against the back wall. Members of the faithful moved quietly about the vast space, praying and lighting candles at various shrines.

Rich and I craned our necks attempting to spot something that might be considered a moon clock, and finally gave up. "Maybe it's outside," I whispered. We tiptoed out and looked up. There, halfway up the central tower, was a large ball painted half black, half yellow, set into the wall and apparently rotating in phase with the lunar cycle.

"Why do you think they were so keen to track the phases of the moon?" I asked. "To know when to plant crops?"

"Maybe it's just a curiosity."

I wondered. The cathedral's name, the Assumption, referred to the belief that when she died, the Virgin Mary was assumed — that is, taken bodily — into heaven. Mary is known as the Queen of Heaven and is often shown standing on a crescent moon, imagery that art historians tell us harks back to the old religions; here in Romania, that would be Bendis, the ancient Dacian goddess of the moon. The Dacians also venerated a god — or possibly an ancestor — who took on the form of a wolf, and they conducted rituals designed to transform themselves into wolves — or, to use the technical term, werewolves. I don't know about you, but if I lived in a district where vampires and werewolves were rumored to roam, I'd be pretty keen to track the moon's phases so I'd know when to lock my doors, hang the garlic, and lay in a supply of wooden stakes and holy water.

Of course, those were medieval superstitions; the Moon Church had been built in the eighteenth century, known in Western Europe as the Age of Enlightenment. But perhaps here in Transylvania the old beliefs weren't so easily replaced by modern critical thinking. Or maybe Rich was right and the church's architects were just having a bit of fun.

The next day we traveled deep into the Carpathian Mountains to the village of Botiza. Cat had stayed at a small guesthouse run by a man named George, and when I emailed him, George responded by extending a warm welcome while breaking the bad news that he had no room for us. He would, however, be happy to arrange for us to stay with a friend of his, an offer which, perhaps a little rashly, we accepted.

He emailed back: "You can take the train IR 367 (departure time from Oradea at 12:06) arriving in Cluj Napoca at 14:42. From Cluj Napoca is the train R4110 to Sighetu Marmaţiei (departure time 15:40), arriving in IZA station at 20:13, where we could pick you up by car and drive you to Botiza." Although we normally tried to avoid spending eight-plus hours in transit on any given day, we fell in with George's plan.

By the time we left Sighetu Marmaţiei we were high in the mountains and the trees were no longer restrained at a respectful distance from the train but crowding in around it, slapping its sides with their branches. Leaves and twigs caught on the open windows of our railway car, tearing free of the branches to land at our feet and drift up and down the corridor.

I looked down as we crossed a gorge and discovered the unnerving sight of a row of derailed boxcars lying on their sides beside the tracks, rusting quietly in place. Apparently moving them required far too much trouble and expense; I gathered that issues such as environmental impact and frightening the passengers were low enough on the priority list to be easily ignored.

We arrived at Iza a scant forty-five minutes late and in pitch darkness. The station — more of a shed, really — was locked up for the night, or possibly the century, for all we knew. Rich and I stood alone on a patch of gravel next to the station, in an island of crepuscular gloom created by a few dim bulbs suspended from wires high overhead. An unpaved road wandered off over the nearest rise. There were no taxis, cars, or even the horse-drawn carts we'd been seeing in villages along the way.

Part of the reason I love railway travel is that it makes me feel like I'm living in the nineteenth century. An era, I now recalled, that had some pretty dark chapters, including a few set right here in Transylvania. Not that I believed in the old tales, of course.

"Are those bats?" I asked, as something fluttered by overhead.

A smiling man appeared suddenly out of the darkness. "I take you!"

"Did George send you?" I asked suspiciously.

The man nodded. Had he understood my question? I repeated, "Did George—"

"I take you!" he said again, and seizing our bags, he rushed off into the darkness. Rich and I glanced at each other, shrugged, and followed him to his car. There are moments when you simply have to trust your instincts, your luck, and whatever saint watches over travelers now that St. Christopher has been debunked.

As we bounced off over the rutted gravel road, Rich asked, "Is it far?" The man held up three fingers, saying, "*Treizeci*—" and something I didn't catch. What did that mean? Three minutes? Three hundred miles? We three had bonded, and now it was one for all and all for one? After that the conversation languished.

I had no doubt that Rich was mentally reviewing every one of our safety protocols and fingering the chain around his neck that carried a small pocket knife and a cross I'd given him to ward off the undead. As for me, I wasn't too optimistic about our chances if it came down to fight or flight. I realized, with a fresh little shock, that we'd actually reached the age where relying on physical strength to get out of a tight spot was not a viable option. A street urchin could take me down in about five seconds, and with Rich's dicey leg, we couldn't outrun anything faster than a three-toed sloth. I could only hope that if we were in danger it would involve a vampire, who could (they said) be fought off with a crucifix and a brisk recital of the Lord's Prayer.

We eventually arrived at a paved road and drove swiftly past fields and a few towns that were utterly dark except for the odd chink of light showing at the edge of a curtain or shutter. Our driver turned onto another unpaved road that got narrower and narrower until branches were scratching the sides of the car. We slid past some dark shapes that might have been low buildings or large haystacks, and finally, about half an hour after leaving the station, the car rolled to a halt in front of a white, two-story house with a wooden door.

The door opened, revealing a bar of golden light and a middle-aged woman in an apron. She stood on the doorstep smiling at us, and I began to believe that we might get through the night without being robbed, killed, or handed over to the family werewolf for unspeakable purposes.

"*Sunteti bineveniti,*" she said in a welcoming manner. Beckoning that we should follow, she led the way into a whitewashed front hall and up a tiled staircase, then opened a door and stood back for us to enter. Inside was a snug bedroom with a flowered bedspread and seersucker cotton sheets sporting lurid magenta roses with lime green leaves. We smiled and nodded to show that we were happy with the accommodations.

She then led us across the hall and opened the door to a bathroom, which I was thankful to see held all the usual amenities; this being Maramureș, I wouldn't have been surprised at an outhouse or a chamber pot. I did note that walking back from the bathroom to our bedroom required going down one randomly placed, curving step, then hopping smartly to the left in order to avoid tumbling headlong down the staircase, which cut into the main part of the upper floor where you'd least expect it. Note to self: bring a flashlight if negotiating this in the dark.

"*Cină?*" asked our hostess.

"Dinner?" translated her husband.

"*Da,*" I said, having boned up on a few useful Romanian words. "Yes, thank you. *Mersi.*"

One of the great things I've learned about Romanian is that it is firmly rooted in Latin (although with a good bit of Slavic, Daco-Thracian, Greek, Celtic, Turkish, and other languages thrown in). My point is that Romanian contains all sorts of familiar-sounding words. Some seem French, such as *mersi* for thank you and *gară* for train station; others are much like Spanish, such as *casă* for house. There are Italianesque words, such as *la revederi*, so close to *arrivederci*, for goodbye; and a few are easy to mistake for something else, such as the word for carp, a common menu (*meniul*) item, which in Romanian is called *crap*. (See, you've been speaking Romanian for years and didn't even know it!)

We went downstairs to a delicious hot chicken stew and mashed potatoes, followed by *horincă*, the local plum brandy. This powerful home brew is as essential to Romanian life as coffee is to Seattle's residents, as tea is to the British, or as yak-butter chai is to Buddhist monks in the high Himalayas. Yes, you might be able to get through a day without it, but why would you? *Horincă* was produced during virtually every social occasion throughout our stay, and I've heard that no Romanian man would go courting, visit a friend, or leave on a journey without a half-liter plastic bottle filled with *horincă* tucked into his coat pocket. It was delicious in an eye-watering way, and we stumbled upstairs afterwards to sleep like the dead.

In the morning, we looked out our window to discover that we had gone back in time some seven hundred years and were now in the middle of a medieval village. Despite the electric wires and cell phone tower that revealed the presence of some modern conveniences, most of the villagers still lived in much the same way as their ancestors did back when Vlad the Impaler was a boy. Here things changed very, very, very slowly.

Most families lived in peak-roofed houses built by hand using wood planks fashioned from trees cut in the nearby forest. Chickens ran about underfoot in the wooden barns they shared with dairy cows, draft horses, and goats. On this mild September morning, small groups of men were heading out in horse-drawn wagons to spend the day scything hay, which they would dry on racks made from cut saplings, then pile into haystacks handy to their barns. Women in skirts and headscarves were busy sweeping, feeding chickens, or walking to the village shop for supplies. Passing one another on the road, the women would usually stop for a brief word and then be on their way, having lots to do before taking the men their lunch in the fields.

Nobody paid the slightest attention to us when, after a breakfast of eggs and bread, Rich and I began wandering about. The village was larger than I had thought; there were several intersecting dirt roads that led off into the hills, and I later read that the population was close to three thousand people. If so, most of them were on outlying farms, since in the course of the day we saw perhaps fifty. Maybe the others avoided the bustle of downtown Botiza, overwhelmed by the hay wagons passing up and down the street, the odd motor vehicle, and the sprinkling of foot traffic heading to the small market at the crossroads. Everyone seemed fully occupied with his or her own affairs. We might as well have been time travelers, given the differences in our lives, but they took our presence in stride and seemed amused rather than offended when I took a few discreet photos.

I noticed a tall, middle-aged man in a cloth cap riding toward us on a bicycle, and I had just decided he wasn't quite quaint enough to try to photograph when he stopped beside us.

"Richard? Karen? I am George."

At last! George seemed pleased to hear how much we liked the village and our lodgings. He apologized for not being able to provide us with the hospitality of his home, as a couple from Spain was currently occupying the guest quarters, but he was free the next day and we made arrangements to meet for a tour of the district. Standing there comfortably beside his bike in the road, George filled us in a bit about village life.

"People here work very hard every day," he said. "And on Sunday, they go to church."

Living in Seville, where people gathered daily in bars and cafés to spend hours socializing and discussing whatever major fiesta was just around the corner, I found it hard to imagine such a nose-to-the-grindstone existence.

"What do they do for fun?" I asked.

George paused to consider the question. "Sometimes there are weddings," he said finally. "They are usually on a Saturday night. There is music and dancing; everyone in the village goes." He came to a full stop. That was it? When I kept looking at him expectantly, he shrugged and added, "Once in a while, if someone is in the home of a friend, he might be offered a beer." Those party animals!

When George had pedaled away to his other duties, Rich and I made our way to the intersection of two roads that marked the center of the village. There was a shop selling packaged goods, a small café, and a large, beautifully carved wooden bulletin board with nothing on it but a few empty staples.

We bought coffees (a rather grisly instant, I'm sorry to say) and sat in the café watching horse-drawn wagons pass by, carrying men to and from their work in the fields and bringing in sacks of feed for the animals. Most people in Botiza lived off the land much as their ancestors had always done, but for the first time in history, they wanted a steady supply of cash to buy manufactured goods. People were eyeing such modern amenities as telephones, indoor toilets, and TVs, and to pay for them, many took part-time jobs in larger towns.

"The traditional, harmless way of life of the Maramureş communities," wrote William Blacker, a young Englishman who'd recently spent several years in a village near Botiza, "had endured for thousands of years, surviving even the forty years of Communism. The modern television, with its insidious advertising, was a threat against which they were defenseless. Money was desperately needed to purchase the new products."

And those most desperate to embrace the new products and the cash economy were, naturally, the younger generation. A teenage girl in snug jeans walked by the café, talking on her cell phone; she looked as if she belonged in a Los Angeles mall. I had no doubt that she and most of her age mates were counting the days until they could head to the nearest city, find a desk job, dye their hair, get tattoos, pierce a few surprising body parts, join a rock band, have sex with inappropriate strangers, and forget they ever came from this nowheresville. How can you keep them down on the farm after they've seen TV?

Older villagers were looking to the future in a different way. Many had already bought their coffins, tombstones, and space in the village cemetery. Despite my resolve to avoid burial places for a while, within an hour after leaving George, Rich and I found ourselves touring the local graveyard. We'd followed a narrow trail that started beside an old, wooden church and led uphill to a small meadow, which was surrounded by wild masses of bright flowers and lush greenery that half covered the simple white crosses and tombstones. In the background rose the fog-wreathed peaks of the Carpathian Mountains. It was blissfully quiet and peaceful. Time seemed to stand still.

But I could tell that even here, alas, modernity was creeping in. A recent gravestone bore an exclamation mark — *dormi in pace!* (sleep in peace!) — which suggested that Facebook and other social media had eroded punctuation standards even here. What was the afterlife coming to?

CHAPTER 12

And a Red String for Luck

"George, why do those cows have red strings tied around their tails?" I asked the next morning.

We were in a vast, green field that was serving as a makeshift livestock market, the rough gravel road in the center being lined with two ragged rows of farm vehicles: eight or ten trucks, a few vans and station wagons, and a dozen horse-drawn wooden carts in various stages of decrepitude. Fluffy, freshly washed sheep poked their heads over the side of one of the carts, and massive pigs stood in sawdust-strewn truck beds, eying us with suspicion. Three beautifully groomed brown cows stood placidly at a manger, munching hay, idly swishing tails that each held a single, bright red strand of string.

"Red is the color of luck," George replied. "It's a tradition to tie red string onto the animals to keep them safe."

All the livestock looked lucky enough at the moment, as safe, clean, and well fed as they were ever likely to be in their lives. The horses drawing the carts were sturdy and muscular, their harnesses hung with thick, red tassels almost as large as their heads, which made me wonder if they needed an extra dose of protection for some reason.

Before I could ask George about it, he stopped to introduce us to a fat, pink-cheeked man standing beside a crate of plump, wriggling piglets. The man scooped one up in his arms, held the piglet's face up beside his own and said, "Look, the big one and the little one!" As George translated, the pig man roared with laughter, and I did too. The resemblance *was* uncanny.

We ambled through the market, stopping to admire the animals and meet their humans. One farmer proudly showed us several small, tidy-looking brown pigs and told us they were raised on a vegetarian diet so they were low in cholesterol. I'd often heard the same thing from Sevillano friends about top-quality Spanish pigs, the ones that grew to their adult weight on an acorn diet. A medical study revealed that this diet made the meat rich in certain antioxidants, giving rise to health claims that eating more Spanish *jamón* could actually lower your cholesterol. Not long after I moved to Seville, my Spanish doctor instructed me to consume plenty of high-quality *jamón* along with dark chocolate and red wine to keep my cholesterol down, and I'd been working to maintain this rigorous regimen ever since.

The real surprise was that anyone in rural Romania worried about cholesterol, a health concern I'd always associated with a more sedentary lifestyle. Nearly all the men and women I saw had the stocky, muscular build of people who labored long and hard every day and ate heartily between tasks. Maramureș men were known for preferring their women to be plump — fat, even — as it was commonly held that a well-upholstered wife was more robust and better able to endure the hardships of farming life.

I saw one strapping, stern-faced woman in a headscarf, tracksuit jacket, down vest, and knee-length skirt of a surprisingly jolly floral print. She looked capable of slinging a full-grown sow over one shoulder and a crying child over the other while chopping meat for the stewpot and quelling the rest of her family with a single glare. She was clearly a force to be reckoned with and I, for one, made a mental note to walk softly around her.

A quiet, gray-haired woman pedaled up on a bicycle, propped it to one side, and put a small tarp on the ground. She began setting out pears, apples, walnuts, and a few homemade socks and trinkets, and before leaving, I bought a bracelet of green beads and a little red and green crocheted flower that I tied on my suitcase for luck. She waved goodbye with a shy smile as we headed to George's car.

Back on the main road, George said, "We will soon be close to Sighet." While Rich and I were still groping for a suitable reply to this enigmatic remark, he added, "There you can visit the Memorial to the Victims of Communism and the Resistance. If you wish."

Did we wish to do this? Although the subject matter sounded rather bleak, something in his voice suggested that George thought it was important, so we said we'd like that very much. A memorial. Surely that would just be some sort of statue or monument. How long could it take?

George drove to Sighet, which turned out to be a town of nearly thirty-eight thousand people and the birthplace of Nobel Prize-winning writer and human rights activist Elie Wiesel. After surviving the concentrations camps at Auschwitz, Buna, and Buchenwald, Wiesel had once remarked, "Human beings should be held accountable. Leave God alone. He has enough problems."

George helped us buy our tickets at the entrance of a three-story building whose sign read *Memorialul Victimelor Comunismului şi al Rezistenţei*; then he left us to make our own way around the museum. It was about as grim as you'd imagine. Built as a prison in 1897, half a century later it became a detention center for enemies of the communist state: political activists, politicians, academics, and outspoken Catholic clergy. It wasn't the massive operation we'd seen in the German-run concentration camps; "only" two hundred men were incarcerated there from 1948 to 1955.

Their photos and those of thousands more Romanians imprisoned during the communist era were posted on the walls, and I stood studying their faces for a while. They looked like perfectly ordinary people who'd had the bad luck to come of age during an era of unbridled intolerance and cruelty. In those days, political prisoners were detained, tortured, and isolated from the outside world, without recourse to legal representation or due process of law. I remembered how proud I used to be that nothing like that could ever happen in my country.

Each cell contained simple exhibits, mostly photos and copies of old documents detailing what went on in the prison, the fate of particular inmates, and the brutal atrocities perpetrated throughout the country by Nicolae Ceaușescu, Romania's head of state from 1967 to 1989. After touring Dachau and Auschwitz, I'd thought I was prepared for anything, but the hour we spent walking through the dimly lit halls of this prison made my flesh creep in new ways.

The most nightmarish spot was the Black Cell, a three-foot-square hole where prisoners who had committed such offenses as glancing at one another or speaking would be chained together, naked, in groups of four and forced to stand up all night, often in water up to their knees. In the bitter nights from October to May the water must have been half frozen. For one hideous moment I imagined what it must have felt like to be forced into the icy water, your legs flinching and shuddering, the cold creeping up your body, the uncontrollable shivering and teeth chattering, knowing you'd be there for hours and hours in the dark . . .

There were two small courtyards, where prisoners had been allowed outside for ten minutes a week. In one there now stood a round, candlelit memorial chamber inscribed with the names of thousands of Romanians who had suffered under the communist regime. In the other was a large bronze sculpture called the Procession of the Sacrificed, showing eighteen figures in agonized postures marching toward a wall which was, as one website put it, "a dead end, just like communism."

Growing up during the Cold War, I'd spent my childhood with the specter of communism hovering over my head, doing air raid drills at school so we'd know how to react if the Reds dropped the atom bomb on us. Of course, ducking under a desk or huddling against the cafeteria wall would not really have been of much practical use against a thermonuclear weapon delivering the equivalent of more than a million tons of TNT, but those drills were very effective in teaching us to fear and hate the communists. The nuns at Sacred Heart made a point of teaching us to distinguish between the leaders of the USSR's totalitarian regime and the people suffering under it, people we'd pray for during Mass on the first Friday of every month. By the time the Berlin Wall came down, marking the official dismantling of the Iron Curtain, I was grown, married, in midcareer, and only too glad to stop worrying about the Red Menace. I was slightly ashamed now to realize how little thought I'd given since then to the sufferers I used to pray for so routinely.

"Well, *that* was fun," said Rich, as we found ourselves back near the entrance at last.

"If there's a gift shop, let's not go there," I said. We stumbled out the doors of the former prison into a day that had turned from overcast to drizzling.

"Okay?" George asked. "Yes? Now, we visit the Merry Cemetery."

So much for my plan to avoid hanging out with the dead. On the other hand, it could hardly be more demoralizing than the *Memorialul Victimelor Comunismului și al Rezistenței*.

"Sounds great!" said Rich.

We drove nine miles north to the village of Săpânța, home to 3,267 living souls and more than 800 of the departed, who rest in what peace they can find beneath loudly painted tombstones and the tramping feet of thousands of sightseers who visit *Cimitirul Vesel*, the Merry Cemetery, each year.

"A man called Stan Ioan Pătraș started it," said George, as we climbed out of the car and paid ten lei, about three dollars, for the right to enter and take photos. "Back in 1935 his brother-in-law died, and being a wood carver, he wanted to make something special for the grave. So he wrote a humorous verse about his brother-in-law's life and carved it in wood, along with images of people and places the man had loved — his family, the village. Everyone liked it so much that when the next person in the village died, he was asked to do one for him too. After that it became a tradition. He carved almost seven hundred of them before he died in 1977. Now his students continue the tradition."

The grave markers were made of sturdy oak, wide planks topped with crosses and little peaked roofs, carved and painted in bright colors on a cheerful blue background. The images might be scenes of daily life

— driving a tractor, baking bread, drinking beer — or show the manner of death — a sickbed, a car crash — or reflect some aspect of the person's character, such as a naked angel (and I can only imagine what inspired that!). Each one contained a humorous, ironic poem about the dear departed, written with an old-fashioned cadence and enough grammatical errors to capture the flavor of archaic, rural speech. Here's one George translated for us:

Under this heavy cross
Lies my poor mother-in-law.
If she had lived even three more days,
I would be lying here and she would be reading this.
You, who here are passing by
Please try not to wake her up
Because if she comes back home
She'll criticize me some more.
But I will surely behave
So she'll not return from grave.
Stay here, my dear mother-in-law!

You just have to love people who exit on a laugh line. I've seen some good tombstones in my time, such as Merv Griffin's "I will *not* be right back after this message," Mel Blanc's "That's all folks," and Rodney Dangerfield's "There goes the neighborhood." Ben Franklin's came closest to the character of the Merry Cemetery: "The Body of B. Franklin. Printer. Like the cover of an old Book. Its Contents torn out. And Stript of its Lettering & Gilding. Lies here. Food for Worms. But the Work shall not be lost. For it will as he believ'd appear once more, In a new and more elegant Edition Corrected and Improved By the Author." Most clever epitaphs stand alone; this was the first time I'd seen hundreds of them in one place. I was sorry we didn't have time for George to translate them all.

The morning's visits to the market, memorial, and cemetery had given us an appetite, and our next stop was lunch at a large, nearly empty restaurant, where Rich and I ordered traditional fare and George had a pizza. The conversation ranged over life in Botiza, George's wife and her work as the village doctor, farm life in Maramureș, and inevitably the Gypsies, who are technically known as Romani or Romany.

This is a rather sore point with Romanians, due to the unhappy coincidence that the name — which comes from the Gypsy word Rom, meaning the man of the house — is easily mistaken for a variant of the word Romanian. The Romani are an unrelated ethnic group with origins in India and a population of millions spread throughout the world, mostly in Europe and the United States. But foreigners don't always make the distinction, causing George to say, rather heatedly, "Romani are *not* the same as Romanians," although Rich and I had certainly not implied that they were.

George and his countrymen had their own term, Tiganii, but when speaking English they use our word, Gypsies, which is a corruption of the word Egyptian. This term reflects an old misunderstanding of their origins; one legend suggested they were exiled from Egypt for harboring the Baby Jesus.

Large numbers of Gypsies were forcibly settled in Transylvanian towns during the communist era, but they had never adapted to the lifestyle and were not popular with their neighbors. Every Romanian we met told us, "Gypsies are lazy and they steal," backing this up with stories about swindles, hoodwinking, robberies, missing livestock, and shady dealings of all sorts. To top it all off, when the profligate Romani ran out of food and money — which happened, it seemed, every winter — they would go, like the grasshopper to the ant, begging for food and aid from their more industrious neighbors.

All this did not sit well with the good citizens of Maramureș, who took pride in their hard work and careful land management. The farms and villages we passed that day had the tidy, self-sufficient look of well-run agricultural communities. Everywhere we went, we saw groups of men and women out scything in the fields and heaping hay onto horse-drawn wagons, like living enactments of a Bruegel painting. Flocks of sheep grazed on the green hillsides under the watchful gaze of grizzled shepherds. Young men with ancient tractors hauled logs to be split for firewood or fashioned into planks and roof shakes to repair homes and churches before the long winter set in.

Nearly a hundred of the traditional wooden churches of Maramureș had survived from the seventeenth century, and each was as quirky as a fairy tale illustration. Most had towers so large they seemed likely to topple the building, some were capped with strangely outsized roofs that came nearly to the ground, and a few had the old "wolf doors," great, curving arches with triangular indents carved into the edges, like canine teeth — the better to eat you with, my dear. All the churches stood on hills, and to reach them we had to climb up steep paths that zigzagged through old, overgrown cemeteries.

"Here we go again!" I thought.

Inside, the church walls were covered with primitive murals of Bible scenes and colorful hangings stitched by the local women. In one we saw a famous block of wood which, when it was being split for firewood, revealed an interior marked with something that looked like a black cross. This was deemed a minor miracle, and the block of wood was proudly displayed in a glass case on one of the altars.

Assuming (correctly) that we'd worked up a thirst climbing about on hillsides and tramping through churches, George suggested we stop by and visit some people he knew who made *horincă*, the local plum brandy. Rich and I instantly fell in with this suggestion.

Our *horincă* host was a ruddy-faced fellow with thinning gray hair topped by one of the close-fitting straw caps favored in the region. His wife was a broad-shouldered, big-busted woman in late middle age, wearing a white headscarf, sweater, ankle-length skirt, and sensible shoes. She invited us to follow her into a large shed; ducking through the door we discovered it was pitch dark and heaving with noisy machinery. When our eyes adjusted, we made out an old piston, driven by a water wheel, pounding woven wool into a dense, felt-like mass, after which, our hostess explained, it would be simmered in hot water, shrinking the fabric and making it into thick, strong, boiled wool. Back outside in the daylight, she showed us warm vests and caps she'd sewn from the heavy material and embroidered with simple, graceful designs.

Her husband offered us samples of various kinds of brandy they'd made, and we enjoyed a pleasant twenty minutes sipping home brew and learning about how the brandy is made. It seems the plums were fermented and then boiled in the huge pots we'd seen in the shed; the vapor, which contained the highest alcohol content, was then distilled into brandy. At least, I think it was something like that; as the level in the bottles dropped, I began to feel a little hazy on some of the details . . .

Our hostess said something in Romanian, and George turned to us.

"Would you like to see the inside of the house?"

Yes, we certainly would.

We all got up from the porch and trooped through the main door into the living room. The colors made me gasp. Light flooded in from windows covered with sheer white cotton curtains delicately edged with embroidered flowers. Every possible surface — tables, shelves, benches, walls — was draped in thick cloths painstakingly stitched with bold red roses and bright green leaves. Even more embroidered household linens were stacked neatly on shelves going up to the rafters. The worn, lined face of our hostess lit up with pride, and for a moment I could see her as a young girl, stitching away on her trousseau, radiant with anticipation of her new, married life.

"Did she do all of this?" I asked George in awe.

"All the women here must do this kind of embroidery before they can marry," he explained. Thank God that wasn't a tradition in my country, I thought, or I would still be single.

At five o'clock, George delivered us back to the Iza train station, where we'd arrived just two days before in what seemed like another lifetime. Now, in the slanting afternoon sunlight, it seemed a perfectly ordinary, even homey sort of place, especially as we now knew there was a village just over the rise, the kind of rural village with which we'd become familiar over the past couple of days. With a dozen words of Romanian on my lips and with a bottle of George's friends' brandy tucked inside my daypack, I felt ready for anything.

It was well past eleven and raining hard when our train finally pulled into the city of Cluj-Napoca, known to its many friends simply as Cluj. Our lodgings were less than half a mile away, but given the weather and the hour, we took a cab instead of walking. The taxi deposited us in front of a tall, modern hotel called the Ary, which as near as I could tell was pronounced "awry"; Rich naturally scoffed at my suggestion that this might not bode well for our stay.

It was nearly midnight by the time we collected our key card from the sleepy young woman at the desk and dragged our bags to the elevator. I remember standing there pressing the button and waiting, pressing the button and waiting, over and over until the desk clerk came over and kindly explained that you had to keep holding the button down if you wanted to call the elevator.

"Really?" I muttered to Rich as the elevator doors closed behind us. "What genius thought *that* was an improvement over the standard model?" I pressed the button for our floor, but nothing happened. Eventually I realized that this button also had to be held down continuously in order to function. "Yes, I'm loving this place already."

We rode up one floor to our room, which turned out to be a small suite with little character but all the modern conveniences.

"Ah, civilization," Rich said.

We were so tired that we *almost* neglected to do a bedbug check. But by now the habit was deeply ingrained, and so, yawning, we peeled back the sheets — nothing — and peered into the mattress seams . . . wait, what was that?

"Rich, get the flashlight," I said. "Come look at this."

We stood peering at the usual ambiguous black specks that were most likely mere lint and at something that looked suspiciously like one of the pale brown egg casings shown in photos labeled 'The Tell-Tale Signs of Bedbug Infestation!"

We were out of the room in ten seconds, hauling our bags down to the front desk and demanding another room. The bewildered desk clerk kept saying, "*Insects*? In the *bed*? What . . .?" Clearly she was unaware that the world was at Defcon Orange in the fight against the bedbug apocalypse. She woke a man, probably her father, who'd been sleeping in the back room, and he leaned, bleary-eyed, against the desk as she accompanied us to a different room on a higher floor.

"You check now?" she suggested. And she stood watching in bemusement as we tore back the bed linens, shining our flashlight into the mattress seams.

"It's fine," I said, and she went away shaking her head. These crazy Americans!

Shuddering at how close we'd come to sharing our bed with a hoard of sex-crazed, blood-sucking insects eager to take up residence in our suitcases and our home, we washed up and climbed into bed.

"We really checked this bed thoroughly, right?" I said to Rich as he turned out the light.

"Good night," he said. "Sleep tight, don't—"

"Don't you *dare* say it!"

And then, at last, we slept.

CHAPTER 13

But Is It Safe?

A week later, sitting around a Transylvania dinner table, one of the British guests told me he'd recently met some Texans in London who, upon learning he was heading to Romania, said apprehensively, "But is it *safe?*"

And we all laughed. Because as wild as Romania was in many ways, we agreed that you'd really have to go out of your way to stir up actual trouble.

It wasn't always that way, of course. Over the past two thousand years, Romania had been dominated by Romans, Carpi, Visigoths, Huns, Gepids, Avars, Slavs, Bulgarians, Magyars, Hungarians, the Ottoman Empire, the Hapsburgs, the Austro-Hungarian Empire, the Nazis, the communists, and now global modernization, to name but some of the highlights. Getting a grip on Romanian history is like trying to unravel the plot of the TV series *Lost*. But with such a turbulent past and transitional present, it was easy to see how any talisman offering luck or protection, such as tying a red thread to your cow's tail, would be enduringly popular, especially in Transylvania.

The very name Transylvania conjures up images of evil, thanks to Bram Stoker's famous book. The author, an Irishman who never set foot in Romania, named the title character after a man who wasn't a count and didn't live in Transylvania. Dracula (or more properly Drăculeşti or Dracul, meaning Dragon) was one of the many titles of Vlad III, prince of the nearby realm of Wallachia. He belonged to the Order of the Dragon, a chivalric Christian military organization defending Europe from the advances of the Ottoman Empire in the mid-fifteenth century. Another of his titles (although you would *never* use it to his face) was Vlad the Impaler, a reference to his favorite method of execution, of which he made widespread use throughout his reign. And while he wasn't a vampire, he was every bit as coldblooded, bloodthirsty, and evil as his namesake.

Vlad the Impaler was spawned in Sighişoara, a charming city perched on a mountaintop in Transylvania. Rich and I went there right after we left Cluj, and as it happened, we stayed in a hotel just around the corner from Vlad's birthplace. One night, over drinks in our hotel bar, a young Romanian named Claudius told us, not without admiration, how Prince Vlad had once held the line against vastly superior Ottoman forces intent on conquering all of Europe.

"When the Ottomans were coming," Claudius said, "Vlad impaled ten thousand of his own people on stakes along the road. He thought the Ottoman army might find it . . . unnerving."

"He killed *ten thousand* of his own people?" I asked, aghast.

"Oh, not just ten thousand," Claudius said, with a certain grim relish. "After riding for miles along the road lined with the impaled corpses, the Ottomans passed through a forest, and when they came out on the other side, there were ten thousand more people impaled on stakes." The young man grinned. "The Ottomans turned around and fled. They could not take it." Gosh, what a bunch of wimps!

Naturally, Vlad's heinous exploits became the stuff of legend, and even today everyone seems to tell a slightly different version of this story. The most common account of the incident places it in 1462, when the Ottomans were marching on the city of Târgovişte, and Vlad ordered twenty thousand Turkish prisoners, taken during an earlier battle, to be impaled on stakes in front of the city. The sight of this sea of his countrymen's rotting corpses repulsed (both figuratively and literally) the Ottoman Sultan Mehmed II, who turned around in disgust and retreated rather hastily back to Constantinople. Christians throughout Europe, including the Pope, celebrated this as a great victory, and even today, Vlad remains something of a folk hero. He may have been a sadistic psycho, but he was a sadistic psycho in a good cause.

That night in the bar of our Sighișoara hotel, Claudius assured us that things had calmed down a lot since then, but he maintained that Romania was still home to plenty of cutthroats and villains.

"We have one entire city here that earns its living hacking into computers," he told us. "We Romanians are so corrupt that even the Devil is surprised."

Somehow it was hard to feel scandalized over that kind of hacking after listening to tales of Vlad's gory exploits.

Rich and I walked past Vlad's birthplace dozens of times, but I was so offended by the cheesy promotion — a large cutout of a cartoon count, complete with huge fangs and a bat-like cape — that Rich and I agreed to add it to the list of things we were skipping on the trip. That list also included Bran Castle, which was heavily marketed as the home of the title character in Bram Stoker's *Dracula*. Like 221B Baker Street in London and Juliet's balcony in Verona, it was pure fakery. Oh, it was a real castle all right, Gothic in style and situated above a dramatic gorge, but no matter how loudly the tourist websites proclaimed it Dracula's Castle, there was no getting around the fact that Bran Castle has nothing whatsoever to do with Bram Stoker, his book, the fictional Count Dracula, Vlad the Impaler, vampires, or anything else from the relevant pages of fiction or history.

So when Rich said, on our very first evening in Romania, "I've been reading about a place run by a Transylvania count—"

I interrupted him before he could finish. "Not Bran Castle. Don't tell me—"

"Of course not," he said indignantly. "As if I'd *ever* consider— No, I've been reading about this guesthouse way out in the country. It's run by a Count—" he peered more closely at the iPad's screen. "Count Kálnoky. It says here, 'Immerse yourself in a forgotten world that you probably believe has ceased to exist in today's Europe.' It looks incredibly rustic. I just hope they won't expect us to milk the cows."

We read a bit further and saw the prices — twice what we'd been paying for our accommodations to date — and learned that the count was a friend of Prince Charles (yes, *that* Charles, Diana's ex). I stopped worrying about milking the cows and started wondering what I'd be expected to wear to dinner. And exactly how did you address a count, anyway? Your Countenance didn't sound quite right . . .

Reading on, I learned the price included all meals and activities, which actually made it quite reasonable, so I fired off an email asking about availability. After a bit of correspondence back and forth, arrangements were made for us to stay for four nights in the main guesthouse. We'd need to take the train from Sighişoara to the city of Braşov; they offered to pick us up there for an extra fee, but as inveterate rail travelers, we chose to take the train as far as possible. In that case, they replied, transfer to a local train in Braşov and disembark at a stop called Augustin.

At the Braşov train station, we discovered the train to Augustin standing on a remote track, packed to bursting with a rough and colorful crowd. Women in vivid headscarves and long skirts sat smoking on the steps of the railroad cars, babies perched on their laps. Climbing past them, we ran into a flock of small children darting past while others slept sprawled on seats or on the sacks of grain piled near the doors. Large, sinister-looking fellows in shaggy country clothing were loading coils of cable, tires, and, in a car further down, a small couch onto the train. In our railway car, men in fedoras and cloth caps were shouting over a card game, cigarettes dangling from their lips. In fact, nearly everyone was smoking, which ordinarily might have been annoying but now provided a welcome counterpoint to the eye-watering scent of unwashed bodies. Babies were wailing, toddlers were shrieking, and somebody was playing tinny folk music on what sounded like a transistor radio but was probably a cheap phone.

"This is *fabulous*," I whispered to Rich as we found places to stand near the doorway. "It's the closest I'm ever likely to get to riding in a

Gypsy wagon." The train jolted to life and we grabbed onto grimy railings to keep from toppling over onto the children sleeping on the grain sacks.

The train stopped at a dozen tiny stations along the way, and often people would run up to our car and chatter briefly with someone in the doorway, at which point a package might be handed in or out, and then the visitor would disappear again. Eventually people started getting off the train, and when a seat opened up in our car, I sat down gratefully, tucking my suitcase under my knees and holding my daypack on my lap. I exchanged polite smiles and nods with my seatmate, a large, stocky man with a thick, black mustache and bushy eyebrows. Across the aisle, four women and a baby were watching me closely. I wondered if I'd broken any taboos by sitting with a man I didn't know. Too late now, I thought.

A couple of stops later, another seat opened up a few rows ahead of me, and Rich sat down next to a man who looked like a hired assassin and was perusing a Bible. Every once in a while, when the noise level rose to a crescendo, Rich's seatmate would look up, shake his head, mutter something, and go back to his reading.

When the conductor came around for tickets, he examined our Eurail documents with the usual suspicion, and once we'd allayed his fears, he asked where we were going and confirmed that this train was, indeed, heading in the direction of Augustin. Our destination now being public knowledge, Rich's seatmate and several other people in the vicinity volunteered to make sure we got off at the right station. This broke the ice, and when Rich began passing around some mints, we all became fast friends — or at least the kind of acquaintances that you no longer worry will rob or kill you.

Eventually we arrived at the Augustin station, and waving farewell to our new *amicii*, Rich and I climbed off the train. We were met by one of the count's managers, an affable, smooth-shaven man named Karsci who asked, a trifle anxiously, how we'd found the train ride. He seemed astonished when we said we'd thoroughly enjoyed ourselves.

"Not everyone — well, I'm *very* pleased," he said with obvious relief. Apparently other guests hadn't always found it quite so diverting.

Karsci drove us out of the little town of Augustin into open countryside and in half an hour we were threading our way down the main street of Miklósvár, a village established in 1211 and currently boasting a population of 512, not counting us. We drove slowly up the main street past centuries-old cottages, built in a boxy style using various combinations of stone, brick, plaster, and wood, their peaked roofs covered with red tile and weathered tin. Karsci turned into a gravel driveway and rolled to a stop in front of a small paddock and a scattering of whitewashed buildings.

The closest building was a barn built of timber and plaster and half covered with vines. On the near side of it stood a wooden lean-to housing an elegant, high-wheeled yellow carriage that looked at least a hundred years old, a stack of firewood, and a tree stump with an axe embedded in it, as if the woodcutter had just that moment ceased his labors.

Beyond the barn was a roomy, two-story house with pleasingly irregular rooflines, its many gables and dormers attesting to how often it had been expanded and altered during its long history. This was the main guesthouse, and Karsci escorted us up a flagstone path, past squat white pillars supporting the low porch and through the front door. Inside, there were more white walls, flowered curtains, soft striped rugs, and carved wooden furniture that looked as old as the house, parts of which dated back to the seventeenth century.

Karsci led us up creaky wooden stairs, past a quaint bathroom fitted with more or less modern plumbing, through a sitting room, to our attic bedroom. This had steeply sloping eaves, a window overlooking the main street, and two wide feather beds with plump down comforters and heaps of pillows. Someone, I was amused to note, had tacked garlic over the door and hung a rosary between the beds.

Downstairs, Karsci gave us a glass of caraway brandy, which was vastly superior to anything we'd tasted thus far, and explained that dinner would be served at seven that evening in the wine cellar beneath the house. For the following day, he suggested a ride in a horse cart and a picnic lunch. Further arrangements for our entertainment would be made on a daily basis. We agreed that it all sounded delightful.

And it was. The wine cellar, reached by a twisting stone staircase, had a ceiling of massive oak beams and walls of rough stone partially lined with wooden wine racks filled with local vintages. Dim electric wall sconces, a crackling fire, and candles standing on the long oak table created pools of light that reflected off the white linen tablecloth and polished silver. There was just enough light to see the heraldic carving hanging on one wall, and even without examining it more closely, I felt sure it came from Count Kálnoky's family, which had lived here in this village, although not in this house, for 760 years.

Rich grinned at me. "These guys don't miss a trick, do they?" he said.

"They're good. They're very, very good," I replied.

The whole experience was exquisitely crafted to be as authentic as possible while meeting every movie-fed expectation we might have. I really had to hand it to the count and his crew.

About now you may be wondering whether a carefully crafted experience can ever be considered truly authentic. I have thought about this a lot, and I have to say that yes, I believe it can. Cast your mind back to the most unforgettable meals, concerts, and parties of your life. You see what I mean.

"Authenticity" is a very modern, first-world term that has lately become the holy grail of the tourist industry; everybody's looking for it, although I'm not always sure that they recognize it when they see it. Google the phrase "authentic travel" and you'll find 242 million results popping up in the twinkling of an eye. So just what is authentic travel and why is everybody so keen to have it?

Back when long-distance travel was slower, more expensive, and less common, it seemed enough of an achievement just to arrive someplace as exotic as France and see the Mona Lisa and the Eiffel Tower with your own eyes. But with today's cheap airfares and abundant online travel information, many places far more remote than Paris are flooded with international visitors. This gives us the uncomfortable sensation of being one of the herd. We don't want to feel like *tourists*; we want to feel like *explorers*. We don't want to simply see foreign people and places; we want to *connect* with them.

But what does *that* look like, exactly?

Rich and I once spent a week in Thailand among the hill tribes, sleeping in bamboo huts, washing in streams, and seeing people make flour by pounding grain with rocks. For the most part they ignored our presence, carrying on with their daily lives as if we were invisible, which I found rather disconcerting. Were they wishing that we'd all just disappear and leave them in peace? One night, a local man returned from an arduous climb down the mountain and back up again carrying a car battery, which he'd recharged someplace and now connected to a black-and-white TV. The entire village gathered to watch an old, dubbed American sitcom they managed to pick up for half an hour. Some of our fellow travelers grumbled that this incident destroyed the purity of the experience. But I was impressed that the villagers had gone to so much trouble to arrange a TV night during our visit. They wanted to show us their modern side. *They* wanted to connect with *us*.

It struck me that I'd been viewing those villagers through a haze of misconceptions and cultural bias. They had been ignoring us not out of disinterest but as a courtesy, leaving us free to roam, observe, and take pictures as we chose. When the time came, they'd gone to considerable trouble to arrange an evening's entertainment geared as closely as possible to our tastes and interests — just as I organize bullfight tickets for bloodthirsty adolescent guests and flamenco nights for musician friends. I make a huge effort to help my guests enjoy themselves and feel at home, and it was clear that our hosts in the Thai village were doing precisely the same thing under far more challenging circumstances. I had to admire their work.

And I reminded myself that when we all talk about wanting authentic travel experiences, that doesn't mean seeing people in some perfectly preserved primitive state, as if their community were some sort of ethnic folk museum. No, it means enjoying people as they *are*, right here, right now. Authentic doesn't mean *old*; it means *real*.

Rich and I once spent a weekend in the Republic of Georgia at a client's family farm, baking bread with the grandmothers, drinking wine with the grandfather, and dancing with the younger generation while someone played a *panduri*, distant kin to a balalaika. The family pulled out all the stops to show us a good time, crafting the best hospitality they could manage to welcome the first Americans most of them had ever met. The deliberate care they took over the details didn't make their generosity or our experiences any less genuine, any more than my fussing over the preparations last Thanksgiving undermined the holiday experience for my guests. It didn't matter that our Georgian friends were wearing machine-made sweaters instead of hand-knitted ones or that we'd arrived in a car instead of on horseback or on foot. The point was not to go back in time and see the place in an "unspoiled" state but rather to have the pleasure of engaging with people who are living a very different lifestyle today.

And that's what Count Kálnoky's staff provided for us throughout our stay. The next morning, as promised, there was a wooden horse cart awaiting us along with a grizzled, snaggletoothed driver named Mihály and a fresh-faced young woman named Imalow who would serve as our guide and translator. The day was warm and sunny and the equine pace was leisurely as we headed up the main road and out of the village.

When we passed a sign reading "Micloşoara Miklósvár," Imalow explained that this area had previously stood on the Hungarian side of the Hungarian-Romanian border, and when it changed hands at the close of World War I the Hungarian Miklósvár was renamed Micloşoara — at least officially. Locally it was still very much Miklósvár and, she implied, always would be.

"Here," she said, "you will find people speak only Hungarian."

This was bad news for me and my dozen or so carefully acquired words of Romanian. I soon learned everyone understood me if I used *mersi* and *la revedere* to say "thanks" or "goodbye," but I had the uncomfortable suspicion that they viewed this as the language of the oppressor, disliking it in much the same way that staunch supporters of Catalan independence resent being spoken to in Spanish. I tried to learn the Hungarian word for "thanks," but somehow *köszönöm* never did trip off my tongue with any ease.

Our first stop that morning was to visit the local beekeeper, who lived on a steep hillside, in a trailer surrounded by rows of colorfully painted wooden hives. A black watchdog announced our presence with a series of sharp barks, and the beekeeper emerged from the trailer to welcome us warmly in Hungarian and help us alight from the cart.

I was pleased to don one of the broad-brimmed, veiled hats our host provided. I'm not particularly phobic about bees, but there seemed an inordinate number of them buzzing around us and crawling on the frames of honey extracted for our inspection. I've never field tested this, but I've read that when bees are feeling defensive, they are attracted to human breath and like to attack the face. Stings there are particularly painful, and trying to extract tiny barbed objects from your own face is an awkward business at best, so stingers tend to have plenty of time to stay in place, continuously pumping venom into your body. I was glad to have a bit of protection as we admired the hives and the specially fitted truck, onto which he loaded his seventy or eighty best hives every spring, driving them to greener pastures to enrich their diet and their honey.

Our host invited us to remove our hats and follow him into a low tent he'd fashioned from tarps draped over cut saplings in front of his trailer. Seated on short stools and upturned crates, we began to sample the honey. It was lovely, rich and sweet and faintly warm from the sun, and he described the flowers that gave each one its flavor as he drizzled one kind after another onto spoons for us to taste.

Random bees made forays into the tent, slipping in through the gaps, and from time to time our host would break off his discussion of the varieties of honey and the diets of bees in order to dispatch a few of his winged workers with a large plastic flyswatter. We emerged unstung and with a jar of his best honey, which apparently had unspecified but powerful healing properties.

As our cart rolled downhill to the road, Imalow, who was sitting up next to Mihály, turned around and asked, "Would you like to meet some shepherds?"

You bet.

Half an hour later we trundled onto a broad, grassy plain to find several huts and a large pen holding four hundred sheep, two dogs, and three humans. Two of the humans — lean, sinewy shepherds in middle age, their faces worn and roughened by decades in the open air — were sitting in an open-sided hut that connected a smaller holding area with the main section of the pen. A gangly fourteen-year-old girl was trotting about the holding pen, chivvying sheep toward a tiny gate in the back of the hut, assisted by two dogs so large, white, and curly haired that they might have been part sheep themselves. As each ewe wriggled through the gate flaps, one of the shepherds would grab her, milk her in about ten seconds flat — squirt, squirt, squirt into the waiting bucket — and then release her to rejoin the herd that was standing idly about in the main part of the pen.

Standing idly comes naturally to sheep. They have the curious ability to vegetate in place, looking as fatuous and dimwitted as a living organism can look without actually being unconscious. Scientific research shows that sheep aren't nearly as foolish as they seem; individually, in fact, they are actually quite intelligent. Give them a problem to solve, such as what color bucket has the food, and they're as quick to find the feed as monkeys or even some humans, easily outperforming mice and rats. A Yorkshire sheep figured out how to roll across a hoof-proof cattle grid eight feet wide to get to tastier food. But in a flock, their intelligence seems to evaporate; if one falls into a hole, the others blindly plummet right down after it. Just now, they were in flock mode and seemed content simply to stand there awaiting further developments.

"The shepherds milk four hundred sheep three times a day," Imalow explained. "They live up here most of the year to guard the sheep from the wolves. The men sleep in these huts."

She indicated two windowless boxes, each about six feet square, standing on short stilts a good fifteen long strides apart from one another. Evidently the shepherds liked their privacy. Perhaps they too had seen *Brokeback Mountain* and knew what had happened when Ennis and Jack were sent out to guard the sheep in Wyoming's grasslands. Eight percent of male sheep are gay, seeking only male sex partners throughout their lifetime; possibly the shepherds were worried it could be contagious.

"What do they do in the winter?" I asked. At this altitude, the mid-September air already held a sharp edge of frost in the morning and evening; the cold came early in these parts.

"The men take the sheep down to a barn and then they go home to their families."

These guys had families?

"The girl in the holding pen is the daughter of one of the shepherds." I looked at the silent teenager with renewed interest. "It's quite unusual for girls to do this work." She glanced at the men and added, "Oh good, they are finished milking. Now they will show you where they make the cheese."

The shepherds carried their tin buckets to another open-sided hut and poured the milk into a larger container, using muslin to strain out the larger impurities such as the bits of wool, dirt, and feces that inevitably fall off the backside and undercarriage of sheep during the milking process. One of the shepherds then poured water into one of the just-emptied cans and washed his hands in the milky water. The demands of hygiene thus having been met, he proudly showed us the cheese-making area. This was a large yellow table topped with a metal sluicing sink, on which stood a plastic-wrapped cheese the size of a pumpkin; another softer cheese, housed in a plastic sack, hung from a nail on the wall. There was naturally no electricity, running water, or refrigeration.

"There are new laws all the time about the conditions for making food." Imalow shook her head sadly. "Soon this kind of cheese making may not be possible."

I have to confess that I had mixed feelings about this. On the one hand, I hated to see a traditional form of food production — and these men's livelihoods — inhibited by persnickety regulations. Traditional shepherds were already likely to become an endangered species in Romania, where the number of sheep had dropped 40 percent in recent years. When government subsidies collapsed along with the communist regime in 1989, the cost of meat, milk, and wool rose sharply, and in the current struggling economy these former staples are becoming less and less affordable. More stringent regulations would make it that much tougher for shepherds like this to survive. On the other hand, there was something to be said for food that was reliably free of wool, dirt, and feces. When the shepherds cut a large hunk off the cheese with a knife and proudly offered it to us in a tin bowl, it was all I could do not to ask Imalow, "Is it *safe*?"

Safe or not, Rich and I ate the cheese, which was light, creamy, and apparently free of the more aggressive forms of bacteria; at any rate, we certainly experienced no ill effects from it.

And then it was time for lunch, which we learned was to be cooked nearby over an open fire. Mihály began unpacking plastic containers of raw chicken and setting a little metal grill over some rocks near the treeline. Clearly this would be a leisurely process.

I noticed a long, wooden horse cart in the distance, making its way slowly across the grassy plain. Imalow exclaimed, "That's the local blacksmith. He comes out here from time to time to feed the wild boars." Really? Why? Wild boars are tough critters that have survived since the Pleistocene era and are currently listed in the not-even-close-to-being-endangered category. But here they need feeding because . . .? "They want to keep the herd strong for times when they wish to hunt them," she explained. Ah, that.

She hesitated, then said, looking across at the blacksmith, "He doesn't usually let people ride with him, but he is a friend of my father.

I will ask." She trotted off across the meadow and stood in conversation for a moment before gesturing for us to join her. When we were within earshot she shouted eagerly, "Yes, he has agreed. Get in!"

The three of us climbed into the back of the cart, which was laden with sacks of grain, and Imalow introduced us to the blacksmith. He was a lean, silent, lugubrious man in jeans, a bright red vest, and the kind of cloth bucket hat favored by old duffers in Florida. He merely nodded in welcome and then returned to his driving, a task that required considerable concentration when we left the grasslands and plunged in among the trees. As we lurched along a rutted dirt track that wound deeper and deeper into the forest, Imalow kept calling out timely warnings to help us avoid being whapped in the face or decapitated by low branches.

We came to a halt in a large clearing, and the blacksmith began to call out. Soon we heard rustling in the bushes, and one or two boars trotted into view, big, yellow-gray brutes with long snouts and small, dark, mean-looking eyes. A few more followed and then suddenly there were dozens pushing and shoving against the sides of the cart. They weren't as huge as the fatted sows I'd seen in the Maramureş animal market, but these were feral creatures and much tougher, crankier, and hungrier than their farm-raised cousins. I felt a momentary twinge of anxiety; boars were omnivores and while they preferred vegetation, they had a taste for meat as well. I made a mental note to be careful not to fall out of the cart.

I needn't have worried. The beasts knew exactly how this worked and kept their eyes firmly on the sack of grain the blacksmith was unloading from the back of the wagon. The pigs milled about, grunting with pleasurable anticipation. Perhaps this is why groups of them are technically known as a sounder of wild boar; personally I preferred the more romantic term, a drift of wild pigs.

The blacksmith threw the grain sack over his shoulder and waded calmly into the drift. Stopping a dozen yards from the cart, he sliced the bag open with a knife and began pouring the feed onto the ground in a rough rectangle. The beasts fell to with gusto. There were several smaller boars, so young that they could almost be considered cute, vying unsuccessfully for some of the food. When he returned to the cart, the blacksmith told us that having been born quite late in the season, the youngsters' chances of surviving the coming winter were very low indeed. Several irascible-looking males stood back from the feast, glowering at us from among the trees; those, I suspected, were the ones most likely to outlive their driftmates when the hunters came around.

All in all it was a remarkable day, and Rich and I thoroughly enjoyed ourselves. Over the next few days, the weather having turned cool and drizzly, we explored the area by car, accompanied by a guide named Monica and an assortment of our fellow guests. At any given time, there were perhaps six or eight other people staying at several guesthouses in the village, and we'd all gather for breakfast in the farmhouse kitchen, head off for the day's excursions in various configurations, and regroup over dinner in the wine cellar. Most of the guests were British and widely traveled, so conversations tended to range over every conceivable topic and proved very entertaining indeed.

One afternoon half a dozen of us visited Viscri, a Saxon village that had been established around 1100 when warriors from the North German Plain were invited to settle there and defend the border between Transylvania and Hungary. The Saxon warriors who took the job arrived with their families, established their own towns, and lived peaceably enough with their new neighbors. But they kept themselves to themselves, speaking only German, holding on to Saxon customs, and staying out of local affairs; there was scarcely any intermarrying, even after more than nine hundred years of living side by side.

Then in the late twentieth century, Germany rather belatedly decided it wanted its citizens back. It negotiated a deal with Romania, paying a fee for each returning Saxon and launching a public relations campaign praising the glories of returning to the fatherland. The fact that many Saxons were leaving centuries-old wooden country houses and close-knit communities for a cramped city flat didn't feature quite so prominently in the descriptions of the plan. But it seemed the practicalities weren't as important as the deep desire to return to their roots. After living abroad for nine hundred years — forty-five generations! — Germany was still home.

As an American, I found this staggering. In my country, known as the great melting pot, new arrivals may cling to the old ways for a while, but in a generation or two most think nothing of intermarrying with other ethnic groups. My own ancestors came over in the early nineteenth century from Ireland, England, and Germany, but after a mere two hundred years in America, no one in my family was likely to be lured into being repatriated to any of those countries, even if they covered moving expenses and threw in an apartment.

But the Saxons left Romania in droves, and soon most of their old strongholds were ghost towns. Viscri was now almost entirely occupied by Gypsies, with a handful of Romanians, a few quaint guesthouses owned by the Prince of Wales, and about twenty Saxons, many of whom were dedicated to maintaining the thirteenth-century church that was the oldest house of worship in Transylvania.

It was a warrior's church, surrounded by two massive bulwarks studded with sturdy, square watchtowers. The church itself was simple, with whitewashed walls, painted wood panels along the sides, and benches running along the walls and standing in tidy rows down the center. During services, the men sat along the outer walls, forming a protective circle around the women and children.

"The young girls sat in the back," explained our guide, Monica. "As they aged, women moved up closer and closer to the altar; the oldest ones sat in the front pews, the ones you see here, with the black angels painted on the walls. Even today, you hear people in these villages referring to older women as 'sitting with the black angels.'"

As fascinating as these outings were, the best part of every day came toward sunset, back in the village of Miklósvár. It usually occurred as Rich and I were dressing for dinner — and by this I mean putting on a marginally cleaner shirt and wiping the worst of the mud off our sneakers; I don't mean to imply that he and I were descending to the wine cellar in formal attire. This was, thank heavens, the country, and my slacks were almost too dressy; for the first time I wished I'd packed a pair of jeans. Anyway, as we were pulling ourselves together for the evening, we'd hear the sound of bells in the street below, and we'd go running to the window to watch the cows come home.

Every morning at sunrise the local cowherd walked through the village, and each family's cow would emerge from the open door of her stable or pen and amble into the road to join the little herd heading into the hills to graze. At sunset, the cows ambled slowly back down the village's main street, each one turning with the ease of long practice into her home gate, where the family waited to greet her.

A pair of goats brought up the rear of the procession, sometimes pausing to snack in various gardens along the way. One evening, the billygoat was standing right in the middle of the road when a truck came zooming up behind him. "Looks like we'll be having goat for dinner," Rich remarked from his viewpoint at the window. But the goat had other ideas. He didn't even deign to glance around, just planted all four hooves and stood firm. The truck honked, braked, honked again, and finally slewed wildly to the left. At the last possible second, the goat trotted off to the right, giving a little kick of his heels as if to say, "Take *that*, modern world."

I loved this attitude and was grateful for the chance to watch the daily comings and goings of the villagers and their herd. It breaks my heart to know that this traditional Transylvanian culture is not safe; it's sitting with the black angels, destined to disappear forever, probably within my lifetime. The change is as unstoppable as the arrival of television and the exodus of the Saxons. But the old ways haven't disappeared yet. And there's a deep comfort in knowing that every evening at sunset, as I close my computer and head out for a beer with friends, the cows of Miklósvár are ambling along the street and finding their way home, where their families are waiting for them.

CHAPTER 14

Pardon Me, Is This Budapest or Bucharest?

Ever wonder where the Pied Piper took the children of Hamelin after he'd lured them away from their homes? According to legend, it was to the city of Braşov, high in the Transylvanian mountains. Oh sure, darker versions of the tale suggest he drowned the kids in the River Weser like the rats or stashed them in a mountain cave for unspeakable purposes. But I favor the theory that the tale of the Pied Piper is really a fanciful, folkloric description of the very real *Ostsiedlung*, the migration of Saxon Germans to eastern parts of Europe such as Braşov and the ghost town we'd visited, Viscri. Rich and I were curious about the Saxon city that continued to thrive, with or without the descendants of the children of Hamelin, so when we left Miklósvár, we took the train to Braşov.

Two nights earlier, Rich had gone on his Airbnb app, typed in Braşov, checked off such must-have criteria as privacy and wifi, and spent some time scrolling through the offerings. He flagged several for us to look over together, and although there were some fancier places a little further from the city center, we decided on one just steps from Braşov's vast central plaza which was named, with greater clarity than originality, Town Hall Square (*Piata Sfatului*).

On the Internet, the apartment had appeared small and cozy. In person, it felt like a pair of cupboards — a slightly larger one into which was shoehorned a double bed, and the miniscule, windowless kitchen that held a sliver of a table and two straight-backed chairs. After the comforts and charm of the count's guesthouse, it felt like Harry Potter's bedroom under the stairs.

However, I soon discovered that its small size had one huge advantage: I could sit at the kitchen table and do everything — write blog posts, watch movies on the computer with Rich, get a glass of water from the tap, pull something from the fridge, even do dishes — all without ever getting up out of my chair.

"Cozy and efficient," I said to Rich. "Ya gotta love it."

The second thing we loved about Braşov — and I know how shallow this will make us sound — was the nearby Gigi pastry shop. We had discovered Gigi two weeks earlier, during our visit to Sighişoara, when we'd noticed locals lining up outside a hole-in-the-wall on a street in the modern section of town. It had turned out to be a pastry shop selling something called *covrigi* through the window. We weren't quite sure what *covrigi* were, but they smelled divine, and when we reached the front of the line we pointed at random in the direction of the pastry rack and held up two fingers. The woman at the window handed us two enormous rings of golden pastry, each as big around as a dinner plate, one filled with cherry jam and the other with soft, sweet, white cheese, both still warm from the oven. "We have died and gone to heaven," said Rich, around a mouthful of cherry-filled pastry. And now, discovering a branch of Gigi just a block from the apartment in Braşov, Rich was licking his lips and grinning from ear to ear.

The third wonderful discovery in Braşov was the White Witch. Within hours of our arrival, we wandered into the tourist office, housed in the fifteenth-century Council Offices in the center of Town Hall Square, thinking vaguely that we should get a map and start hitting a few points of interest besides Gigi. There, sitting behind the desk, was a black-clad, white-haired woman with a sweet, grandmotherly smile and a ghoulish delight in sharing hair-raising tales about the city's history.

She gave us a map and glossy brochures showing photos of the major monuments, and then she leaned forward with a confiding air and said, "Vlad Tepes lived here, you know, the one they call Vlad the Impaler." She beamed at us. "He was a great hunter. And he was very fond of dogs.

Not many people talk about that, but it's true. Yes, he loved his dogs."

What? There was a softer side to Vlad the Impaler?

Our new friend showed us a grainy photo of a stone statue of a warrior in chain mail, with a bow and arrow slung over one shoulder, a hunting horn at his lips, and a hound at his knee.

"He used the dogs to hunt poachers; the dogs were very fast and always ran them down. And when he caught them, of course," she gave an indulgent little chuckle, "he impaled them. This statue of Vlad Tepes is on a church dedicated to hunters." No doubt the congregation found it inspirational. I wondered if it was still legal to hunt down poachers in these parts. Surely they'd outlawed impaling?

We were still blinking from the dog story when she added, "Would you like to see his bank?"

He had a bank? Apparently there was a *lot* more to Vlad than I'd suspected.

"Come with me." She stood up and led us out the front door, her long, black skirt flowing behind her as she walked. She wasn't wearing a costume, but something about the old-fashioned cut and midnight hue of her clothing conjured up images of medieval robes and the illustrations in *Grimm's Fairy Tales*. Her long, silvery hair sparkled in the sunlight, and already I was thinking of her as the White Witch.

"Vlad Tepes," she explained, "was very interested in financial power — in money and moving money around. When people called him a vampire, it was actually a metaphor for being a bloodsucking banker. Look over there."

We obediently gazed across the street at a large, three-story bank painted a cheerful pink with white trim. I'm no expert on architectural styles, but even I could tell it had been constructed four hundred years after Vlad was running around impaling poachers.

"The bank was built soon after the book *Dracula* came out. The decorations were a sort of homage to Vlad Tepes. Look at the windows." Peering more closely at the windows, I realized that the carvings above them, which I'd taken to be ancient deities, had large, white fangs protruding from their upper lips. "Yes," said the White Witch complacently. "This is Vlad Tepes's town, all right."

We thanked her for her help, and when she 'd gone back inside to await the next innocent victims — sorry, I mean tourists — I said to Rich, "If someone told me she lived in a gingerbread house and tried to stuff Hansel and Gretel into her oven, I wouldn't be at all surprised."

During the next few days, as we wandered around Braşov enjoying the sights, we dropped in on the White Witch every so often to collect printed information about the city and hear more grisly tales of its history.

"Oh yes," she said comfortably one afternoon. "There are still wolves and bears in these parts. Not like the old days, though. Back then the bears used to come down out of the forest, right to the city dump, and rummage around for food. But then the Gypsies started picking over the same waste piles, and there were some . . . unfortunate incidents." Her lips thinned in disapproval. "The city decided the bears had to go." It was pretty clear she thought the Gypsies should have been the ones airlifted out to a remote mountain wilderness and left to fend for themselves without the rich pickings of a garbage dump.

Braşov marked the halfway point in our trip, and after a month and a half of travel, Rich and I were thinking that maybe we needed to slow down a trifle. As railway nomads we'd kept on the move, spending three or four days in most places with a few one-nighters to break up longer train journeys between major destinations. Now we decided to spend an entire, restful week somewhere, and somewhat arbitrarily, we chose the Romanian capital. We booked a promising-looking Airbnb apartment, made one last trip to Gigi's to buy *covrigi* for the train, and headed south out of Transylvania to Bucharest.

Having spent three weeks enjoying the storybook beauty of Romania's smaller cities and rural villages, my first, second, and third impressions of the nation's capital came as a hideous shock. The city was jammed with brutal, Soviet-era architecture: massive, featureless, gray, concrete behemoths formed of countless identical cells, designed as a constant, dehumanizing reminder to workers that they were just cogs in the State machine. The buildings would have been bad enough in their heyday, but now, sprouting hazardous tangles of electrical wires and leprous with dirt and graffiti, they created a distinctly dystopian atmosphere. If this were a movie set, you'd know instantly that this was a post-apocalyptic world where people lived on the edge, fighting over water, eating rats — and possibly each other.

As the taxi carried us deeper into the heart of the city, I fought the impulse to tell the driver to turn around and take us back to the train station. A whole week here? What were we *thinking*? In the shadows, jammed up against one of the concrete monstrosities, I saw a genteel, old Victorian apartment house with filigree, turrets, and an air of being appalled to find itself in such rough company. I knew exactly how it felt.

The taxi driver let us out in front of a large, drab, pre-Soviet building with a dental office on the ground floor, deposited our bags on the sidewalk, and took off.

I said, "We *can* get out of this contract with Airbnb, right? I mean, if we decide not to spend a whole week here."

"Well, they can't *force* us to stay," Rich said, eying the scabrous stains on the concrete walls opposite, half hidden by torn posters, city grime, and generations of spray-painted social commentary.

At that moment a wiry, young man popped out the front door rather breathlessly to welcome us into the apartment building. Speaking rapid-fire English with only a faint Romanian accent, he escorted us inside, past the dentist's door, to an old-fashioned, wire-cage elevator.

"The apartment has been completely redone," he said, wrestling the door closed and jabbing at buttons. As we lurched upwards, he added, "Everything is very new, very comfortable."

It was instantly apparent that somebody with taste, style, and access to an Ikea had been given free rein in the renovations. The look was clean, bright, and contemporary, perfectly color coordinated throughout in shades of gray and cream with cheerful red accents. And the space! There were two ample bedrooms, two full baths, a living room, a dining room, a kitchenette, and a laundry room. We could go for days without seeing one another if we so desired.

"And here," said our host, making a sweeping gesture toward the living room windows, "is a view of the Museum of George Enescu!"

George who? In my ignorance, I assumed the museum was a tribute to some forgettable local mini-celebrity. It was only later that I learned this Romanian composer was, as the preeminent cellist Pablo Casals put it, "the greatest musical phenomenon since Mozart." Yehudi Menuhin, arguably the twentieth century's greatest violinist, said, "Enescu gave me the light that has guided my entire existence." Being a total musical illiterate, I knew none of this at the time. However, it seemed tactful to evince some interest, so I exclaimed, "What? Right next door? How convenient!" I joined him at the window, glanced out, and gasped.

Next door was a fin-de-siècle palace crawling with gold-leaf cherubs, urns, curlicues, escutcheons, balustrades, and tchotchkes of all kinds. It was a monument to wealth and power and self-indulgence, a soaring tribute to artistic excess and elitist ego. I was amazed the communists hadn't torn it down in an effort to cleanse the community of its riotous decadence.

"Nice view," Rich said. He accepted the keys from our host, walked him to the door, and came back to me.

"I take it we're staying?" I said.

"Let's give it a day or two. Maybe the city will grow on us."

The George Enescu Museum and our apartment gave me hope that Bucharest might contain some shreds of non-Stalinist ambiance, so as soon as we'd unpacked, we took off to explore the city. Rich had read that a good place to start was Lipscani Street, an old mercantile pedestrian area in the heart of the city. As promised, it was old, mercantile, and pedestrian, but the ground floors of all the vintage buildings had been converted into fast food franchises, retail chain outlets, strip clubs, and cheap bars filled with drunken louts. It was utterly cringe-worthy, like seeing a long-admired actor cavorting about in an embarrassingly crass comedy.

Aghast and dispirited, Rich and I headed back to the apartment. On the way, we attempted to find a market where we could stock up on food, but the best we could discover was a convenience store, where we bought cheese, crackers, apples, and beer. This simple picnic in hand, we retired to our spacious apartment for the night and hoped that the next day, Bucharest would come closer to meeting us halfway.

We were up early the next morning, our natural optimism reasserting itself as we headed back downtown to take a free walking tour. There was a sizable group — what *were* all these people doing here? — assembled around Mihaela, our young guide.

"Good morning," she said. "First, I want to make sure you all know where you are right now. What city is this?"

We all eyed her suspiciously. Was this a trick question?

Someone said, rather tentatively, "Bucharest?"

"Congratulations. You're doing a lot better than most. Some of you may have heard that when Michael Jackson came here in 1992, he stood up on the balcony of the new parliament building — you can see it there—" We all turned our heads to the east, where a colossal, white building topped a rise in the far distance. "Michael Jackson stood there, surrounded by thousands of fans, and called out, "It's great to be here in Budapest!""

The King of Pop wasn't the first to mix up the names of *Budapest*, the capital of Hungary, and *Bucharest*, the capital of Romania and the place he happened to be standing at the time. Nor was he the last. It seemed that just about everyone — from the lead singers of Iron Maiden, Metallica, Whitesnake, and Morcheeba to Ozzy Osbourne and Lenny Kravitz — had stood up before cheering throngs and misidentified the city. Just the year before, four hundred Spanish sports enthusiasts chartered a plane to attend the Europa League final but found themselves 397 miles from the action when they landed in Budapest by mistake. A British sports announcer, who had managed to arrive at the correct location for the game, started off his program with an enthusiastic, "Good evening, Budapest!"

Clearly something had to be done, and a firm of Romanian candy makers called ROM decided to step in to clear up the confusion — and, not incidentally, to make their product a household name in the process. They launched a "Bucharest Not Budapest" campaign with T-shirts, billboards, and the name of Romania's capital clearly stamped into each chocolate bar. When a certain well-known singer was scheduled to appear, an enormous billboard was put up in the main square, saying, "Hello, Bruce! How was your flight? Kind reminder for tonight: it's 'hello, Bucharest,' not Budapest. You didn't start the confusion, but maybe you can help end it. Thanks." He got the message.

I was beginning to warm to this town. Anybody who could turn that lemon into lemonade earned my admiration.

And there was much more to like, as the walking tour took us through the better parts of the old center, the ones happily free of strip clubs and drunken louts. We saw the most ancient medieval monument in the city, an old court known, inevitably, as the Old Court, built by our old friend Vlad the Impaler. "He was fond of dogs, you know," I remarked casually to some of our fellow tourists as we stood in front of his statue. They didn't seem too impressed.

There was an astonishing diversity of architecture crammed together in the downtown area: ancient churches, glass-walled modernist cubes, curvy art deco apartments, neoclassical theaters, staid Victorians, and the ubiquitous Soviet hulks. As we followed Mihaela past some grandiose nineteenth-century buildings into Revolution Square, I saw something that made me stop in my tracks, grab Rich by the arm, and say, "And what in the name of God is *that*?"

That was a skinny, white marble spike, rising 82 feet into the air, with some sort of blob stuck onto it near the top. The blob, which was an oval-ish tangle of dark metal, had on its bottom edge a splash of vivid red that looked like dripping blood.

"Another monument to Vlad the Impaler?" Rich hazarded.

"That is the Memorial of Rebirth," said Mihaela. We all gawked at the gruesome object. "It commemorates the overthrow of the communists and the rebirth of Romania as a free country. The original name was *Glorie Eternă Eroilor şi Revoluţiei Române din Decembrie 1989*, or Eternal Glory to the Heroes and the Romanian Revolution of December 1989." I could see why they went with the shorter title. The populace had, of course, come up with their own names for the bloody (and I mean that literally) thing: the potato skewered on a stake, an olive on a toothpick, the potato of the revolution. Physics and engineering majors liked to call it "the vector with the crown," vector sounding so much like victor yet being a technical term meaning (and I'm paraphrasing roughly here) a linear shape; apparently the pun sounded a lot funnier if you happened to be a rocket scientist. The monument had proven so wildly unpopular that it was guarded around the clock, yet a performance artist managed to slip past security to add the blood-like red paint — the catsup, if you will, on the potato of the revolution — and in my eyes, the work was the better for it.

By the end of the morning, I had abandoned my image of Bucharest as being sunk in post-apocalyptic gloom. I liked its spunky irreverence and began to think the town had real possibilities. It was time, Rich and I decided, to get to know some of its citizens.

As it happened, the Bucharest branch of the expat network InterNations was throwing a cocktail party that night, and Rich and I emailed the hosts to let them know that we were visiting from Seville and would attend. The party was held at a glamorous, old club downtown, and we arrived to find it packed to the rafters with a noisy international crowd. Although InterNations gatherings were usually free, that night there was an admission charge that covered one drink and a buffet of hors d'oeuvres, so we paid up and began wriggling through the crowd in the direction of the bar. Drinks in hand, we then struggled on through the mass of bodies to the buffet, only to find it had been picked clean by the ravening hoards.

I was staring dispiritedly at a large, silver platter containing nothing but half a bread stick when someone behind me said, "Hi!" I turned to find a young Bulgarian dressed in a suit and proffering his business card. "I'm in marketing. My wife has a jewelry shop. I wrote the name and address on the back. Just show her this card, and she'll give you a discount." And with that he disappeared back into the crowd.

"Let's introduce ourselves to somebody," Rich shouted over the noise. We chose a thin, middle-aged man who was standing alone. He handed us each a card, explained that he was a Canadian there on business, and launched into a lugubrious monologue about the shortcomings of Romania in general and Bucharest in particular. "Efficiency? Don't expect to find any here. Once I put an order in on a Tuesday . . . or maybe it was a Wednesday . . ." It was like having cocktails with Eeyore, Winnie the Pooh's woebegone donkey friend. "And I said, 'Well, you *told* me that you could . . .'"

When we finally managed to break free from Eeyore on the pretext of needing fresh drinks, Rich shouted to me over the din, "Let's split up and mingle." I nodded and he stepped away to be instantly swallowed up by the crowd.

I spent the next half hour circling the room and accepting business cards; nearly everyone seemed to be looking for work in marketing, consulting, or marketing consulting. Like the man whose wife sold jewelry, they had a tendency to pop in and out of view like the Cheshire cat, staying just long enough to introduce themselves and then disappearing, leaving behind nothing but their shiny, white business cards.

Eventually I ran into Rich again at the bar, talking to a stocky, middle-aged Austrian, who handed me his card and let me know that he was exceedingly well connected and could be of tremendous assistance to us during our visit to his adopted city. A tall, thin woman in a skimpy dress had one arm draped languidly over his shoulder. The Austrian winked at me and hinted broadly that he'd had sex with all the best women in Bucharest. Not for the first time, I reflected that one of the enormous advantages of getting older was not having to worry that he would attempt to add me to his collection, requiring all sorts of tedious, defensive maneuvers on my part. There wasn't nearly enough left of my drink for me to waste any of it on his face.

Rich, who'd made himself scarce during my conversation with the

Austrian, now showed up again with a young Romanian-Canadian in tow. "Hi, I'm Calin," said the newcomer, and to my astonishment he didn't give me his card or offer any marketing consulting services. He actually seemed — like us — to be there just for fun, and we spent a pleasant twenty minutes chatting together. Eventually Rich and I were overcome with hunger pangs and left in search of food; no likely-looking eateries presenting themselves along our route, we wound up dining on cheese and crackers back at the apartment.

Over the next several days, Rich and I explored the city with mixed results. We'd read glowing reviews of the Museum of the Romanian Peasant, but after wandering through the exhibits for ten minutes, we realized that the collection consisted in large part of objects identical to the ones we'd been sleeping on, eating from, and seeing all around us in Maramureș and Miklósvár. Looking at them under glass soon palled, and we made our departure.

Stepping outside, we noticed a hop-on-hop-off tour bus discharging some passengers nearby, and we decided to come back the next day and take a ride around the city. This proved more complicated than expected, as the stops weren't marked, and the buses seemed to pause randomly at the curb, usually somewhere that was separated from us by six lanes of traffic. Finally one stopped within sprinting distance, and we raced over to it and leapt aboard.

In our haste, we nearly bypassed the large, uniformed woman sitting by the door. She glared at us and held out her hand for the fare. Rich dug out his money clip and began extracting local currency, muttering to me, "Do you remember what the charge—" The woman reached over and snatched fifty lei, about seventeen dollars, out of Rich's hand. Okay, thanks for clearing that up! I looked past her to a large rack of audio headsets, pointed, and said, "English?" She shot me a look of outraged disbelief, as if I'd asked her for kinky sexual favors or offered her a syringe full of heroin. She jerked her head toward the back of the bus. No headsets. No commentary. No backtalk. Go.

We went.

Sitting up top in the open-air section of the bus, we kept saying to one another, "Hey, that looks interesting. Wonder what it is . . ."

Eventually we began making up our own commentary. "Look, there's the old church where Vlad the Impaler had his first exorcism!"

"Isn't that the bar where Ceaușescu used to sing karaoke with Michael Jackson?"

I tried to take photos, but with the bus alternately lurching forward and braking sharply, most of my shots were blurs or peculiarly angled close-ups of the back of the seat in front of me.

After twenty minutes of this, Rich said, "Are we done?"

We went downstairs and asked to be let off at the next stop. The woman who had refused to give us headsets shot us a withering glare, and the driver pointedly ignored us. The bus continued onward for quite a long time, passing intersections I was certain I had seen listed as stops on the bus company's website, moving ever further away from the neighborhood of our apartment. Obviously I wasn't about to risk saying anything, as I didn't want to be banished back upstairs or possibly to the Gulag. When the driver finally — grudgingly — pulled over, stopped, and opened the door, Rich and I flung ourselves off the bus without even looking to see where we were.

"Well, that was a complete waste of fifty lei," said Rich. "I haven't had so little fun since the Kafka Museum in Prague."

"Nonsense," I replied. "It was a slice of history, a recreation of the old Soviet days. Bureaucratic stonewalling, brooding menace, the whole nine meters. At the Kafka Museum, we'd have had to pay extra for that kind of abuse."

During the long walk home, we happened to run into Calin, the young man we'd met at the InterNations party. He seemed pleased to see us, and we formed a plan to meet the following night for dinner. Rich and I were pretty excited, as that put two items on tomorrow's social calendar! Before our dinner with Calin, we would be meeting up with Erika and Julian, Bucharesters we'd met at the count's guesthouse. They had kindly made arrangements for the four of us to tour Bucharest's most infamous landmark, the parliament building we'd seen from a distance at the start of our walking tour, known locally as the Palace of the People.

The Palace of the People was even more intensely unpopular than the Potato of the Revolution. "We'd tear it down," one Bucharester told me bitterly, "only that would cost us millions." He sounded as if he'd do it with his bare hands if he could.

But the hostility people felt for the Palace of the People was nothing compared to their loathing for the man who built it: Nicolae Ceaușescu. He started life as one of ten children in a poor peasant family, went to work for a shoemaker with communist leanings, joined the Party, and rose through the ranks to rule Romania from 1967 until 1989. He was brutal even by the standards of the other Stalinists in the Soviet bloc, and I'm only surprised that he didn't reinstitute impaling as the preferred form of execution. Possibly there was a shortage of suitable wooden stakes. There were shortages of everything in Romania in the latter part of his dictatorship. Ceaușescu ran up a huge foreign debt and decided to pay it off by exporting virtually everything produced within the country's borders, leaving his people without food, fuel, medicine, and pretty much everything else required for human survival.

Obviously, what starving, freezing, sick people need most is a morale boost, and yet, inexplicably, Bucharesters failed to become noticeably jollier upon learning that their beloved leader had embarked on one of the most extravagant building projects since the pyramids of Egypt. Ceaușescu wanted to build the world's biggest administrative center, so he hired two thousand architects and put a million people, including thousands of soldiers, to work around the clock. The site he'd chosen occupied about a fifth of the old city center, so he ordered the demolition of nine thousand homes, giving residents just days to pack up and clear out. Incredibly, morale in the city continued not to improve.

Ceaușescu "was demented," said Valentina Lupan, one of the architects, in an interview which, wisely, was only published after the dictator's death. "Why did he want the biggest building? Like Hitler, like Mussolini, dictators love architects. Trust me on this. They, the dictators, imagine themselves as architects of the new world." Nearly a quarter of a century after the palace was completed, Romania's accountants were still totaling up the receipts, but it was looking as if the final tally would come out to around four billion dollars, which represented about 40 percent of Romania's wealth at the time.

Naturally I was agog to see what four billion dollars, a million workers, and one demented ego could produce. It didn't disappoint.

We approached by taxi, up a broad avenue Ceaușescu had insisted must measure one meter wider than the Champs Elysees in Paris. We pulled up in front of a mountain of white marble that managed to be both austere and excessive; I could see why people called it the Stalinist wedding cake. The building was breathtakingly huge, covering nearly four million square feet. I'm told it can actually be seen from space, like the Great Wall of China.

Inside, the overblown, pseudo-neoclassical style made me feel as if I were walking around inside a sarcophagus. The four of us spent hours trailing after our guide, who showed us reception halls the size of cathedrals, corridors so long I could barely see the people standing at the other end, and the vast balcony where Michael Jackson committed his famous faux pas.

Most of the palace was empty, the current occupants — the Romanian parliament, a modern art gallery, and several other organizations — taking up just a tiny fraction of the space. As for its carbon footprint, just the essential functions (heating, cooling, lights, water, etc.) required as much energy as a city of two hundred thousand people. We only saw a fraction of the eleven hundred rooms and were allowed only the briefest glimpse of the subterranean sections, which supposedly included four more floors, tunnels big enough for cars, and a nuclear bunker.

We heard story after story about Ceaușescu's obsession with detail. The main staircase, for instance, was rebuilt three times so that it would more precisely match the size of his feet. The staircase came out perfectly, but the timing was off, and in 1989, before the building was completed, Ceaușescu was deposed and promptly executed. More than two hundred soldiers volunteered to be on the firing squad.

And the building turned out to be only the *second* largest administrative building in the world, surpassed by the Pentagon. I guess four billion dollars doesn't buy as much as it used to.

Over dinner that evening, we enjoyed exchanging snarky remarks about the Palace of the People with our new friend Calin. We also covered such important topics as the Potato of the Revolution, the hop-on-flee-off bus, and Calin's plans to leave Bucharest soon for a job and a girlfriend in Switzerland. As the congenial evening drew to a close, he invited us to join him two nights later for a gathering he was hosting for a group called the Hash House Harriers. Neither Rich nor I had any notion what that might be, but as usual we decided to leap first and ask questions later, so we accepted. Calin mentioned something about a run but — and here's another huge advantage to being older — he suggested we could skip that part and join them for the afterparty. We aren't runners at the best of times, and with Rich's (improved, but persistent) leg problems, to say nothing of the forecast calling for rain, we were happier joining Calin and his friends for the post-run portion of the festivities.

I had heard the name Hash House Harriers but had to go home and look them up on the laptop to find out what they were all about. I discovered that the organization, often referred to as HHH, is an international club founded in 1938 by young British army officers who felt a brisk Monday evening run would help them work off the excesses of the weekend. After that, they thought a little hair of the dog was a better bet than going cold turkey, so beer drinking was added to the evening's agenda. Today HHH is, as they are fond of saying, "a drinking club with a running problem."

Beer swilling and jocularity were, I read on the Internet, among the hallmarks of the HHH experience, along with the use of outrageous nicknames, various forms of good-natured teasing, and "punishments" for silly infractions that often involved either drinking beer or pouring it over your own head. Basically, it was the British army's version of beer pong night at a frat house. Today there are thousands of HHH chapters around the world, all loosely adhering to the format but taking plenty of liberties too, because hey, it's that kind of club.

We arrived at Calin's around sundown, beneath drizzly gray skies, just as the runners came straggling in. Most were in their thirties, men and women of various nationalities who all spoke English and had the most extraordinary nicknames: GutterSlut, SofaSucker, PaperAss, and others far more unprintable. A slightly older Scotsman called the PiyedPiper seemed to be serving as the master of ceremonies.

"Do you want to be in the circle?" the PiyedPiper demanded as Rich and I came into view.

"I don't know," I said, in a moment of unaccustomed caution. "What is a 'circle'?"

"A two-dimensional shape whose boundary consists of points equidistant from the center," he said.

I laughed and said, "I'm in." Rich nodded gamely. We stepped into the ragged circle and the ritual began.

It seemed to be the PiyedPiper's job to take people to task for various transgressions, which were delineated with a great deal of joking and wordplay. One woman had borrowed her mother's brand new running shoes, and — as I soon learned — the traditional penalty for wearing new shoes was having to drink beer out of one of them. That couldn't have been tasty. And I don't suppose it was easy explaining a soggy, beer-scented shoe to her mother the next day, either. But traditions were traditions and had to be upheld.

When our turn came, Rich and I were told that as newbies, we had to sing a song. Now, as I may have mentioned, Rich and I are about the least musical people on the face of the earth. Some years earlier, we had been horrified when, at a barbecue thrown by Spanish friends, our hostess suddenly announced, "And now, the Americans are going to sing us a song from their country." We quavered our way through "For He's a Jolly Good Fellow," and while generously applauding our effort, they carefully refrained from demanding an encore. Since then, Rich and I have been asked to sing so often that out of sheer necessity, we now have a go-to song: "Deck the Halls." We teach our audience the "Fa-la-la-la-la-la la-la la-la" chorus, so for at least that much of the performance, our underwhelming efforts are drowned out by other voices.

The seasonal inappropriateness goes unnoticed by our non-English-speaking friends, and now it seemed to be taken in good part by our new pals in the Hash House Harriers. As usual, people enjoyed chiming in on the chorus, if not listening to our solo section. Afterwards, PiyedPiper told me to dump a beer on my head. To be honest, I've been expecting that response ever since I started singing in public. I complied in such a slapdash manner that most of the beer went over my shoulder and he — bless him — let it go.

The demands of tradition having been met, we went indoors to Calin's apartment, shaking the rain and beer out of our hair. A neighbor of his was waiting for us in the kitchen with *ciorbă de perişoare* (sour soup with meatballs) and *sarmale* (stuffed cabbage rolls), and we fell to with gusto. The next few hours were spent getting to know the HHH crowd, who seemed like such mature, responsible, and normal adults that it was hard to reconcile them with the crowd that had so recently been calling each other raunchy names, urging us to dump beer on our heads, and drinking out of running shoes.

Around eleven, Rich and I rose to take our departure, explaining that we had to be up early in the morning to catch a train to Bulgaria. Calin asked if we had a sufficient supply of *horincă* for the journey. When I confessed that we had none, he exclaimed, "But you must take some with you!" He ran to fetch an empty plastic water bottle and filled it from his own stash of home brew. We thanked Calin for all his kindness toward us, said our final farewells, and walked out into the crisp night air.

"Did you have fun?" Rich asked.

"I did," I said.

"Was this night everything you wanted it to be?"

"Rich," I said, "I cannot think of a nicer way to have spent my sixty-second birthday."

CHAPTER 15

Tough Guys

As you may have guessed by now, I do not consider myself an overly timid traveler. But I confess that I did have just a smidgen of trepidation about our next destination: Bulgaria.

A lifetime of watching cheap action movies had imprinted vivid, if largely inaccurate, images on my brain, and I half expected everyone I met there — male or female — to turn out to be a ruthless assassin, the bodyguard of a criminal mastermind, or a shifty-eyed, tattooed informant with a life expectancy of under twenty minutes. Wikitravel did not entirely dispel this image by noting, "In general, organized crime is a serious issue throughout Bulgaria, however it usually does not affect tourists." *Usually?* Could they be more specific about the odds? How many tourists, in a typical week, were likely to run afoul of underworld figures and wind up sleeping with the fishes in the Yantra River?

My other and more immediate concern about Bulgaria — or, as it liked to call itself, България — had to do with the language. Give me a Romance language, such as Italian or Romanian, and with a bit of effort I can usually master a few useful phrases, common menu items, and the local spelling of destination cities posted at railway stations. But Bulgarian was a Slavic language (meaning very, very few words would sound familiar) and used the Cyrillic (кирилица) alphabet, so when it came to oral or written communications, we were basically screwed.

I remembered my struggles many years earlier in rural Japan, where I never could remember whether the ladies' room sign was made up of the characters (and I'm translating loosely here) flying X, drunken Y, running man, coffee maker, and apartment house, or if I wanted the door that read tango move, man decorating Christmas tree, eyeball loop, coffee maker, and apartment house. Usually I just loitered about until someone went in or out of one of the doors to give me a clue.

In one Osaka restaurant a waiter, seeing my confusion, kindly escorted me to the restroom door. When I stepped through, I discovered that I was now standing directly behind a man using a urinal; I'd have to walk past him (eyes carefully averted) to get to the women's room. That might work in law-abiding Japan, but I felt pretty sure that surprising a Bulgarian crime syndicate boss at such a delicate moment could be bad for both of us.

Rich, who had evidently been turning the language problem over in his mind for some time, came up with his own solution. While we were still in Romania, some ten days before we were due to head south to Bulgaria, he said to me suddenly over breakfast, "Karen, you have to learn the Cyrillic alphabet."

"Yeah, right. I'll get back to you in a couple of years."

"Nonsense," he said bracingly. "I'm sure you can do it in no time."

Rich, who has (and I say this lovingly) absolutely no ear whatsoever for languages, holds an exaggerated opinion of my ability to pick up foreign lingo. Spanish had always been easier for me than for him, I'd learned a bit of French in grammar school, and I'd enjoyed acquiring a smattering of Italian, German, Czech, and Romanian on this trip. Alphabets, however, were a bit trickier. During our volunteer work in the Republic of Georgia, I'd struggled mightily for many months to master the Georgian letters, whose squiggly forms continued to seem less like phonetic guides and more like random scraps of cooked spaghetti flung against a wall. I was not optimistic about learning Cyrillic in less than two weeks.

Springing to the laptop, I soon found an article that claimed it could teach you the Cyrillic alphabet in five minutes, and after only ten days of strenuous effort, I managed to grasp a few of the essentials. Seven letters were like the ones we use in English, four came from the Greek (and even I knew π, or pi, which is pronounced like our letter P), and the others . . . well, that's where things got complicated. By the time we boarded the train for Bulgaria, I could identify a few vital words, such as кафе (coffee), ресторант (restaurant), and Pyce (Ruse), the name of the first Bulgarian town on our itinerary.

As our train pulled into the station at Ruse (or Pyce), Rich and I gathered our luggage and started down the corridor. But before we could disembark, a large, stern-faced man in clothing of vaguely military cut leapt on board, blocked our path, and demanded to see our passports. We handed them over, and he began slowly thumbing through the pages, regarding each stamp — and then us — and then the stamp again — with a deeply suspicious glare. But as hardened veterans of Bucharest's hop-on-hop-off bus, we took the hostility in stride, and simply stared back at him. A couple of white-haired ladies chose that moment to attempt to climb up the steps into our railway car, and the fellow turned and barked at them so ferociously that the poor dears fled in terror and confusion. Eventually, with the air of doing so against his better judgment, the man handed us back our passports, nodded curtly, and stepped off the train. We were free to go. For now.

"Welcome to Bulgaria," I muttered to Rich once we were out of earshot. "Who was that guy?"

"Obviously organized crime would be my first guess, but I suppose he *could* be an immigration officer," he said.

The railway station was a huge, gray stone building, built in an austere, pseudo-neoclassical style vaguely reminiscent of Romania's Palace of the People. Despite the enormous amount of floor space, it managed not to have a café where we could stop for our usual arrival coffee. I reflected that the Bulgarians must be tough customers indeed if they could manage long train rides without infusions of caffeine.

"Take my taxi!" shouted a voice at my side. I jumped and turned to see a little, grizzled man with an expression that attempted, without much success, to look engaging and trustworthy.

Nearly everywhere in the world, legitimate taxi drivers are obliged to wait outside of train stations and airports, and guidebooks are quick to warn you about scam artists who accost foreign tourists inside transportation hubs. Even without such warnings, we had only to look at this fellow to know we wanted no part of whatever he was offering. We shook our heads and moved away.

But he began following us, repeating, "My taxi. You go my taxi. Is just outside. My taxi . . ."

Rich said sharply, "No. Go away."

But this only made our new acquaintance more persistent. Pretty soon he was dancing around us in circles, shouting that we had to go with him. I began to fear he'd become so enraged that, like the Devil in Munich, he'd stamp hard enough to leave a permanent footprint in the pavement.

Ignoring him as best we could, Rich and I walked briskly out the main doors of the station to find several taxis drawn up haphazardly at the curb. Our pursuer was now in a paroxysm of fury, and as we stepped closer to one of the cabs, he shouted, "You no go that taxi. He is no even Bulgarian. You must have Bulgarian driver. You go my taxi. That man Romanian. You no want him." That was a good enough recommendation for us. Rich and I dove into the Romanian's taxi, told him the name of our hotel, and we were off. I didn't look back to see whether or not our pursuer had stamped his footprint into the sidewalk.

This was the only time in the entire trip that we had skipped the ritual coffee upon arrival, and halfway to the hotel, I suddenly realized what we'd done. The ritual coffee is, of course, less about coffee than about catching our breath, making sure we know where we're going and how to get there, and — let me underscore this point — figuring out where there's a cash machine so we can get enough local currency for our immediate needs. We had not obtained any Bulgarian lev and were now in the awkward position of hurtling toward our destination without the ability to pay our fare.

Luckily our driver, being a Romanian working in a town close to the Romanian border, was willing to accept his country's currency, especially when Rich sweetened the deal with a bit extra for his trouble. I dug into my little store of Romanian vocabulary and gave him a *"mersi"* (thank you) and *"la revederi"* (goodbye) for good measure, and he drove off happily enough.

It did not take me long to figure out that our hotel, while modestly priced and close to the train station, was intended for a very specific clientele, and we did not fit the profile. The walls of our room were red, the thick carpeting richly patterned in purple and gold. The enormous bed was accented with gold satin, purple tassels, flower petals of orange polyester pretending to be silk, and little, purple boxes of chocolates. A fruit plate wrapped in a huge swath of stiff, red paper stood on a side table. Apparently the champagne and oysters had to be ordered separately, but other than that small omission, this suite was all ready for a night of headbanging sex. Anticipating this, the management had thoughtfully chosen headboards thickly padded in sound-muffling white leatherette.

I naturally assumed that half of our fellow guests would be underworld figures enjoying a well-earned vacation to celebrate a successful heist or hit, and the other half would be attractive but impoverished young people out for a bit of fun and/or profit. I knew that I'd have to wait a while to find out if my predictions were correct. The kind of clients who patronized our hotel would, I felt certain, prefer to arrive under the cover of darkness. We saw no one as we made our way outside and set off to explore the town.

Ruse was a fairly typical mix of sweet, old buildings and grimly modern apartment blocks. But the townspeople had done a very clever thing. Somewhere around the time the communist regime collapsed, they'd planted trees along the streets that were blighted with ugly, modern apartment blocks. Now these mature trees were tall and leafy, creating lovely, shaded boulevards that tactfully concealed the architectural monstrosities looming overhead. Well done, Ruse!

Rich and I wandered along nearly deserted streets past shops, through parks, and beneath the canopy of trees until we'd worked up an appetite and then found an Italian-themed restaurant near our hotel. We dined in solitary splendor, seated on ornate purple and gold chairs at a gold and glass table in a room with lots of mirrors and crystal chandeliers. Clearly this was where the local big spenders took their dates to dazzle them into bed at our hotel.

"You had me at 'Oh good, they serve spaghetti,'" I informed Rich.

It wasn't until the next morning that I finally caught a glimpse of our fellow hotel guests. Breakfast was served in a room with blue lighting that turned the sponge-painted gray walls purple, added a slick sheen to the black granite tabletops, and coordinated nicely with the fluorescent glow of the fish tanks embedded in the walls. I collected some muesli and yogurt from the buffet and sat down in an armchair upholstered in golden crushed velvet tufted with diamond buttons. The guys tucking into their *printessi*, the local breakfast sandwich of melted cheese, looked more like businessmen than mobsters. But then, so did Don Corleone.

"You know what impresses me?" said Rich, looking about the room. "All these men taking their daughters to breakfast. It is really heartwarming."

We didn't linger in Ruse but left late that morning for our next destination, Veliko Tarnovo, which had once been the home of those toughest of Bulgarian strongmen, the Tsars. The city had served as the nation's capital during the Second Bulgarian Empire, which, in case you're a tad rusty on your history, lasted from 1185 to 1396. Being Tsar in those days was no job for lightweights; you had to rule the country, dominate all of the Balkans, and fight off the Byzantine Empire, the Mongols, and the Ottoman Empire.

One of the more unusual Tsars was a swineherd named Ivaylo, known as "the Radish," who in 1277 led the first successful peasant uprising in history. Unfortunately, by 1279 he was in exile and soon after that he was assassinated, but still, he made his mark on history as few swineherds before or since have done. Hats off to you, Tsar Radish!

The Tsars had chosen a remarkably inconvenient location for their stronghold, no doubt in hopes of discouraging would-be invaders. Our train crossed vast plains then climbed into the thickly forested mountains for hours. When we finally arrived at our destination, the City of the Tsars utterly failed to enchant.

On that cold, gray afternoon, the small city looked drab and dispirited. We took a taxi to our hostel, and its exterior — a high, windowless stone wall — looked about as welcoming as a prison. I'd had a few misgivings about the hostel from the start and now, although I was comforted by the knowledge that we'd managed to secure the only private room (with its own bathroom!), I realized that I hadn't specifically checked to see if there would be heat and hot water. Here in the high mountains, as September slid into October, the days had a nasty bite; after dark, temperatures would drop below freezing. I hoped they'd be a bit warmer in our room. I rang the bell at the wooden door and we were buzzed in.

Like everything in this mountain city, the hostel was built on a steep slope, and we hiked up a very long outside staircase. Halfway up, I caught a glimpse of a small, rustic dining room through a windowed door. At the top, we found a tiny lobby and a large common area furnished with colorful rugs and floor cushions. The young woman at the front desk certainly didn't fit my stereotype of the sinister, underworld Bulgarian; she looked like a schoolteacher and chatted pleasantly in English as she showed us down a narrow corridor to our room.

This was pretty basic: a wide-planked, knotty pine floor; a window with striped curtains; and two twin beds shoved together, sheets and blankets folded on top. An extra twin bed stood against one wall, and it was here (once we'd checked for bedbugs, of course) that we dumped our suitcases. I'd certainly stayed in worse, but I was beginning to see why some women would consider sex a fair trade for a night at our hotel in Ruse.

"Doesn't look like we're getting a fruit basket or chocolates on the pillows," I said to Rich as he peered into the miniscule bathroom. It was so small that he could reach in and test the sink's tap without actually stepping into the room.

"No, but you'll be glad to know there is hot water," he said cheerfully. Rich has always enjoyed roughing it a bit. It makes him feel bold and exciting.

"What did the woman who checked us in say about the heat?" I asked, hoping I'd misunderstood her. "There is heat, right?"

"Of course there's heat," he said. "In the common areas."

I sighed and began removing the orange and green plaid wool blankets off the extra bed, adding them to ours.

The centerpiece of Veliko Tarnovo was the medieval citadel of Tsarevets, which stood on a peak surrounded on all sides by the winding Yantra River. It took much of the following day just to explore the grounds, which held the ruins of the Tsars' palace, a reconstructed cathedral, and the remains of four hundred homes, twenty-two churches, and four monasteries. The entire citadel was well protected by guard towers, walls that were twelve feet thick, and the Yantra River, which looped around the hill creating a natural moat at the bottom of a dizzyingly deep gorge.

"I would really hate to have to take this castle," remarked Rich, whose military acumen was developed during his service in Vietnam (which he freely admits did not actually involve storming a lot of castles) and honed by twenty years in the Naval reserves, reading countless military biographies, and watching every episode of *Game of Thrones*. "First you'd have to hike all the way up here through the mountains — in armor. Then you'd have to climb that wall." He gestured to the surrounding hills, where a high stone wall ran along the slopes, encircling all three hills of the old city. "And even then the Tsars could defend themselves with just a few good swordsmen placed here on the drawbridge."

I peered way, way down into the gorge, where no doubt many a hopeful invader had fallen to his death.

Despite the difficulties, plenty of armies had marched on Tsarevets over the years, and the citadel had managed to hold out against all of them until 1393, when it fell to the Ottomans after a three-month siege and was thoroughly sacked and burned. It lay in ruins until the middle of the twentieth century, when the government launched a reconstruction project to mark the anniversary of Bulgaria's founding in the year 681. The results of the project were, in my humble opinion, distinctly mixed. The sections rebuilt from the original rough, gray stone had a great deal of crumbling Gothic charm, while the modern reproductions, in starkly angular fresh-cut yellow stone and brick, would have looked at home in a strip mall and struck me as anachronistic and considerably less romantic.

At the very peak of the hill stood the shiny new Patriarchal Cathedral of the Holy Ascension of God. Built on ground that had been considered sacred since Roman times, it was the latest in a series of massive houses of worship to grace the site. The interior was covered with modernist murals showing crowds of droopy, distorted, black-and-white figures with huge, gnarled hands and flaccid, morose faces. A Madonna rendered in color held a Christ Child that appeared to be dead, although I suppose he might have been asleep or possibly just wishing he were elsewhere.

"What *were* they thinking?" I said, when confronted by this dreadful spectacle.

"This is what happens when you let communists decorate a church."

Rich was right; the style wasn't as robust or colorful as the old propaganda posters I'd seen in Prague's Museum of Communism, but it made the same strenuous effort to show that a person's value — their *only* value — lay in serving as part of the laboring masses; it was the hands, not the faces, that counted.

For some, that made it great art. Later I would read, on a blog called *Stalin's Mustache*, high praise for the murals' "earthly bodies, fully rounded, muscled, sensual . . . Not quite the church's tradition of desexualized bodies from the Bible and the saints . . ." Seriously? Reading that, all I could think of was one particular Spanish Renaissance painting I'd seen, where a voluptuous Virgin Mary was pulling open her gorgeous blue and scarlet robes to reveal a plump breast, from which she was squirting milk into the mouth of a blissful saint kneeling at her feet. If Stalin's Mustache thought religious art was desexualized, he had obviously been going to the wrong churches. Compared to the passionate Spanish religious art I was used to, the murals in this church of the latter-day communists was anemic and gloomy stuff.

"It's a good thing they don't use this place for worship anymore," I said. "Looking at this every Sunday would make me want to throw myself off Execution Rock." This was a natural stone outcropping over the river gorge from which the Tsars liked to have prisoners flung to their doom. How many people had taken flight off that rock and crash landed in the Yantra River? I didn't want to know.

We spent the next several days exploring the town, which was apparently something of a tourist destination during the warmer months but now had the deflated air of a summer resort in the off-season. Restaurants stood empty, museums were closed, and many old churches could only be visited during the hours of prayer services. The stores, however, remained open, which was good news for me, as I'd decided to buy a sweater.

Buying any article of clothing was a major decision, given the tight space in my suitcase. But my fleece top and thin rain jacket, even with a scarf and long-sleeved shirt, had proven no match for the icy October air this high in the mountains. I had in mind a thick, hand-knit, wool pullover like the ones Irish fishermen wear; in the end, the best I could find was a machine-made synthetic from China. It was pretty clear that the stores carried high-quality clothes only for the summer tourists; this time of year, they stocked cut-rate goods for the locals.

Thin as it was, my new sweater made me reasonably comfortable, and we tramped around during the daylight hours enjoying the breathtaking landscape and finding surprisingly good lunches at the local restaurants. My favorite dish was *shopska* salad, made of cucumber, tomato, fresh parsley, maybe a bit of green pepper or onion, and red-wine vinaigrette, topped with lots of crumbled feta cheese; it was much like a Greek salad without the olives or lettuce. Rich fell in love with some succulent lamb that, he swore, tasted just like his Irish mother's.

A recent street art competition had sparked a spate of fresh, colorful, and whimsical painting on city walls, trash bins, and utility boxes. The subjects were eclectic: a mustachioed accordion player, a beatnik, a grinning cat, and a porcupine whose quills turned into a forest in which stood the Patriarchal Cathedral of the Holy Ascension of God. I reflected that if only the restorers of the cathedral had hired these artists to spruce up its walls I, for one, would be singing hymns of thanks and praise.

But my most vivid memories of Veliko Tarnovo are of the hostel. Yes, it was pretty chilly in our room at night but tolerable enough if I wore several layers of clothes and piled five thick wool blankets on the bed. True, the weight of the blankets made it difficult to move and nearly impossible to roll over, but that was a small price to pay in order to stop my teeth from chattering. Luckily the hostel's common areas were always comfortably heated, and I spent many happy hours sitting on the dining hall's wooden benches, sipping cups of tea, writing my blog, and chatting with our fellow guests. Everyone gathered morning and evening for meals provided by the hostel, and as there wasn't much nightlife in the town, most of our fellow guests were only too happy to linger in the warm dining hall after supper. Someone always seemed to have a bottle to pass around, and everyone had stories to share.

And they were stories worth a listen. Veliko Tarnovo was not on your average tourist's short list of must-see destinations; by the time people made it to Bulgaria's City of the Tsars, they had usually been on the road for months, if not years. Most of the hostel's dozen or so guests were European or Australian, and ages ranged from twenties to sixties. If they'd all been from the United States, I would have expected the group to organize itself along generational lines. I've found many Americans, especially younger ones, have never acquired the knack for conversing with people outside their own age group; they assume they'll be bored and uncomfortable, and so they are. Those who have grown up mingling with people of different generations at home, work, and play find it much easier to overlook the differences and find common ground. And so it proved at the hostel. We compared notes on everything from travel to history to what makes for a good life. Like those at the count's guesthouse in Transylvania, meals at the hostel were never dull.

It was there in the hostel's dining room that I first heard the expressions "time rich" and "time poor" from Robert, an Australian who had been on the road for six months.

"Most people feel time poor," he said one night after dinner, as we passed around some eye-watering Flirt vodka and the bottle of brawny Romanian brandy Calin had given us in Bucharest. "They have the idea that they have to jam as much as possible into each day because there are so few hours available to them. Doing less opens up your day. You realize that you really are time rich. It's true luxury."

And that's especially true when you're on the road. "By far the most important lesson travel teaches you," says Rolf Potts, author of *Vagabonding*, "is that your time is all you really own in life. And the more you travel, the more you realize that your most extravagant possessions can't match the satisfaction you get from finding new experiences, meeting new people, and learning new things about yourself." In fact, according to Potts, "Time = wealth." By that measure, Robert was a very rich man.

One morning at breakfast I asked Robert what he did when he wasn't on the road. He gave me a sideways smile and said, "I stock shelves in a supermarket." He shrugged. "My boss makes a tiny bit more money than I do and is always worrying about the job. Me? When I walk out that door I am free to think about whatever I want, whatever interests me. That's worth a lot."

As he spoke, he was scratching absently at some insect bites on his jaw, and Rich said, "Let me see those . . . You know, when there are three bites in a row like that, it usually means bedbugs."

"I think you may be right," said Robert, and the next thing I heard, he'd packed up and gone.

Rich and I did another even more exhaustive bedbug check of our room but found nothing to make us move up our departure. We left as planned the following day, heading south to the capital. I was curious to see the city of Sofia, about which I'd heard highly conflicting reports.

Eight months earlier we'd had dinner with Theo, who grew up in the Bulgarian capital and was now a quintessential San Franciscan: witty, urbane, *au courant*. When we told him about our plans to visit his native land, his reaction was not quite as positive as we'd hoped.

"Why would you want to go to Bulgaria?" he asked incredulously. "Sofia?" He shuddered. "It's the armpit of the world." We explained about The Experiment and getting *out there*. He didn't seem convinced but finally said, "Well, if you must go, you should meet my brother, Sany."

He alerted his brother that I would be in touch, and Sany's reply to my first email began: "Honestly I wouldn't like meeting you, I would love to. Seeing Theo's friends and/or Americans is a great pleasure for me. You guys are usually a little bit more left-leaning in politics for my taste but it is completely fine to exchange views on so many topics. The thing is that I am simply very suspicious with all social justice/ equality/security ideas and proposals because I saw what such rhetoric had brought to my country and to countless numbers of people all over the world as well. Of course, you shouldn't feel hesitant to share your views on anything with me trying not to be offensive or insulting. I find this Western politically correct sensitivity repulsive because it reminds me of the communism. So I wait for you both to talk on anything you like."

Clearly, conversations with Sany were going to be pretty strenuous. I felt as if I should go into training; maybe take a quick course in geopolitics and another in debate to enable me to keep up my end of the conversation. Of course, I never got around to anything of the kind.

Between Sany's enthusiasm for his city and Theo's disparaging remarks, I had no idea what to expect. I was bracing myself for squalor and depravity, hoping for a model democracy emerging phoenix-like from the ashes of communism, and still keeping my eyes peeled for the crime lords and strongmen the movies had led me to expect. But as our taxi rolled into Sofia's bustling downtown, I mostly saw trendy home décor shops, upscale coffee houses, and Europeans in smart business suits or brand name blue jeans.

After days of roughing it in the mountains, I began to nurture hopes of relaxing with such civilized luxuries as central heating, comfortable furniture, and good coffee. When the taxi dropped us in front of our lodgings, I wasn't particularly daunted by the graffiti-covered front door; Bucharest and other cities had taught me that fabulous apartments often lie behind underwhelming, even frightful exteriors. I idled on the sidewalk, waiting in pleased anticipation for the owner to arrive with the keys to our new temporary digs.

Fifteen minutes later, she came roaring up in a compact car, parked rather precariously with two wheels on the curb, and escorted us inside in a breathless rush. She swept us upstairs to the apartment, unlocked three deadbolts, and shoved open the door for us to enter. The place was enormous, with lots of windows, almost no furniture, and a pervasive scent of raw sewage.

"Sorry about the smell," she said offhandedly in her heavily accented English. "There is nothing we can do about it. It might get better if you run the shower." She flung open a window, and the room's chill nosedived toward arctic. "Unfortunately there is no heat. Heat is controlled by the building, and they have not yet turned it on for the year. Let me know if you need more blankets." I caught a glimpse of two thin blankets folded on a shelf; there were none on the bed. Temperatures were predicted to drop below freezing during the night. "I must hurry; I am parked illegally." She pressed the keys into Rich's palm and was gone.

Rich and I stood in the middle of the cold, smelly apartment — which I'd already dubbed "The Stinker" — regarding our new, prepaid digs with dismay. The apartment was huge, as advertised, but it was shabby, grubby, and almost completely empty. A few pieces of modern, uncomfortable-looking furniture huddled disconsolately in the corners.

A cheap, fake-wood coffee table with a missing leg leaned against one wall like a dying bug.

"It's a flop-house for nightcrawlers," I said. "If we're going to be this cold and uncomfortable, we might as well sleep in the train station."

We left our bags in the flat, attached to the radiator (a basic security precaution which seemed doubly advisable there) and went out in search of alternatives. It took us about ten minutes to find a nearby hotel that was perfect. Well, maybe not perfect unless you like smoky glass, glitzy wallpaper, and breakfasts of instant coffee and cardboard muesli, but the room was cozy, warm, comfy, and smelled of roses.

The young man at the front desk was the first person I'd encountered — aside from the immigration officers, if that's what they were — who truly lived up to my movie image of a Bulgarian. He was a thin, sleek, impatient youth who spent a lot of time standing in the hotel's door-way, smoking cigarettes, jiggling his keys, and glancing furtively up and down the street. I immediately pegged him as a low-level member of a crime family, the kind who thinks he knows better than his boss and makes the fatal mistake of trying to prove it. Still, I felt my chances of survival were higher here with Fredo Corleone than in the Stinker.

The Stinker's owners bucked and snorted a bit, but in the end they gave in and agreed to give us a full refund. One of the beauties of renting through Airbnb was that both guests and hosts provided evaluations, enforcing fair play for anyone who wanted to continue using the system. Guests who made endless frivolous complaints found fewer people willing to rent to them. Hosts who returned unhappy customers' money promptly and in full were spared a negative review. As satisfying as it would have been to air our complaints to the world, fairness and the Airbnb rules prevented us from posting comments about any place in which we had spent less than twenty-four hours.

"The clues were all there," Rich said, poring over the Stinker's Airbnb listing on his iPad. "We should have looked at the description and the reviews more closely. We got too relaxed, too confident."

"We got sloppy," I said. "We won't make that mistake again."

Rich and I spent a warm, comfortable, peaceful night at the hotel, and the next day, at long last, we met Sany. He turned out to be as charming and energetic as his emails, knowledgeable about his city and passionate about the democracy that had been forged in the aftermath of the communists' departure. He proudly showed us the government offices where he worked, and then took us next door to see the Sofia Synagogue, a majestic neo-Moorish building that was the largest synagogue in Southeast Europe and the only one still functioning in Sofia.

"We saved *all* our Jews during World War II," he told us with more than a touch of pride. "There were forty-eight thousand of them living here. When the Nazis took over, they told us that we would have to round them up for deportation to concentration camps. We knew we were not strong enough to oppose them directly, so we said, 'Yes, absolutely, we will send them to you. Do whatever you want with them. But first, we have jobs for them to finish here.' And we kept stalling until the end of the war." He grinned. "This is how we Bulgarians like to fight. The indirect way."

Not one single Bulgarian Jew was deported or murdered by the Nazis, and later Israel's leaders officially thanked the Bulgarian government, the Tsar, and the Church for their efforts — which, to be fair, included more formal diplomatic means and a huge public outcry as well as the evasions and foot-dragging Sany described. Naturally the Soviets covered up the whole story afterwards; they didn't want anyone saying nice things about such enemies of the state as the Bulgarian government, church leaders, or most especially the Jews, nearly all of whom sensibly departed for Israel when the communists showed up. The details only emerged after the Cold War ended in 1989, and outwitting the Nazis and saving the nation's Jews had now become a source of national pride.

This was just one of many stories Sany told us about the region, its history, and its pre-history, which extended back an impressive 1.6 million years. That's when our common forebears, who weren't even Neanderthals yet, let alone *Homo sapiens*, began passing through the area on hunting expeditions. One of these proto-humans left behind in the nearby Kozarnika cave a bone on which some simple lines were carved; archeologists believe this is the oldest record of symbolic thinking ever. Not bad for a species just getting the hang of fire and tool use. Good thinking, proto-humans!

Sany didn't show us anything nearly that old, but we did visit ruins of the original city, known as Serdica, founded by a Celtic tribe in 400 BC. The stubby, broken remains of ancient Serdic walls surrounded a fourth-century Roman building that was repurposed in the tenth century as the Church of Saint George and currently squatted rather prosaically in the shadows of the Sheraton Hotel towers.

"And this," said Sany, "is St. Nedelya, where the communists tried to blow up the dome and kill the Tsar." We were standing in front of a three-story brick church topped with an impressive dome that had been the centerpiece of an elaborate assassination plot back in 1928. Bulgaria had recently outlawed communism, and the comrades were spoiling for a fight. For a while they concentrated on individual assassinations, but then they got the bright idea that it would be more efficient to stage a mass murder of all their political enemies, even the Tsar himself, if only they could get them together in one spot — say, for a funeral. They recruited the sexton at St. Nedelya, brought in twenty-five kilos of explosives and a 50-foot extension cord to ensure their own personal safety, and when all was in place they assassinated a general so important that even Tsar Boris III would have to show up to pay his respects.

Sadly for the comrades and luckily for the government leaders, the plot didn't quite work out as planned. The Tsar arrived late, being elsewhere attending another funeral of bystanders killed during a separate attempt on his life, so he wasn't in the church when the explosives were detonated. One hundred and fifty people were killed, but by chance or poor planning on the plotters' part, all the major government leaders survived.

Nearly five hundred people were wounded that day in St. Nedelya, and no doubt many of them relied for their recovery on the healing properties of the city's legendary hot springs, which had been used for thousands of years to treat every sort of illness and injury. The water also (allegedly) helped you live longer and even grow younger. Sany explained that the old public baths had been closed for years so we couldn't go soak in the stuff, but he showed us the public spigots where locals came daily to drink and fill bottles to take home. Naturally Rich and I had to try it too, leaning over to slurp from the faucet in the traditional manner. The water was warm and tasted, not unpleasantly, of minerals. Afterwards, we still seemed to be sexagenarians.

"I wonder what's in this stuff," Rich mused, wiping his lips and chin with the back of his hand.

"How hard do you think it would be to have a few thousand gallons shipped to us at home?" I said. "It's probably just a silly superstition, but still . . ."

As the afternoon slid toward evening, Sany suggested that we go drink something else.

"I know from reading your blog that you like beer, so I have arranged to meet my girlfriend in the pub Five Corners. We can go by bus."

When the bus pulled up, it turned out to be so old that it was made entirely of metal and wood. We climbed aboard and stood gripping handrails layered with countless generations of flaking paint (along with an equal number of layers of germs and grime, although I made an effort not to think about *that*). The bus rattled and wheezed up the street for ten minutes, then we alighted and walked another few blocks until we came to a door that was so discreet that I would never have suspected it of leading to a commercial establishment of any kind, let alone a very popular pub. Sany opened the door and in we went.

Five Corners was my kind of pub, noisy with the sound of a dozen boisterous conversations and redolent with the scent of sausages on the grill. A young woman with long brown hair and a wide smile waved to us from one of the tables, and Sany, leading us to her, made the introductions. Irena's English wasn't as fluent as his, so she didn't speak much at first, but she seemed to understand a good deal, and as the evening advanced, her reserve gave way, and she jumped in with more comments and plenty of laughter.

As soon as we were settled, Sany leaned forward and said, "You must try their special potato chips. You've never tasted anything like them." I was too polite to say so, but having lived for ten years in Seville, which prides itself on its world-class artisanal *patatas fritas*, I was not prepared to be impressed. But Sany was right; the chips were hot and crisp and salty and — yes, I freely admit it — even better than Seville's. As platters of sausages and roast meat arrived on the table, our conversation ranged over everything from history and politics to children (Irena shyly passed us photos of her smiling, fresh-faced kids) and travel. I needn't have worried about brushing up for the conversation with Sany; by the second round, the four of us were chatting away like old friends.

Rich and I spent two more days in Sofia, mostly roaming the streets, drinking coffee at trendy cafés, and doing a little shopping. When you're on the road for months at a time using travel-sized containers of toiletries so they take up the absolute minimum of space in your bag, you constantly need to replenish your supplies. In Sofia, I stocked up on a few necessities and then, throwing caution to the winds, I decided to purchase a new pair of trousers. My comfy old tan slacks, veterans of many an adventure on the road, were finally losing their elasticity, the fit shifting from relaxed to downright comatose. I wasn't quite prepared to toss them, but I needed a backup.

I spent a pleasant hour strolling around the shops, eventually buying a comfortable, stylish pair of black trousers. I felt sure it was the beginning of a beautiful friendship. Luckily, with the cooler weather, I wasn't worried about fitting them in my suitcase, as I was wearing half my wardrobe at any given time.

And then we were packing up again, in preparation for the following day's departure on the overnight train from Sofia to Belgrade, Serbia.

"It looks like a pretty nice train," Rich said, scrolling through the information on his iPad. "I think they have private compartments, maybe even ones with their own bathrooms."

That represented a breathtaking level of luxury; it was never fun to make a late-night excursion — alone, half asleep, and sketchily dressed — down a dark, drafty corridor to a toilet that was all too likely to be very nasty indeed. I began to imagine a cozy compartment like the one we'd booked many years earlier on a train from Los Angeles to Chicago, which had seats that rearranged themselves into a double bed and a cunning little bathroom where you could even take a shower if you didn't mind sitting on the toilet while you washed.

"Let's go now and get our tickets for tomorrow night," he suggested, and in the gathering twilight, we walked companionably through the town to the train station.

"Private compartment?" said the ticket seller, barely managing to contain her derisive laughter. "No, there is no private compartment. All compartments have six bunks for six people. You share."

"Forget it," I said to Rich. "I am *not* sleeping in a compartment with a bunch of strangers."

"You do it on planes all the time," he pointed out.

"Yes, but not shut up in a small, dark room with them. Doesn't that strike you as creepy?"

"Look, if the people in our compartment are creepy, we can go to one of the regular cars and sit up all night."

I turned back to the ticket seller. "Is there another train? A day train?" But it transpired that there was not, the day train having been discontinued some months previously. This left us with few options. The buses apparently took longer and were even more uncomfortable. And to hire a car and driver or (perish the thought) take a plane — well, that would fly in the face of everything we'd agreed upon when we decided to embark on The Experiment.

"Come on," Rich said. "It will be an adventure. You'll see. We'll have fun. It'll be something to laugh about later." And then, because he knows me very well, he added, "Just think of the blog post you'll be able to write . . ."

The ticket seller, watching our little drama with interest and a certain amount of amused sympathy, added helpfully, "The train is not full.

Perhaps you will be alone." And with this slender reassurance I had to be content.

"Okay," I said grudgingly.

Rich beamed. "We'll take two tickets on tomorrow night's train." As the ticket seller handed over the tickets, Rich said to me, "Don't worry. It will be *fine*."

What he based that assurance on, I cannot imagine. Because — as I found out much, much later — he had been reading all sorts of harrowing posts about this particular stretch of rail travel, mostly along the lines of glad-I-survived-I'll-certainly-never-do-that-again. Here's a typical example from a blog called *The Art of Adventure*:

"The compartments and train itself were designed during communism, and the last time it was cleaned was around the same period. My bed was at a 45 degree angle, which made it impossible to do anything besides sit on it and crouch down to not hit my head on the bunk above. Train conductors do nothing but yell at you in Serbian and make aggressive hand gestures in the direction of every foreigner. The train stops at least 4 times during the night for passport control officers to shine bright flashlights into your eyes and demand your papers. You are provided with a pillow, a scratchy blanket and one grimy sheet that you need to creatively figure out how to wrap yourself in so as to have both your head and feet covered at all times to avoid touching the pillow with questionable stains or the filthy, smelly blanket. Instead of double bunk beds, the beds are stacked in threes, so 6 of us had to fit in an incredibly narrow compartment. It was freezing cold. The beds squeaked and I kept envisioning the bunks toppling down on me because they rocked with every train bump. Dark, dirty green and gray defined the color scheme of the train. The windows had cracks, the blankets had holes, every aspect of the train dated back to before I was born."

Now, my husband and I have a thirty-year relationship based on mutual honesty and trust, due in large part to Rich's total inability to lie convincingly or keep a secret. If he had been entrusted with the plans for D-Day, we'd all be speaking German right now. However, on this one occasion, he managed not to blurt out the truth, convinced that it would only add to my anxiety. I suppose it was partly my own fault for not asking him more direct questions about what he'd learned or for not checking the Internet myself. I was so busy worrying about the disagreeable prospect of sharing a confined space with bizarre and sinister strangers that I hadn't really paused to consider the full range of other physical discomforts and hazards to health and safety that I might encounter.

"Quit fussing, it will be *great*," Rich kept saying as we left the train station. "You never mind roughing it a little."

"A little, sure. I can't believe you don't mind sleeping crammed into a tiny space with a bunch of strangers. When did you get to be such a tough guy all of a sudden?"

"I've always been a tough guy," he said, steering me into a bar. "You just never noticed before."

The bar was reassuringly civilized. The décor was chic, modern, and comforting, with soothing lighting and well-padded chairs. The clientele looked like office workers and other respectable professionals, including a small group of laughing young women drinking — goodness, were those cosmos? — on what was obviously a girls' night out. In next to no time, a very generous pour of white wine was placed in front of me, followed closely by a hot meal. I began to think that maybe I'd overreacted. Rich was a sensible guy who'd done his research, and he wasn't worried. Besides, this was the twenty-first century. How bad could the night train be?

I was soon to learn. We arrived around ten o'clock to find the station dimly lit and nearly deserted, with a few lost souls wandering about in the shadows, dragging their suitcases behind them like Marley's ghost hauling his chains in Dickens's *A Christmas Carol*. When we got to the platform, I discovered that our train was so battered, stained, and rusty that the masses of graffiti actually improved its appearance.

The almost complete lack of signage made it hard to identify the sleeping car and even harder to find our assigned compartment. When we finally worked out which one was (probably) ours, via careful counting and the process of elimination, I beheld with dismay a space approximately six feet by seven feet with six narrow bunks, three to a side, and a skinny center aisle where presumably all six of us would be piling our luggage. Rich and I had reserved the two lowest bunks, just in case we had to make a quick exit, and I soon discovered, as had so many before me, that the only way to occupy them was to lay flat on my back or sit hunched forward awkwardly, haunches on the bunk, feet on the floor, elbows on knees, head sticking out into the aisle. Even this would soon be impossible if roommates showed up with any luggage more extensive than a toothbrush.

"A little Vitamin G, my dear?" asked Rich, passing me the mini bottle of gin he'd wisely purchased that afternoon.

"You bet." I had to stand up to drink it.

After a couple of swigs, I stepped out into the corridor to see who else might be joining us on Hell's Railway. Two enormous, red-faced men, speaking a language I eventually identified as an obscure dialect of English (rural Welsh, maybe?), took up residence in the compartment next door. A chattering group of Chinese passengers went by. A party of Mexicans moved in on the other side of us. Clearly the locals were opting to sit up all night in the regular railway cars rather than spring for the luxury of a sleeper like the crazy foreigners. If there were any criminal masterminds or shifty, tattooed informants, they were evidently bedding down elsewhere. As near as I could tell, I was the only woman on the train; should I read anything into that? Oh well, too late to worry about it now.

A pair of young American backpackers came bumbling down the corridor, complaining to one another as Rich and I had about railways that failed to properly label the compartments so that customers could find their assigned sleeping quarters in a timely fashion. I called out a cheery greeting, and the two boys looked over at me, astonished and aghast, as if they'd discovered their mother — or grandmother — on board. I had momentarily forgotten that American kids often cherish the mistaken belief that grand adventures are only for the young; to these guys, the very presence of a couple of sexagenarians redefined their bold escapade as an insipid outing suitable for old-age pensioners. They dove into their compartment and shut the door, terrified that I might actually want to talk with them further.

I decided to face up to the worst and trudged down the corridor to inspect the toilet. It was, all things considered, not nearly as revolting as you'd expect. The space was, naturally, cramped and dimly lit, with decades of grime imbedded in every surface, but the door locked properly, and the toilet's mechanism seemed to be working, delivering its contents efficiently onto the tracks below. And it hardly smelled at all. No, all in all, it was far better than I'd dared to hope.

I returned to our compartment, noting with relief that the head count hadn't increased during my absence, and two minutes later a tall Bulgarian entered and asked to see our passports. He was not dressed in any kind of uniform nor did he show us any ID, but he carried himself with such an air of authority that we meekly handed over our most precious travel documents.

"I return them tomorrow," he said, disappearing down the corridor.

"Hey, wait a minute," I said. "What just happened? Who was that guy?"

"I *think* he was the porter or something," said Rich. "We'll be crossing the border in the middle of the night. Maybe this means they won't wake us up to show our documents to the Serbians."

Or maybe it meant we would find ourselves awakened at two in the morning by sleep-deprived Serbian authorities demanding to see passports we no longer had. Time would tell.

The porter, or whatever he was, returned a few minutes later with folded stacks of bedding: pillow, blanket, and rather astonishingly, crisp, clean, white bed linens. True, there was just one sheet, but it was plenty large enough to double over and slide inside. And the blanket, although as scratchy as a horse blanket, was plenty thick enough for the cold night, not smelly or obviously soiled, and appeared not to be harboring bedbugs or other vermin.

We made up our beds, boldly appropriating the middle bunks on either side of the aisle, as they were at a more convenient height, knowing we would quite likely be forced to move down to our own bunks at some point during the night, possibly to be trapped there by a barricade of luggage. After that, we stretched out and stared up at the underside of the bunks overhead.

"Hey, there are little reading lights!" Rich said, playing with the switch.

"Great," I said. "All the comforts of home."

And then the train gave a tremendous shudder and heaved itself out of the station and into the night. Fifteen minutes later it lurched to a halt at another station. I found myself tensing. Would this be where our new roommates appeared, demanding their rightful bunks and filling the aisle with large suitcases and the room with snoring or worse? The whistle blew, the train lurched onwards, and no one appeared in our compartment. Slowly I relaxed, and soon I began to feel drowsy . . . Twenty minutes later, we stopped again.

"Rich, how many stops does this train make?"

He groped for his iPad and called up the iRail app. "Thirteen," he said. I sighed. It was going to be a long night.

At every one of the eleven stations that followed, I braced myself for the arrival of roommates, but they never came. Maybe fewer people traveled on a Monday night, perhaps we were just lucky, or just possibly the ticket seller took pity on us. At any rate, we had the space entirely to ourselves the whole way.

I would have sworn that I didn't sleep a wink, yet somehow I was abruptly awakened every time we jolted to a stop. Shortly before dawn, the porter reappeared with our passports, which had been duly stamped during the night by Serbian authorities. And at half-past five, as the first pale rays of light began to illuminate the heavens, we stopped for the final time.

"Hello, Belgrade," I said.

"See?" said Rich. "That wasn't so bad, now was it?"

[CHAPTER 16]

The More You Learn,
the Less You Know

Arriving in an unknown city at 5:30 in the morning is always a bit surreal. The silence, the odd half-light, and the subtle strangeness of the scene always make me feel as if I might still be dreaming. Yawning, Rich and I made our way toward the central hall of Belgrade's train station. Our fellow passengers quickly melted away, and I noticed that the American backpackers were nowhere to be seen. I could only suppose that they had climbed out their compartment's window rather than risk another encounter with me. A bar of light from an open doorway drew us into the café, a brightly lit room with yellow walls and air that hummed with the hiss of the coffee maker, the rattle of crockery, and the subdued, not-quite-awake-yet conversation of travelers huddled over half a dozen tables.

Sitting on chairs against the far wall, feet planted firmly on the floor, were two strapping American males in cowboy hats and plaid shirts who looked as if they'd just moseyed in after a cattle drive across Montana. Rich and I ordered coffee and toast and soon struck up a conversation with them. To my astonishment, one of them actually hailed from Montana, and the two were on their way home after visiting an old Navy buddy who had become the U.S. ambassador to one of the Balkan countries. They seemed to find this part of the world vastly entertaining, and no doubt the locals viewed them in much the same light.

When we'd waved so long to our new cowpoke pals and walked outside, Rich said, "We can't check in to the apartment until two o'clock,

ADVENTURES OF A RAILWAY NOMAD ❖ 211

so we'll have to find someplace to hang out until then. What about getting a hotel room? Whatever it costs, it would be worth it to get a little shuteye now."

"You're on, pardner."

We moseyed across the street to a big, old-fashioned hotel to enquire about availability and rates.

"Will this be an overnight?" asked the woman at the front desk. "Or the day rate?"

There was a day rate? It turned out the hotel offered short-stay accommodation for passengers arriving on early morning trains. If those same, short-term rooms were later rented for more carnal purposes, I didn't want to know about it. I cheerfully paid the equivalent of thirty-four dollars for a half day and accepted the key. Five minutes later I was climbing between clean sheets in a bed that was blissfully stationary. Five seconds after that I was asleep.

Hours later, rested, showered, and having partaken of a substantial breakfast at the hotel, we set out to explore. There was a steepish climb to the city center, which Rich accomplished without complaint. His leg, while never quite comfortable, could usually sustain at least a couple of hours of walking each day, and that morning he didn't seem unduly aggravated by the ascent. Nearing the top of the slope, we were greeted by the sight of an imposing, century-old building with a sign reading Хотел Москва, which I painstakingly deciphered as Hotel Moscow.

"I've read about this place," Rich said. "They recently fired the entire staff due to gross incompetence. Replaced every single one of them." Obviously their PR staff wasn't any more capable than the chambermaids if the whole world knew about that mess.

Not far from the Hotel Moscow we came upon the long, broad shopping street popularly known as Knez Mihailova Street or Prince Mihailo Street, although it is more properly called Kneza Mihaila; to Serbians it's Улица Кнез Михаилова or Улица Кнеза Михаила, which means Ulica Knez Mihailova or Ulica Kneza Mihaila. As I would soon learn, just about everything in Belgrade had multiple identities, and the more you learned about something, the less you really knew.

Strolling up Knez Mihailova Street, I saw such familiar names as Zara, Mango, Nike, and the Gap mingled with local boutiques and cafés, all housed in impressive nineteenth-century buildings. From what I'd glimpsed thus far, much of the rest of the city was twentieth-century bland, although there were some graceful older sections and a few stellar historical buildings.

The most notable feature of the landscape was the citadel that stood on the high ground at the far end of Knez Mihailova Street, overlooking the junction of the Sava and Danube Rivers. The complex was known as the Belgrade Fortress, Београдска тврђава or *Beogradska tvrđava*, and included the old citadel (Upper and Lower Town) and Kalemegdan Park (technically Large and Little Kalemegdan). Got that so far? I admit that I was finding the multiple identities rather slippery but felt sure I would soon get the hang of them.

We made our way back to the hotel, collected our bags, and presented ourselves at our new lodgings promptly at two o'clock. The building was a large, solid, nineteenth-century apartment house painted a sober gray but enlivened at ground level by dashes of colorful graffiti. We were renting a small, beautifully appointed studio with a large, sunny window, period architectural detail, and a charmingly eclectic décor. It was like living on a boat; everything was there, but compressed to its smallest possible form. There was a two-burner stovetop, a mini fridge, and even a tiny washer-drier combo. Like the apartment in Braşov, it struck me as cozy rather than cramped, although I'm not sure I would have enjoyed an extended stay in either place.

We spent the next few hours settling in and doing laundry. And that was when tragedy struck. Unfamiliar with the controls on the combined washer-drier, I accidentally set it to wash and automatically proceed to dry. By the time I noticed that the sound had changed from the whoosh of the rinse cycle to the rhythmic tumble of a drier, it was already too late. I rushed over and stopped the machine, but when I pulled out my new black trousers, which I'd worn almost nonstop since their acquisition, they'd shrunk to a size that would have been snug on an under-weight ten-year-old.

"Don't say a word," I told Rich. "I am officially in mourning."

By the next day I'd recovered from my loss and was ready to set out for a free walking tour of the city. Our guide, Jakov, was a lean, edgy youth with firebrand tendencies. He started off conventionally enough, escorting us along Knez Mihailova Street where he pointed out the ro-mantic, Renaissance, and Balkan architectural styles. After detouring to show us various neighborhoods, bars, and old churches, he wound up back on Knez Mihailova, which led us to the Belgrade Fortress.

Jakov filled us in on the various groups that had fought for suprem-acy on the site: the Thracians, the Dacians, the Celtic Scordisci tribe, the invading Goths and Huns (Attila's grave is said to lie under the for-tress), the Byzantine Empire, the Bulgarians, the Hungarians, the Otto-man Turks, and possibly the Martians and the Moonies, for all I know. Under the deluge of factoids, my brain quickly glazed over and soon I was staring glassy-eyed across the river at the forest on Great War Is-land, named for all the wars-to-end-all-wars that had been fought over this strategic bit of high ground.

Describing these ancient military campaigns naturally inspired Ja-kov to add some impassioned remarks about the 1990s and Serbia's role in the series of conflicts that were variously known as the Wars in the Balkans, the Conflicts in the Former Yugoslavia, the Wars of Yugoslav Secession (or Succession), the Third Balkan War, and the Yugoslavian Civil War. Whatever you called them, they formed a particularly vicious and ugly chapter in human history and added up to the deadliest conflict since World War II.

Serbia's president at the time, Slobodan Milošević, managed to stand out even among the other brutal warlords on the scene. He was later indicted for genocide and crimes against humanity but died in his cell during the trial, leaving the war crimes tribunals and everyone else still arguing about what actually happened. In fact, there were so many hotly contested and sharply conflicting accounts of every aspect of the war years that, to paraphrase the famous remark about quantum mechanics attributed to physicist Richard Feynman, "If you think you understand it, that shows you don't."

The essential facts, as best as I can grasp them, are these. The troubles officially started in the early nineties when Yugoslavia broke up, creating half a dozen new nations that promptly went for each other's throats in four separate but inter-related wars. Not only was everybody competing for political and economic power, but there were ancient scores to settle, rancor over who had collaborated with the Nazis, and bad blood among the various ethnic groups that included Bosnian Muslims, Catholic Croatians, Eastern Orthodox Serbians, and Kosovo Albanians.

Some political leaders, with Slobodan Milošević in the vanguard, declared that the world would be a better place if certain ethnic groups were removed from it altogether and launched a form of genocide that became known as "ethnic cleansing." It was open season on civilians, and every neighborhood was on the front lines. The resulting war crimes on all sides were enough to make you weep. Eventually NATO bombings helped force the combatants to the negotiating table, and the last of the peace accords was signed in 1999.

Standing on the clifftop beside the Belgrade Fortress, Jakov showed us the communications center NATO had bombed, then flung out a hand toward the river. "You see that bridge?" We all nodded to show we did, indeed, see the large, traffic-clogged bridge a few miles away. "During the war, we were so afraid that NATO would bomb our bridge, our lifeline, that all the young people in the city went out and stood on the bridge. If the NATO planes wanted to bomb our bridge, they would have to bomb us as well!"

I had to admire their spirit, although using the human body as a shield to protect an inanimate object against bombs in a war zone struck me as a dubious strategy at best. Clearly Jakov felt that his country was the victim of unwarranted aggression on NATO's part, and I'm sure I'd have felt much the same if someone were dropping explosives on my town.

But in the overall scheme of things, it was hard to position Serbia as the innocent victim. Slobodan Milošević fought hard and he fought dirty. How dirty? Well, here's one example: there were official orders for Serbian soldiers, police, and paramilitary to rape young women as a form of ethnic cleansing. In that part of the world, a child's legal ethnic status came from the father's side, so the raped women, largely Bosnian Muslims and Kosovo Albanians, bore children who were classified as Serbs. Although the sanctioned rapes could — and did — happen everywhere, there were special government-run camps where women would be repeatedly violated, then detained until late in their pregnancy. When they were finally released, the pregnant women were often outcasts, homeless and left to fend for themselves in the middle of a war zone. This happened to tens of thousands of women and girls over nearly a decade, and the impact was devastating, not only to the individual women, but to their children, their families, and their communities.

If I were in charge of NATO, would I have authorized bombings to end such atrocities? I don't know. I do know that I am profoundly grateful that I've never had to make that kind of judgment call.

All in all, I felt exhausted and rather subdued by the end of the tour. Rich thought a beer might help us recuperate, and he managed to find his way back to a bar that Jakov had pointed out in passing, one whose name was simply a question mark.

The bar named ? was across the street from the Cathedral Church of St. Michael the Archangel, and in 1892, when the bar changed hands, the new owner caused a furor when he announced he would rename it "By the Cathedral." Apparently the local clergy felt using the name of a sacred edifice for such a worldly establishment was bordering on sacrilege. I gathered that there was a spirited exchange of opinions on the matter, but eventually the bar's owner capitulated and agreed to come up with something more suitable. To give himself time to mull over the matter, he posted the question mark as a temporary solution, and it's remained in place ever since.

Belgrade loves its quirky bars, and ? is among its most popular.

Rich and I discovered countless other eccentric watering holes around town, including colorful bohemian dives, flashy modern nightclubs, and an outdoor café with dozens of open umbrellas suspended overhead, forming a colorful canopy. I'd read numerous references to a district called Silicon Valley and assumed the city had some sort of high-tech industrial zone until I found out the nickname was a sly pun referring to the silicone implants favored by many female patrons of the glitzy bars in one particularly slick, upmarket district.

Silicon Valley wasn't really our scene, but we soon discovered a more congenial nightspot in the Klub Knjizevnika. Founded in 1946 as the Serbian Writer's Association, this private club soon became the place to see and be seen by the city's literary figures and journalists, along with a lively collection of artists, politicians, and diplomats. Needless to say, it became a hotbed of spies and informers, and a single careless remark inside its walls had been known to cost people their liberty and sometimes their lives.

The Klub's lavish basement dining room later became a public restaurant, attracting such international celebrities as Alfred Hitchcock, Elizabeth Taylor, Richard Burton, and Samuel Beckett. When the UN embargo in the 1990s kept foreigners out of the city, the Klub became the favorite haunt of well-heeled warlords and crime bosses. Željko Ražnatović, the most powerful and infamous military leader in the Balkans, took his wife there for a romantic Valentine's Day dinner on the night he was assassinated.

Our introduction to Klub Knjizevnika came via Slavica, the mother of an editor I know. Slavica and I had corresponded before the trip, and in her last email she had suggested meeting up for an evening at the Klub's underground dining room. She was a slender, energetic woman about my own age, a wise and witty dinner companion, and a brilliant economist who had served as advisor to high government officials for decades. At her recommendation we ordered the lamb, which was easily the best I've ever tasted — in my opinion, better than even the lamb in Veliko Tarnovo, although Rich begs to differ. Sitting in the opulent dining room, I savored the excellent wine, the succulent lamb, and Slavica's stories about working with some of the most powerful people of her generation. She touched lightly, almost casually, on the dangers of Serbian public life.

"I remember once, at a time when relations with Croatia were . . . delicate," she said with a wry smile. "I was invited to go there for a conference, one that I particularly wanted to attend. I knew I couldn't enter the country by plane or train; if they became aware that I was there . . ." A small shrug. "Well, I didn't want to be killed just to attend a conference. So I hired a car and a driver and slipped across the border without anyone noticing. And back again after, safe and sound." She smiled and drank some more wine.

I reflected, briefly and thankfully, on the singular lack of death threats in my own career. The worst danger I'd ever encountered on a business trip was driving through bad weather.

"So what's next?" I asked her.

"I am trying to decide on a new direction. I would like to spend more time writing. Like you. Tell me more about your book . . ."

As we discussed the business of writing and publishing — she had produced numerous books with such weighty titles as *Economic and European Perspectives of Western Balkan Countries* — I reflected that this was one of the great benefits of traveling when you're older. Twenty-something backpackers, like the boys who had recoiled from me on the train, have plenty of adventures on the road, but they're unlikely to include the sophisticated pleasures of that kind of dinner.

The next day, I decided it was time to replace my late, lamented black trousers and returned to Knez Mihailova, the main shopping street. I eventually found a pair of trim stretch jeans, which struck me as the right attire for the following night's activity: going in search of a speakeasy.

The search wouldn't be easy. This particular underground bar went by at least two different names and was located on a street that had ceased to exist years before. My only guide was a map with standard

Roman lettering, which didn't help much as there were almost never any street signs, and the few we did see were written in Cyrillic. Naturally almost none of the buildings had a visible street number. However, such is the power of the Internet that I managed to discover that Улица 29 новембра (29 Novembra Street) was the older (and still preferred) name for Булеван Деспота Стефана (Bulevan Despota Stefan), and by counting carefully we eventually arrived at an apartment block with a big, black, unmarked, wrought-iron gate. Beside the doorbell was a discreet label that read "Federal Association of Globe Trotters." We were pretty sure this was the place, even though we'd been looking for the World Travelers' Club. Translations were always a bit slippery.

After that we simply had to press the doorbell, wait for the gate to buzz open, walk through the echoing lobby of the apartment building, make our way down some dimly lit stairs, find the yellow door standing slightly ajar, push it open, and enter. Inside was one of the coolest bars I've ever seen, dimly lit and gorgeously decorated in around-the-world memorabilia and family attic castoffs. The fact that it was one of the city's secret drinking dens added a small, clandestine thrill.

The speakeasy atmosphere harked back to the war era, when it was imprudent to be overheard expressing anti-Milošević sentiments at public places like the Klub Knjizevnika, and hip, young dissidents wanted to gather to discuss their political views in safe, congenial surroundings with a fully stocked bar. Nowadays, in the free and democratic Republic of Serbia such secrecy was no longer necessary, but the habit of flying under the radar seemed deeply imbedded in the local psyche. This wasn't the only speakeasy in town, and we regretted that there wasn't time to visit them all.

When I posted photos of the Federal Association of Globe Trotters/ World Travelers' Club on my Facebook page, several people wrote in asking how I managed to find such clandestine gin joints. So I am going to let you in on a closely guarded trade secret: I looked on the Internet. Lonely Planet had a short description, Google led me to their website (yes, even speakeasies have websites nowadays!), and the *Financial*

Times online edition mentioned it and others in a story called *Belgrade's Secret Bars*.

I felt sure that Belgrade had deeper secrets it had managed to keep hidden even from these shrewd investigators, and I hope someday to return and unravel a few more of the city's mysteries.

Belgrade is clearly a city that believes, as Sir Arthur Conan Doyle once had Sherlock Holmes say, "there is nothing more deceptive than an obvious fact." When it came time to make our departure from Belgrade, I had a ticket clearly stating the number of our train compartment, yet that number didn't exist anywhere, and eventually I found a car marked with three other numbers — a large 430, an upside down 431, and an even larger 864 pasted below that — which, inexplicably, turned out to be the right place. Cryptic to the last, Belgrade offered this final reminder that there, the more facts you had, the less sure you could be about anything.

[CHAPTER 17]

Not Quite What I Expected

One of the reasons why I love railway travel is that unlike other forms of long-distance transportation, it does not invariably reduce me to a brain-dead zombie. The thrumming vibration of planes, the mesmerizing view of an endless ribbon of highway unspooling before me, the elephantine acceleration and deceleration of public buses — these all induce a sort of languor that soon morphs into a mindless stupor. And I'm not the only one; on long car trips, for example, I've noticed everyone's wits tend to slow to a crawl, reducing the conversation to such fatuous remarks as "Oh look, there's a cow" and "Yes, I see that cow."

But on trains I tend to feel as alert and alive as I do with my feet on solid ground. It could be the fresh air coming in through the open windows, or the ability to get up and move around, or having new seatmates arrive and depart at unexpected intervals. Whatever the cause, when I'm on a train, I generally feel like myself, able to enjoy such civilized pursuits as thinking, talking, and reading without motion sickness.

A Eurail pass provides the added luxury of making ordinary trains into hop-on-hop-off transportation. Throughout the trip, whenever we'd been faced with an excessively long stretch — Bucharest to Sofia, for instance — we had broken up our journey by stopping for the night in a town that seemed interesting or at least conveniently placed. So at first I wasn't particularly worried when, toward the end of our stay in Belgrade, Rich mentioned that our next destination, the capital of Montenegro, was ten hours and twenty minutes away by rail.

"So where can we stop overnight?" I asked. "Are there any interesting towns along the way?"

"The only town of any size seems to be a place called Užice." He consulted his handy iPad. "It's in the mountains, in an area called the Dinaric Alps."

"That sounds rather nice," I said, picturing Swiss-style chalets, exhilarating walks in *Sound of Music* meadows, a fireplace to warm ourselves during the chilly autumn evening . . .

"It appears to be a mining town. And it has just this one hotel." I peered over his shoulder at the photo on his iPad's screen.

"That's not a hotel; it's a death star," I said.

Užice's only concession to the demands of human hospitality was a massive, dark tower with a flared base, rather like Darth Vader's helmet. Looming over a dreary residential landscape of unpainted concrete and cheap aluminum, its incongruous size and featureless exterior managed to suggest the careless brutality of a place you'd be sent to await reprogramming or execution. Photos of the interior showed narrow, metal-frame beds with thin mattresses, the kind you see in prison movies. It looked like the sort of place where you'd be well advised to sleep with a shiv under your pillow.

"Okay, so *not* stopping there," I said, as Rich flipped through more photos of the hotel, several showing brown stains on the bare walls above the beds, where inmates — I mean guests — had leaned their exhausted, despairing heads. Were these grim shots really the best the hotel could disseminate to the online public? I began to suspect that they'd hired the same marketing people who'd presided over the PR disaster surrounding the mass firings at the Hotel Moscow.

"There's really nothing else," Rich said. "The other stops don't even have that much."

"I guess we're going straight through, then." I sighed. "It's going to be a very long day."

"There *is* a night train . . ."

I shuddered. If that's what their hotels looked like . . . "I think not."

On the morning of our departure, when we'd finally managed to decipher the cryptic numbering system on the train cars, I settled into our compartment, setting out my Kindle, some snacks, and a bottle of water on the empty seat next to me. Yes, it would be a long day, but at the end of it we'd be in Montenegro, a country that countless people had assured us that we would absolutely adore.

I recalled the words of Denise, the Irish woman I'd met back in August on the train out of Český Krumlov in the Czech Republic: "At this point for me to say a place is special, it would have to be dipped in gold." Now, after months of travel, I knew just what she meant. Every few days Rich and I had been hauling out the map and Googling destination options. And I often found myself saying things like, "Well, it's got a twelfth-century cathedral, an old town that's a UNESCO World Heritage Site, the miraculously preserved dead body of a saint, opera in a Roman coliseum, and a fountain that does light shows to Bach and Beatles tunes . . . but nothing *special*." I had a feeling that this train ride was going to redefine my concept of "nothing special."

At first, I was glad to have the chance to simply stare out the window and think. Leaving Belgrade marked a major turning point in the trip. We had made a giant, irregular loop, heading northeast from Seville into Italy, then north by northeast as far the Czech Republic, heading south as far as Bulgaria, and angling a bit to the northwest to reach Serbia. Now we were moving southwest into Montenegro, bringing us back to the shores of the Mediterranean.

The homeward journey had begun.

We'd been on the road just shy of two and a half months, and it looked like we'd be back home in Seville within a couple of weeks. I was so used to being on the road that the idea of coming to rest anywhere, even in such a familiar and beloved place, left me feeling a trifle disoriented.

I leaned back against the tough, fuzzy, old fabric of the train seat, closed my eyes, and thought about the last two and a half months. Was The Experiment a success? Had it been worth all the effort? Was I any different from the person who had stepped on the high-speed train from Seville to Barcelona? If so, how?

On the most basic level, I was very relieved that we'd managed to go the distance. We had now almost completed the route roughed out on the map that had been taped to our kitchen wall for so long, and we had never seriously considered turning back or flying home. Rich had managed well and traveled cheerfully, despite an often-painful leg. Somehow we'd avoided falling victim to ruthless villains, unsafe transportation vehicles, savage beasts, vampires, and whatever other hazards Enrique had in mind when he remarked, all those months ago, "Well, it's been nice knowing you." I suppose the most basic benchmark for any long journey has to be the one used by aviators who, when asked what makes a good landing, often reply, "One you can walk away from."

And I'd gotten *out there*. I'd traveled to remote, rural areas and strange cities, hobnobbing with shepherds, philosophers, economists, political firebrands, Hash House Harriers, and countless others. I had seen spectacular beauty, architectural horrors, and once-gorgeous locales reduced to strip clubs and theme parks. I'd visited places where acts of unspeakable cruelty and heartbreaking tragedy had taken place. And it was those places, the ones where I'd stood in the Devil's Footprint, that had changed me the most.

How? In a way, it all came down to having a new understanding of the word "us." I'd always considered "us" to be one of the sweetest words in the English language, suggesting the love between parents and children, friends, lovers, football fans rooting the home team on to victory. It feels good to be part of something larger than ourselves, whether it's a family, a religion, or a country. The problem is that the minute you talk about "us" there's a "them" standing outside the magic circle, and that's where things get sticky. Anyone who went to high school knows how nasty in-groups — the mean girls, the bullies — can be to outsiders.

The hard truth is that we all have a touch of mean kid in us. It's human nature. Most of us are just lucky enough that our circumstances don't encourage our inner meanie to come out and play too often. But that can change fast, sometimes without our realizing it. This was dramatically demonstrated in a notorious experiment that took place in 1967 at a high school near mine, among students of my own grade. It all started when one kid asked his history teacher, Ron Jones, the inevitable question about where all the good Germans were during the rise of the Nazis.

Jones decided to get creative in answering that question, and he constructed a classroom experiment that began the next Monday with a description of the role of discipline in fascism. To illustrate his point, he had his students adopt more formal postures and manners. The kids loved the game. Jones began coming up with slogans and lectures praising community over individuality and started treating his students like an elite group.

The response was astonishing.

In days, most students were exhibiting blind obedience to Jones and a superior, sometimes hostile attitude toward non-members; worse, Jones found himself acting more and more like a dictator. To end the experiment, he told students that the project wasn't an exercise but a real-life movement in support of a political candidate. The students were more enthusiastic than ever, and on Friday morning they eagerly assembled to meet their new leader.

Then Jones revealed there was no leader and no movement. He explained that in less than a week they'd been duped into acting like fascists, and played a video of Germans marching in disciplined ranks saluting Adolf Hitler.

The kids were shocked speechless. Lesson learned. Where were all the good Germans? Just look in the mirror.

I'd always been a bit haunted by that story, knowing that it was only by the sheer luck of school districting boundaries that I wasn't a member of Jones's class. Would I have been transformed into a fascist in less than a week? I liked to think that I would have been smarter and stronger than that. But I couldn't be sure. Jones conducted his experiment at a high school in Stanford University's hometown of Palo Alto, with above-average students, just an hour south of San Francisco in the spring before the famous Summer of Love ushered in the full flowering of the resist-authority sixties — and almost no one questioned, protested, or refused to participate.

Now, sitting on the train speeding out of Serbia toward Montenegro, I thought about how much easier it must have been to convince members of earlier generations, in cultures that emphasized respect for authority, to view "us" with pride and "them" as beneath contempt. If I had grown up under, say, Nicolae Ceaușescu, and been part of *that* social experiment, could I have ended up capable of sending people to stand all night naked in freezing water in the Black Cell of a communist prison? I liked to think I would have been smarter and stronger than that too.

I would never know what might have happened if I'd been in Jones's classroom or had come of age in a fascist dictatorship. But I felt that now, going forward, having traveled to so many places where "us" vs. "them" thinking had run so tragically amok, I wanted to take a hard look at what I meant by those terms. Could I learn to think of "us" as including everybody?

The Dalai Lama once said, "Today, as the world becomes smaller and smaller, the concept of 'us' and 'them' is almost outdated. If our interests existed independently of those of others, then it would be possible to have a complete winner and a complete loser, but since in reality we all depend on one another, our interests and those of others are very interconnected." I think the Dalai Lama is on to something here, and I have to respect the opinion of a man who's had fourteen incarnations to work out this stuff. So what exactly did that mean for me, in my daily life? "My religion," said the Dalai Lama, "is kindness." Maybe that would be a good place to start.

Rich, who had dozed off in his seat — how I envied his ability to sleep anywhere, at any time! — now awoke, and after passing him the water and cookies, I asked him, "How do you think this trip has changed you?"

He said thoughtfully, "Well, for one thing, it really took my mind off this problem with my leg. For a while there, back in California, it was just about all I could think about. I needed to deal with it, but I didn't want it to become the permanent centerpiece of my life."

"Do you think all the walking made it better or worse?"

"Better."

"So I was right, back at the start, when I told you that you should man up and walk it out?"

He laughed. "Not really. I needed to go through all that therapy and learn the exercises — they really help a lot — and how to pace myself."

"But you don't think you should have stayed longer in California to get more treatment?"

"Definitely not. You can always think of a reason to delay a trip and find excuses that might be important or pretty slim. It would have been easy to say, 'Let's put this off' for another month or a year. But I think I had taken the treatments about as far as I could. If we'd stayed much longer, it would have been the wheat-free diet and medical marijuana. I think hitting the road was more effective and more fun."

The train made seventeen stops that day, and at each one Rich and I rose to go out in the corridor and lean out the window, checking out the station and observing the activity, if any, on the platform. Most of the stations were square, concrete boxes that appeared unattached to any human settlement, and it always struck me as slightly surprising that a few hardy souls actually got on and off the train at these places. Occasionally a newcomer would wander into our compartment, sit down, and attempt to make conversation with us, although usually the complete lack of any language in common made this a short-term proposition.

At one o'clock in the afternoon the train pulled into an actual town, and even before I saw the sign that identified it as Užice, Rich said, "Hey, there's the Death Star Hotel!" Directly opposite the station, the hulking mass of the hotel dominated the cheap apartments and dismal shops that surrounded it. The reality looked even more forbidding than the photos. I shuddered to think that we had, even for a nanosecond, contemplated staying there.

"All it's missing," I said, "is a sign reading, 'Abandon hope, all ye who enter here.'"

The train lingered for a while, no doubt needing to catch its breath after the steep climb, giving us plenty of time to inspect the town. Užice might not look like much now, but it did have its moment in the limelight. Back in 1941, communist partisans liberated the town from the Nazis and declared it the capital of a brand new mini-state called — drumroll, please! — the Republic of Užice. Sadly for the partisans' hopes, the fledgling nation lasted literally as long as the average life span of a flea; within a few months the Nazis rolled in, crushed the upstart nation like said flea, and regained control over the region. A chastened Užice went back to work and had been keeping its collective head down ever since. There were resort areas as close as sixteen miles away, but it was pretty clear that tourism had not made inroads into this no-frills town.

I was glad to leave Užice behind and continue onward. The train soon rolled across the Serbia-Montenegro border. Another million or so trees flew past our window. It began to rain. Again.

"Remember when we were kids and the nuns taught us about limbo?" I asked.

In catechism class, we'd learned that unbaptized babies went to a special place where there was no suffering but they were forever denied the joy of entering God's presence. It had seemed to me rather hard on the poor babies to be condemned, through no fault of their own, to spend eternity in a state of bland nothingness. Recently the Catholic church had downgraded limbo from a doctrine to a hypothesis, explaining that the concept was used in medieval times to motivate people to get baptized, but now, a mere thousand years later, we could all forget about it. It was hardly the most shocking news about the Catholic church to emerge during the early twenty-first century, but the sudden reversal had left me with a bit of mental whiplash.

"Limbo? Didn't they get rid of it back in 2005?" said Rich.

"They said they did, but they were obviously wrong, because that's exactly where we are right now."

Eight hours into the trip, I woke from a fitful doze and had my first good idea in what felt like days.

"There's been nobody in the compartment with us for a while," I said to Rich. "Why don't we watch a movie on the laptop?"

We'd brought a few along for just such emergencies, and it was but the work of a moment to don our headsets and boot up a film. As the incredibly handsome onscreen protagonists started firing off snappy one-liners and bullets with equal insouciance, I took a deep breath and thought I just might survive the last two hours of the trip without falling into an irreversible coma.

At that moment, a flash of gold outside the window caught the corner of my eye, and I turned my head slightly and gasped. It was sunset, and we'd just topped a rise and started down into a valley where the leaves had turned color in earnest. The warm, slanting afternoon light caught a vast sweep of brilliant yellow foliage, illuminating each leaf with a radiance like holy fire, casting long shadows deep into crevasses, where tendrils of fog were collecting into swirling drifts. It was, quite literally, breathtaking.

I grasped Rich's arm and pointed. He turned his head and his jaw dropped. "Just when you thought you'd never get excited about scenery ever again," he said, and paused the movie.

"It's what Denise said," I told him. "This place is *dipped in gold.*"

We stared out the window at this blaze of glory for several minutes, and then the train passed into another valley with less sun and more fog and shadow, and we put our headsets back on and went back to the movie.

It was after nine and raining steadily when we pulled into Montenegro's capital, a city so obscure that my computer's spellchecker didn't even recognize the name; in case you don't either, it's Podgorica. The blogging community, in a rare show of unity, dismissed it as a lackluster town, and without much further research, Rich and I decided to make it a single, overnight, convenience stay en route to the coast. We took a taxi to our hotel, a modest place on a tree-lined street in a quiet neighborhood.

Our room's single most noteworthy feature was that the en suite bathroom had a wall dispenser containing paper toilet seat covers, something I hadn't seen in months. I could only hope it was due to a fast-talking salesman or some personal quirk of the owner's, rather than some alarming public health issue that I would have known about if only I'd spent a little more time researching Podgorica.

After settling into our hotel, Rich and I took a stroll around the neighborhood, which held a desultory collection of small shops and cafés, a plaza with a modest fountain, and not much else. The next morning, having four hours to kill before our train, I asked the desk clerk for a map so we could explore the city.

"There is no map," she said.

No map? Wasn't this the nation's capital? "Okay, then could you direct us to the center of the city?"

She looked at me strangely. "This *is* the center of the city."

Seriously? "Oh," I said rather blankly. "Well, then, could you recommend anything for us to do? Are there any important buildings or museums we might want to visit?"

She thought for a moment. "You could go to a café and have a coffee." Let the good times roll . . .

After that underwhelming buildup, I was pleasantly surprised by Podgorica's geography. The city center was built around a winding river flanked by lush parks, and in the distance steep hills provided a dramatic backdrop. In between, however, the urban landscape was crowded with soulless concrete buildings that ranged from dull to hideous. I was particularly struck by one low-slung bunker, half buried in a hillside, with dark slits for windows; it looked like the set for a cheesy sci-fi movie, the place you'd hole up as a last resort while fleeing the undead (who would, of course, turn out to be in there with you).

"The setting is really quite nice," I said to Rich. "If they ever figure out how to exploit the natural beauty around here, tourists will flock to

Montenegro."

I soon learned the Montenegrins were way ahead of me on this. Arriving that afternoon at the wonderfully picturesque medieval port of Kotor, Rich and I could hardly squeeze through the town's gate, so thick were the throngs of sightseers from the massive cruise ship anchored just offshore.

"This? This isn't crowded," a local boatman told me later. "Sometimes we have as many as four big cruise ships and several smaller ones — they bring maybe 10,000 people a day to the town." With just 13,500 people living in Kotor, that made it practically a one-to-one tourist-to-resident ratio.

"I think they've figured out how to exploit the natural beauty around here," Rich said.

Kotor had been a lovely port town from Roman times up until the early days of our own century, when the desire for tourism revenues outweighed quality-of-life considerations, and massive, low-fare cruise ships were welcomed with open arms by the town's civic leaders. Kotor was one of the most physically attractive towns I'd ever seen, filled with quaint, red-roofed stone buildings and enclosed by medieval fortifications that zigzagged at improbable angles up the steep, rocky slopes, around the city, and down to the placid blue waters of the bay.

In its long history, Kotor had suffered the usual vicissitudes, including war, plague, earthquakes, and invasion by a large number of Renaissance literary luminaries. Now the ancient streets rang with shouts of, "Look at this *darling* little souvenir shop! Did you ever *see* anything so *adorable*?" Americans, Germans, Australians, Japanese, French, Spaniards, Chinese, Italians — it was always the same. The women shopped for trinkets, the men stood around discussing how the fortifications would protect the city from invaders, and then everyone chose one of the cookie-cutter tourist restaurants for a quick lunch before returning to the ship.

By the time we'd found the shop where our landlady worked, fetched the key, and shouldered our way through the crowds to our apartment just a few short blocks from the main gate, I was ready to hop on the next train out of town.

Ever since Prague, I'd felt that I was heading further and further *out there* into lands ever more mysterious and exciting; it had been rather like going deeper and deeper into Narnia. Arriving in Kotor was like stepping through another wardrobe and finding myself in Disneyworld, where every flowerpot and set of shutters had been carefully chosen by decorators to provide the cutest possible background for snapshots. I was deeply disappointed. I'd had such high hopes of one more exciting and challenging town, one more place that felt truly foreign, before we hit familiar territory again.

"Welcome to Orlando, Florida," said Rich.

We unlocked the door to our new digs and stood surveying the dark, slightly musty apartment without much enthusiasm.

"We prepaid for four nights here, didn't we?" I asked.

He nodded glumly. "We should have known better."

"How? Everybody raves about Kotor."

Not only had many friends spoken warmly of the town, but the Internet was full of breathless articles singing its praises. Even the normally reliable travel guru Rick Steves called Kotor "a time-capsule retreat for travelers seeking a truly unspoiled Adriatic town. The town, with 3,000 living inside the old town walls, has just enough commerce to keep a couple of restaurants and hotels in business." No doubt it was like that during his visit some years earlier, but by the time we got there, Kotor was about as unspoiled and natural as a child beauty pageant.

"Well, we're here now," I said. "Maybe there's another section of town that still feels more authentic."

But a quick walk about town dashed even these modest hopes. Every part of Kotor that lay within the old city walls was entirely devoted to tourist restaurants and hotels, which had apparently spread like kudzu since Mr. Steves's delightful visit. Spotting a pair of colorful laundry lines strung across a back alley, I couldn't help wondering if someone from the tourist office had added them for effect.

Later, when we went outside the walls of the old town, we found modern neighborhoods where ordinary Montenegrins were going about their daily affairs, eating at fast food restaurants, shopping at supermarkets and working in chain stores, but within the walls, virtually everyone we saw was a tourist or working in the tourist industry.

The harbor housed a few fishing boats, lots of visiting yachts, and half a dozen commercial boats offering half-day cruises around the bay. There were naturally no walking tours, Kotor being small enough to circumnavigate on foot in less than fifteen minutes, so there being little else to do, we signed up for a boat trip the next morning.

The day dawned gloriously warm and sunny, and as we climbed aboard the tour boat and left Kotor behind, I felt my spirits lift. Our first port of call was the exceedingly pretty Our Lady of the Rock Island. According to local legend, the island had been an insignificant rock until someone found an icon of the Virgin Mary there on July 22, 1452. Everyone got pretty excited about it; the word "miracle" was bandied about, and soon the rock was considered sacred ground. Fishermen began to drop stones around its outer edges to build up the holy spot, and eventually the rock became an island large enough to hold a church, a tower, and a small museum. Every year on July 22, the locals held a *fašinada*, a festival for adding more stones to shore up Our Lady's island.

The boatman gave us half an hour on the island, which, although extremely picturesque, could be thoroughly explored and photographed in about ten minutes. After that, Rich and I wandered into the museum.

"Be sure to see the tapestry of Jacinta Kunić-Mijović," advised the woman at the museum's tiny front desk.

I had read about this famous object, described by one gushing website as "one of the most valuable religious tapestries in the Mediterranean." Making my way past the seashells, barnacle-encrusted lanterns, and paintings of storm-tossed ships, I found a small, framed linen rectangle showing the disembodied heads of Mary and the infant Jesus floating in a sea of gold thread surrounded by cherubs. Created by a woman in the nearby village of Perast, the object's main claim to fame was that the cherubs' heads were embroidered using strands of the artist's own hair, golden brown in her youth and fading to gray then white as she aged. Jacinta worked on the tapestry for twenty-five years, whiling away the long, lonely nights waiting for her husband to return from the sea, which he never did.

It was a heartbreaking story. I wouldn't want that tapestry on a wall in my home, bearing its mute testimony to twenty-five years — 9,125 nights! — of loneliness and increasingly forlorn hope. But was it among of the most valuable religious tapestries in the Mediterranean? Only in the minds of the local equivalent of the chamber of commerce public relations department.

The second — and last — stop on our tour was the village of Perast, home of the ill-fated embroiderer. It was as photogenic as Our Lady of the Rock Island, with charming old stone buildings, an ancient fire truck parked in front of the quaint little station, and brightly colored laundry fluttering from shuttered balconies. The streets were almost entirely devoid of local residents; presumably they were all in Kotor, selling chicken Caesar salads and coasters that read "I (heart) Montenegro." We were back at our apartment by midafternoon, still debating whether a quick escape would be worth sacrificing the money we'd prepaid to rent it.

"There must be more to this area," I said. "What was the town that Ang and Ryan liked so much?" These were friends who ran a small, online business and, being location independent, roamed the world working, playing, and writing about their adventures on a blog called Jets Like Taxis. They'd choose a place, explore it until their ninety-day tourist visa was about to expire, and then zip off to another country — as one friend put it, taking jets like taxis. I remembered them telling me that they had thoroughly enjoyed the several months they'd spent in another town on Kotor Bay, which was called . . . It was on the tip of my tongue . . .

"Got it," said Rich, thumbing through his massive Evernote files. "Herceg Novi. We can go there tomorrow and see if we fall in love with the place."

That night, Rich suggested that we try a funky little mom-and-pop eatery we'd seen outside the walls of the old city, not far from the bus station. It was our kind of place: rickety tables, blue-checkered plastic tablecloths, and somebody's mother cooking out in the kitchen.

"It smells wonderful," said Rich. "Whatever she's making, that's what I want for dinner."

"If I were you, I'd find out what it is first," I cautioned.

There's an oft-told family story about our early days in Seville, when Rich's imperfect grasp of Spanish led him to order the day's special, which turned out to be tripe, a dish he loathes above all others. His attempts at explaining to our host why he couldn't eat it only entangled him in further misunderstandings, and we slunk out of the café in disgrace, not daring to show our faces there for months. Needless to say, Rich has never lived down the incident and still takes a certain amount of ribbing about it in situations like these.

Rich loftily ignored my cautionary remark, but he did wander back into the restaurant's nether regions to check out what was in the stewpot. He was promptly shooed out of the kitchen by the indignant cook, but not before he'd managed to convey, in pantomime, that he wanted some of that, please.

"Did you see what it was?" I asked.

"No, but my sniffer tells me it's going to be incredible." He sat back in his chair with a sigh of pleasure. "It's so great to get off the tourist track to someplace authentic with real home cooking."

Rather to my surprise, the café had a printed menu, and I ordered the only thing I recognized, *sarma*, a delicious dish of cabbage leaves stuffed with minced pork and rice. The Ottoman Turks had introduced it to the region as they marched through invading and pillaging, and *sarma* had stayed around much longer than they had. I'd eaten plenty of it in Romania and Bulgaria and greeted it as an old friend now.

When the cook carried out our food and deposited it on the table, Rich stared down at his bowl, aghast. It was tripe soup: thick, rubbery strands of cow intestines heaped in a richly seasoned broth. He'd done it again! I laughed so hard I bent double in my chair and almost brained myself on the tabletop.

Possibly drawn by my whoops, a gray-haired matron who looked like she might be the cook's mother, or possibly her grandmother, emerged from the kitchen and stumped over to sit at a nearby table, darting uncertain glances in our direction.

I fought down my laughter and wiped my eyes. "You're welcome to some of my *sarma*," I told him.

But Rich was still staring in horror at the long strips of bovine bowel swimming around in his bowl. "I can't eat this," he said. "You know that. I really can't." I nodded as sympathetically as I could and managed to suppress a snort of laughter. "But I can't leave it," he went on. "That would insult the cook." He glanced over at Grandma, who was still staring in our direction.

"Just sop up the broth with the bread, push the rest to the side, and leave it."

But Rich was shaking his head. "We have to get rid of it. *You* have to get rid of it."

"Me? Why me? I didn't order the tripe."

"That's why they won't suspect you," he wheedled. "You're good at this stuff."

"Oh, for heaven's sake. What are you, twelve? Fine. Wrap as much tripe as you can in a napkin and slide it to the center of the table. *Not yet!* Wait until Grandma isn't looking." The old woman turned around to say something to the cook. "*Now!*" I hissed.

He dropped half a dozen paper napkins over the tripe pile and scooped the soggy mess out of his bowl, plopping it into the middle of the table just as Grandma turned back to us. Maybe she was wondering why I was snorting with laughter again.

A few minutes later, when I had myself under control, I casually wrapped my hand around the sodden little bundle, got to my feet, and walked toward the rest rooms. I held the oozing wad down at my side, as if I were carrying a half-forgotten tissue in my hand, and gave a few nasal sniffs for verisimilitude. I was just a woman with a cold heading to the ladies' room. Nothing to see here, folks. Luckily, Grandma kept her eyes fixed on Rich, whom she'd evidently pegged as the more dangerous member of our little party. I slipped past her into the ladies' room, tossed the horrid mess into the waste basket — the local plumbing clearly not being equal to the task of disposal — and lingered for a few minutes before emerging.

"You owe me big time," I said to Rich as I slid back into my seat.

"Damn right," he said, grinning. It's amazing how freeing himself from a few pieces of cooked cow innards can cheer up a man.

The next afternoon we took a local bus along the coast road to Herceg Novi, which stood at the mouth of Kotor Bay. Naturally such a strategic position had brought an endless series of invading armies to its shores, but nowadays its biggest battle was establishing its reputation as a tourist attraction. There were some rather rocky beaches and several spas offering baths in *igaljisko blato*, a local sea mud much admired in some circles for its healing properties. It also contained the usual assortment of monuments: fort, clock tower, churches. Fortunately or unfortunately, depending on your point of view, the big cruise ships needed a more sheltered harbor, so the majority of vacationers were bypassing Herceg Novi in favor of Kotor.

As Rich and I stepped off the bus, we heard riotous singing coming from a small bar adjacent to the station. Someone at the Orange Caffe-Bar was playing recordings of Montenegrin folk music, and half a dozen men were raising their glasses and their voices in a haze of patriotic fervor. It sounded like the party was well advanced.

Rich and I made our way to the center of town and spent a couple of pleasant hours admiring the scenery — which was truly spectacular — and visiting the fortress, the clock tower, and the Church of St. Michael the Archangel. Sadly St. Michael's was closed, but the nice little outdoor café across from it was open, and Rich and I settled down to reboot our energy levels with fresh, grilled fish and a glass of a very respectable local chardonnay.

When we eventually arrived back at the bus station, we were surprised and rather impressed to find the men still singing away lustily in the Orange Caffe-Bar.

"These are hardy folk indeed," I remarked to Rich. "If I were drinking at that rate, I'd have passed out hours ago."

With half an hour to wait and the bus station lacking such frivolous extras as benches or rest rooms, we repaired to the Orange. Within two minutes of our arrival, the party animals bought us a round, and after that it seemed only courteous to buy them a round and join them in singing and pounding out the songs' rhythm on the bar with our hands and glasses.

"*Hoopa! Hoopa!*" shouted the impromptu DJ. And somebody jumped up on top of the bar and started dancing.

Eventually our bus arrived, and — it being the last one of the night — we had to tear ourselves away. But not before several of the men shook Rich's hand and kissed me on the cheek. One fellow asked, "Where you from?" When I told him, he said, "Go and tell them. Tell all the people about what you saw here!"

And that's what I'm doing this very minute. Thanks to Herceg Novi and these hardy and exuberant men, I do have cherished memories of Montenegro. *Hoopa! Hoopa!*

[CHAPTER 18]

Wild Rides

It was a dark and stormy night on the Adriatic. "'The sea was angry that day, my friends,'" said Rich, quoting from the *Seinfeld* episode where George pretends to be a marine biologist. "'Like an old man trying to send back soup in a deli.'" We were reeling about the pitching ferry, trying to find our mini-cabin in its lower depths. "You do realize," he added in his normal voice, "that we're actually below the cars and cargo? We're in *steerage*."

We had departed from Kotor a day early and taken a bus to Dubrovnik — a city I was staggered to discover was even more crowded with tourists than Kotor — to catch the overnight ferry to Italy. The ferry was huge, able to accommodate thirteen hundred passengers and three hundred cars, and designed much like a cruise ship, with spacious first-class cabins that included en suite bathrooms, double beds, and windows offering views of the sea. We did not get one of those. By the time we made our reservations, the only cabins left were in the dark underworld maze once known as steerage. When we managed to locate ours, we discovered a closet containing two narrow, stacked bunks, a sink no bigger than a salad bowl, and scarcely enough floor space for our suitcases. The toilets were four dimly lit corridors away in another part of the labyrinth. On the positive side, at least we wouldn't have to worry about sharing the compartment with other passengers. You couldn't possibly get anybody else in there with a shoehorn.

"A beer?" suggested Rich.

We climbed several flights of stairs, passing the first-class cabins (wistful sigh) and third-class lounges crowded with people wrapping themselves with blankets in preparation for sitting up all night in chairs (sympathetic shudder). Eventually we arrived at the bar, which was doing a brisk business. Outside, rain lashed against the windows, and even with the ship's stabilizers working overtime, we could feel the sea roiling beneath us. We collected our drinks and fell into conversation with Ce-Ann and Howard, a couple of Americans of my generation who were touring Europe on a motorcycle. We passed a pleasant hour or two swapping road stories, and then Howard asked, "So what's your next destination?"

"We're thinking of Pompeii," Rich said.

Neither of us had ever visited the city so famously preserved by the volcanic eruption of Mount Vesuvius in 79 AD. We had been casting about for one more exciting stop en route home, something that would end the trip's adventures on a higher note than Kotor. Everyone — from history professors to hipster travel writers to hard-drinking yahoos on package tours — raved about Pompeii. My only concern was that being one of the most popular tourist destinations in Italy, with 2,600,000 visitors a year, Pompeii might have more tourists per square foot than I could tolerate. I didn't want to have to stand in long lines to view each of the thousands of plaster casts that were all that remained of its residents.

"Oh yeah, Pompeii's cool," he said. "Any idea where you'll stay?"

"We *had* been thinking of doing it as a day trip from Naples," I put in. "But everyone's been warning us not to go there. They say the city is dirty and dangerous."

He and Ce-Ann exchanged one of those glances all long-married couples develop (the one that says, "Do we go there?" and replies "Oh, yeah."). And then Howard leaned across the table and said, "Look, I don't know you guys that well, but I have to say, from what you've been telling me, I think you'd like Naples. It's . . . different. A little rough around the edges, sure. Dirty? Yes, unbelievably. Dangerous? Not so much, if you don't do anything stupid. But Naples is . . ." He paused, and his face softened into a grin. "It's a fun town. Kinda crazy."

Soon after that, it was time to make our way back down to steerage and the cupboard in which we'd be sleeping. Well, *sleeping* turned out to be a bit of an exaggeration. We spent the night there, dozing fitfully, praying the tiny half railings on our bunks would hold and we wouldn't find ourselves hurtling to the floor. The ferry pitched and yawed and shuddered, fighting its way across every inch of the storm-tossed Adriatic by sheer brute force.

Around two in the morning, when a trip to the bathrooms became necessary — damn those beers! — Rich and I lurched through the warren of heaving corridors together, stumbling about and crashing into walls, hoping fervently that we wouldn't be flung bodily through anyone's door. If it hadn't been for the handrails that lined the passageways, we'd have been crippled or dead long before we made it to our destination. I shuddered to think about the sufferings of those who might have to negotiate this route in the throes of serious seasickness.

"Imagine weeks of this on the Atlantic," I gasped.

"Now I know why my grandmother vowed she'd never cross the ocean again," Rich said.

Somehow we made it to the facilities and back to our closet, where Rich instantly dropped into a deep sleep and I clung to my bunk rail, bracing myself against the roll and toss of the ship. We were on deck at dawn, thrilled to see solid land on the horizon, even the unlovely harbor of Bari, Italy.

The massive cranes and silos lining the docks made it clear that Bari had long since thrown quaintness and charm under the bus and embraced the more tangible benefits of shipping and petrochemical profits. We disembarked among stacks of rusting metal containers and took our arrival coffee at an ugly, modern café filled with dockworkers and bleary-eyed business travelers. We'd been warned that there wasn't much to see in Bari, but having hours to kill before our train up the coast, we left our suitcases in lockers at the railway station and walked into the old center of town.

Following the night's storm, the morning was bright and windy, and early as it was, the industrious housewives of Bari had already hung out their washing. Every balcony was aflutter with flapping clothes and snapping sheets, and I had the giddy sensation of constantly walking beneath a ship's unfurling sails.

Doors stood wide open to the sunshine, and we saw cobblers tapping on boot heels, tailors stitching, and women gossiping as their fingers shaped the "little ears" of pasta known as *orecchiette*, forming them with astonishing speed and spreading them on mesh trays to dry outside in the sun. All the warmth and charm that were missing in the harbor could be found in the city's back streets. I was sorry I didn't have more time to spend in Bari, but we'd already booked our night's lodging in the small coastal city of Barletta.

We'd picked Barletta almost at random as a convenient place to rest up after the crossing, checking only to be sure that there were enough noteworthy monuments to keep us entertained and relatively few tourists crowding the streets. It was a short train ride with multiple stops, and at the outskirts of each town — especially those with delightful sandy beaches and pretty Mediterranean architecture — we wondered aloud whether this might be our destination. When the train slowed to a crawl in an area crowded with high-rise apartments and grain elevators, a combination that managed to be both gritty and sterile at the same time, I remarked, "How perfectly hideous. I hope this isn't—"

"Welcome to Barletta," Rich said, as the station sign came into view. With somewhat less than our usual enthusiasm, we collected our bags and got off the train.

But as I'd found in Bari, as soon as we left the industrial wasteland of the harbor behind, the town began to grow on me. The high-rises gave way to smaller, older buildings with shops at ground level and apartments above, their tiny balconies made colorful by flowerpots and painted shutters. Arriving at our bed and breakfast on a side street in the old section, I found it sweetly old-fashioned, as if the owner had inherited it from his grandparents and had the wisdom to leave everything just the way *nonna* and *nonno* liked it.

As soon as we were settled, Rich and I went to pay homage to the town's most famous resident, the Colossus, an ancient bronze statue standing sixteen feet tall. No one was quite sure who he was (a fifth-century Roman emperor maybe?) or how he got to Barletta (washed up on shore after the sack of Constantinople perhaps?). But everyone agreed that he was the hero who had saved the city back in the day.

According to ancient legend, when the dreaded Saracens were about to invade Barletta, the Colossus went down to the harbor and stood on the shore weeping. "Why are you crying?" the Saracens asked. "Because I am so much smaller and weaker than everyone else in this city," he moaned. Terrified at the prospect of fighting an army of giants, the Saracens rowed back to their ships with all due haste and left Barletta in peace. And I am sure every word of that is true . . .

Barletta offered good weather and pleasant, undemanding points of interest just a short stroll apart, but we weren't inclined to linger. By now we were beginning to feel the gravitational pull of our Seville home. Winding down any long trip creates a certain tension; you're still on the road, but now you're heading *back there*, rather than *out there*. The fizz is starting to go out of the champagne. It's at this point that we usually try to think of some way to pep up the final days of the trip.

Over a glass of wine in an old stone *trattoria*, Rich said, "What the hell, let's go to Naples. We can book a room for two nights. If it's awful, we'll do Pompeii as a day trip, and then move on. But who knows? Naples might be fun."

I had my doubts. "I know that couple on the ferry said we'd like it, but the city does sound a bit dicey."

This was putting it mildly. Googling Naples, the very second listing I found (after the ubiquitous *TripAdvisor* site) was an article titled "79 Tips on Naples Warnings or Dangers — Stay Safe!" There, recent visitors waxed eloquent in their descriptions of the city, and the terms "pickpockets," "street scams," "seedy," and "filthy" cropped up with alarming frequency. Many complained bitterly about "helpful" residents who turned out to be thieves, often working in concert with other nefarious characters. Nearly everyone commented on the extraordinary amount of garbage strewn on the streets, apparently due to a standoff in landfill disputes involving the Mafia.

As for personal safety, one writer strongly recommended that future visitors "SHOW NO FEAR," using all caps to make sure that everybody GOT THE POINT. Another had written, "Naples in general is a horrible horrible place. With no redeeming value. Avoid it at all cost if possible. Your time and money is better spent someplace else. The major industry in Naples is cheating and robbing tourists." Yes, who wouldn't want to go to Naples after reading all that?

"Look at it this way," Rich said. "All those warnings will keep the tourists away. At least you won't have to worry about ending the trip with another Kotor or Dubrovnik."

"No, but I don't want to end it in the seventh circle of hell, either," I said. "Or dead, for that matter."

There was an oft-quoted comment by Johann Wolfgang von Goethe, author of *Faust*: "See Naples and die!" In the context of his praise of the city's beauty, it was clear he meant that you'd want to stay there until the end of your days, but that was in 1787; his words seemed to have a new, more sinister ring now.

However, we did find some favorable comments by contemporary writers. A few months earlier, Rick Steves had written in the *Huffington Post*, "I just spent two days in Naples, and loved it. It's one of the most fertile, churning, exuberant, and fun cities in all of Europe. And the entire time, I wondered, 'Where are the tourists?'" That sounded considerably more promising. Although, Mr. Steves *had* led us astray about Kotor . . .

In the end, we decided to take a chance on Naples. "If it turns out to be ghastly," I told Rich, "at least it will be *colorful* and ghastly."

It took us a while to find suitable accommodations, but eventually we booked a room in a bed and breakfast in the old section of Naples

— or Napoli, to use its proper name. The website mentioned an on-site spa, and I began to happily picture myself sipping wine in a hot tub after a relaxing massage. We got the only room available, which was being offered at a last-minute discount of twenty euros below the usual rate. So far, so good.

As our train sped toward Italy's west coast, I felt that we were now heading home in earnest. Much as I loved Seville and was looking forward to returning to my friends and my life there, it was hard to think about ending the journey and declaring The Experiment over. This made me feel a trifle melancholy, and I found myself looking forward to Napoli, hoping it would at least provide some distraction.

Once Rich and I commit to visiting a place, we rarely rethink or second-guess the decision. However, it was just possible that in this case, our subconscious minds were not 100 percent on board with the plan, and that's why the screw-up occurred. As to *how* it happened, I can only suppose we must have typed "Napoli" as opposed to "Napoli Centrale" in the destination section of the iRail app.

For months I had placed absolute faith in the app's nearly mystical powers to divine the best routes and stations. It had, for instance, easily separated the sheep from the goats in Bucharest, letting us know that the station we wanted was Bucureşti Nord and not Bucureşti Obor or Bucureşti Basarab. So on the train to Naples, when we consulted the iPad and saw that iRail wanted us to get off at the next station, we obediently gathered our things and started toward the doors.

As the train rolled into the station, which bore a sign saying Napoli Something-or-other, Rich turned to one of the nearby passengers, pointed, and said, "Napoli?" The man nodded. "*Sì, sì*. Napoli."

So we got off the train.

I was surprised that almost none of the other passengers followed us out the door.

"Wasn't Naples the end of the line?" I asked in some confusion.

The few people who had disembarked disappeared briskly up the stairs, and in moments Rich and I were alone in the drab, modern station.

We began to walk, our footsteps and the sound of our suitcase wheels echoing hollowly as we crossed the empty platform, climbed the stairs, and made our way toward the outer doors, passing various empty kiosks and ticket offices along the way. The entire station was deserted.

"This is *so* wrong," I said. "This *can't* be the central station. Let's go back down and take the next train. We must have gotten off too soon."

"Let's not be hasty. Why don't we look around a bit and see where we are?"

Pushing through fly-specked glass doors to step outside, I saw a street lined with closed-up warehouses and defunct businesses. A few empty beer cans, cigarette packets, and scraps of newspaper lay on the sidewalk, but it was hardly the ankle-deep litter I'd been warned to expect. There were still no people to be seen.

"What do you figure?" I asked, as we started walking up the street. "A nuclear holocaust while we were on the train? We're the only people left alive on the planet?"

"No," he said, rounding a corner. "*There's* somebody. Several people, in fact."

Up ahead I saw a long, dark pedestrian tunnel, the kind all moviegoers instantly recognize as the setting for an imminent mugging or murder. To make the image complete, three teenage boys loitered by the entrance.

"Well, of course, *they* would survive Armageddon," I muttered. "Shall we just throw them our wallets and beat ourselves up to save everybody some time?"

"Oh ye of little faith." Rich shook his head in mock sorrow. "Come on. I'm sure it'll be *fine*."

By now a few more people had appeared from the other direction. They looked like ordinary, respectable adults, and they walked into the tunnel without even glancing at the three kids. Rich and I followed closely on their heels. As I passed, the boys ignored me completely, and I reflected, not for the first time, on the practical advantages of being beyond the age that makes street gangs feel honor-bound to leer and engage in one-sided sexual banter. As for attracting attention as potential robbery victims, by this point in the trip our belongings — to say nothing of our persons — were looking distinctly the worse for wear, and no doubt even fledgling criminals would be discerning enough to seek richer pickings elsewhere.

As my eyes adjusted to the gloom of the cavernous tunnel, I saw the usual graffiti and had my first sight of the Napoli street garbage I'd heard so much about. The floor of the tunnel was almost entirely covered with broken glass, rotting food, and various lumps, mounds, and oozing blobs that I felt disinclined to examine too closely. "Whatever you do, don't trip and fall in here," I said, more to myself than to Rich. I suspected there were diseases lurking in this tunnel that had never seen the light of modern science, and I didn't want to take one home as a souvenir. "See Naples and die!" could be interpreted a lot of ways.

We emerged into bright sunlight and a bustling intersection. Dozens of people were dashing about in every direction, carrying groceries, pushing baby carriages, leaping off and on motor scooters, all talking and gesticulating at full tilt. I stood, blinking, for a long, dumbfounded moment, then began searching for a street sign that might, with the help of the iPad, let us figure out where we were.

A silver-haired stranger approached, saying in excellent English, "Where are you trying to get to?" He was so handsome, well-groomed, and smooth-spoken that I immediately assumed he was one of Napoli's famous scam artists. But Rich was already telling him the name of our bed and breakfast, even pulling out his notebook to show the stranger the address. Was he *insane*? Hadn't he read the seventy-nine warnings and safety tips on that website?

"You want to go back to the train station," the stranger said kindly but firmly. I had to admit this seemed like excellent advice. He went on to explain that we should take the next train onwards, and while we could get off at Napoli Centrale, the main station, and take a taxi, it would be cheaper to continue on for another few stops to the neighborhood where our bed and breakfast was located. Rich thanked him and we set off back through the tunnel.

As I carefully skirted one of the more virulent-looking objects on the tunnel floor, I suggested that perhaps we shouldn't put too much faith in the silver-haired, silver-tongued stranger. He might, of course, be a Good Samaritan, but it was equally likely that he was sending us to some other deserted station where his accomplices would be waiting for us. Rich agreed that it would be safer to disembark at Napoli Centrale and find a cab.

The fare from that station, our hostess at the bed and breakfast had written, should be no more than twelve euros, about fourteen dollars; she warned us not to let the local taxi drivers scam us. By now we'd had plenty of practice negotiating with taxi drivers at train stations, and we were confident that we could handle those at Napoli Centrale.

Fifty million people a year flow through Napoli Centrale — about 137,000 each day, some 5,700 per hour — and we emerged from our train into the thick of the throng. This was more what I'd expected! We elbowed our way to a café and swallowed some coffee, although the frantic bustle and bedlam all around us made this ritual a bit less soothing than usual. We then fought our way to the taxi stand, showed the driver the address, and Rich said "Twelve euros."

"Fifteen!"

Rich shook his head. "Twelve!"

"Fifteen!"

"Twelve!"

The driver didn't seem prepared to budge, so we walked off down the street. Seeing another taxi parked a little way beyond the station, Rich showed the driver the address and asked the cost.

"Fifteen euros!"

"Twelve!"

The driver shook his head. We shrugged and trudged on.

A car screeched up behind us, and a man leaned out the window, shouting, "Okay, I take you, twelve euro!" It was the first cab driver, with a thin, mustachioed man in the back seat. "You share. Twelve euro."

He leaped out, grabbed our bags, and threw them in the trunk. Rich raised his eyebrows at me, shrugged, and climbed into the back seat with our fellow passenger. I sat up front next to the driver, who shot away from the curb with a speed that slammed me back against the seat like an accelerating rocket.

Our driver was a magnificent road warrior. He drove at breakneck speed, shooting into impossibly small gaps, riding up on sidewalks, flying past stop signs, going against the flow of traffic on one-way streets, and at one point, zooming up trolley tracks in the wrong direction. All the while, he kept up a running commentary on the shortcomings of his fellow motorists. They were mouse-hearted chumps who drove like old ladies on their way to church. Look at that bonehead who was trying to butt into our lane! And what the hell was that bozo doing (loud honk, shouted curses) stopping at a red light? Hey buddy, if you wanna sleep, go home (more honking, more curses, highly creative hand gestures)! The commentary may have been in Italian, but the meaning was abundantly clear.

To keep up my end of the conversation, I nodded sympathetically, rolled my eyes in disgust, shook my head, and shrugged my shoulders, suiting my actions to the tone if not the details of the driver's remarks. The rest of the time I was busy clutching my daypack to my chest, wondering how effective it would be as an airbag in the crash that was beginning to seem inevitable.

The city flew by in a blur. I had fleeting impressions of tall, modern buildings, a busy port, and drivers cursing and shaking their fists. We zipped off the trolley tracks onto a wide main boulevard, then dove into an alleyway so narrow even our gonzo charioteer was forced to slow down. Here the buildings were smaller and older, the walls layered with centuries of scabrous grime and peeling paint, the sidewalks and streets covered with debris and thronged with people and buzzing Vespas. It was *Mr. Toad's Wild Ride* as filmed by Fellini. It was a pure adrenaline rush. I loved it.

Suddenly our intrepid chauffeur stomped hard on the brake; the car

gave a sickening lurch and stopped dead in the middle of the street. There
was no sign for a bed and breakfast or anything else, just a massive, old,
wooden door big enough to ride horse and carriage through. No matter
how I craned my neck, I couldn't find a street name or building number.
Rich took out his notebook again and leaned forward, pointing out the
name and address of the bed and breakfast, and the driver yelled "*Sì, sì.*
Yes! Here!" He leaped from the cab, ran around to the trunk, grabbed
our bags, and flung them onto the sidewalk. We jumped out after them.
The driver thrust forward his hand.

Rather unfortunately, Rich didn't happen to have exact change; he
produced a five and a ten, which the driver pocketed and then turned
away. "No," said Rich sternly. "Twelve euros!" The driver dug around
in his pocket, produced a single euro coin, pressed it into Rich's palm,
leapt behind the wheel, and was gone.

"Hey," Rich began. "That guy—"

"Let it go," I said. "That fifteen minutes was worth the price of the
entire trip."

He grinned. "It was, wasn't it?" He looked at the big, wooden door
and then up and down the street. "I wonder if we're anywhere near our
bed and breakfast. Did you happen to catch a street sign as we turned
in?"

"Are you kidding? I was too busy praying to St. Christopher that
we'd get out of the taxi alive. I didn't really care where."

The gigantic, wooden door had a smaller, human-scale door cut
into its middle, and this opened suddenly to let a youngish, dark-haired
man step out onto the sidewalk. Rich greeted him — I think in Spanish,
which we tend to lapse into in Italy — and said the name of our bed and
breakfast. The man smiled, shook his head, and walked away.

"It's not here," said Rich dejectedly.

"Maybe he didn't understand your question," I said.

"Yeah, right." But he grabbed the door before it swung all the way
shut and we stepped inside.

We found ourselves in a once-grand courtyard, flagged in stone and open to the sky. Directly across from me was a broad staircase, flanked by elaborate pillars supporting vaulting arches picked out in grimy yellow and white paint. Various low-budget additions jutted into the courtyard, including a glass-walled elevator that looked as if it had been installed — and last serviced — around the time Mussolini rose to power.

"If it *is* here and we're supposed to use that thing," Rich said, eyeing the elevator with deep suspicion, "we are finding somewhere else to stay."

"Let's try up there," I said, pointing to some metal steps that led to a wooden door ten feet above ground level in one of the add-on sections. "At least we can ask for directions." Climbing up to the door, we were dumbstruck to discover a small placard with the name of our bed and breakfast.

"I am never going to doubt St. Christopher again," Rich said, as he rang the bell.

"He was working overtime today," I agreed as we were buzzed through.

The woman behind the desk confirmed our reservation and explained that we would be staying in a *very special* room. She then led the way back down the stairs, out through the little inset door, and along the street to a small storefront with a white metal grate. This looked *very special* all right. I was beginning to see why this room was offered at a discount. She unlocked the grate and ushered us inside.

Our "room" turned out to be a defunct massage parlor. The "spa" mentioned on the website had evidently been less successful than the management hoped, and the massage table had been hauled away and replaced with a double bed. Right beside it was a blue-tiled shower stall fitted with a light that constantly changed colors, red-green-blue-red-green-blue. I really, really hoped there was an off switch somewhere.

"*Very special*," our hostess repeated, showing us the miniscule powder room and the foyer, which held a small, round table, two chairs, things for making tea, and cookies that I would soon learn were very stale indeed. I wondered how long this "spa" had been closed, and how much longer it would be before anyone thought to remove all mention of it from the web page. "No other guests here. All for you." She handed us the keys, beamed at us, and disappeared.

"A massage parlor?" asked Rich. He started to laugh. "How do we get ourselves into places like this?"

"There *are* no places like this," I said. "This is Napoli. Everything's an original."

The wild cab ride, the crazy lodgings — this town was certainly not going to be dull. Fifteen minutes later, having done a particularly thorough bedbug check, lashed our bags tightly to a sturdy pipe, and (hallelujah!) found the off switch for the shower light, we went back out in the chaos of the city streets.

"Is that *graffiti* on a *church?*" Rich said incredulously, staring at the red, purple, and turquoise names spray-painted on the venerable gray stone.

"They are *so* going to hell for that," I said. "Their souls are *toast.*"

But as I looked more closely, I realized that it wasn't the usual random graffiti but pairs of names, often accompanied by hearts and the words "*ti amo,*" which even I knew meant "I love you" in Italian. It hit me that this was a twenty-first century, Bizarro-World, street-punk version of the ancient tradition of posting the banns. Napoli's young people were still going down to the church to declare their love publicly, in front of God and everybody, just in a slightly different way than their ancestors had. It was really rather sweet — for sacrilegious vandalism.

Progress along the sidewalks was slow, as we had to negotiate our way past the larger mounds of rubbish, sprawling café tables, and clusters of motor scooters chained to streetlights. Kamikaze motorists roared up and down the streets, ignoring lanes, lights, stop signs, and stray pedestrians with sublime nonchalance. I reflected that Napoli seemed to pride itself on not being intimidated by the constraints of ordinary society. The city's robust, free-for-all atmosphere demanded that you embrace the chaos or (sometimes literally) be run over by it.

On the heels of that thought, I found myself dodging into a doorway to avoid being trampled by an onrushing parade. The boisterous crew came charging down a hill toward us: a handful of costumed characters and a dozen musicians, all mixed in with a small mob of people who might have been part of the troupe, locals on their way home, bystanders, tourists, or members of the Mafia checking on how the street garbage campaign was progressing.

The costumes were those of stock characters from the sixteenth-century street theater known as the *commedia dell'arte*. The most striking figure was a large man dressed in white and sporting a black mask; this was Pulcinella, the crafty and untrustworthy trickster. Napoli, recognizing a kindred spirit, gave him a permanent place in the city's popular culture. (England adopted him too, giving him a wife and making him Mr. Punch of the *Punch and Judy* shows.) Pulcinella's trademark raspy yet squeaky voice, somewhere between Donald Duck and a kazoo, was made by a swazzle, a small device soaked in beer and held in the performer's mouth; apparently you're not considered a veteran of the craft if you haven't swallowed your swazzle at least twice. If this Pulcinella was using (or swallowing) a swazzle, we certainly couldn't tell in the general hubbub.

That evening, relaxing back at our massage parlor, Rich shared an email he'd received from Kathryn and Peter, American friends vacationing in Venice, who'd sent a photo of a parade they'd just attended. The picture showed an immaculately uniformed band marching in orderly ranks through well-tended streets, watched by a respectful crowd.

"They call that a parade?" Rich said scornfully.

He sent them my photo of Pulcinella flailing his arms, surrounded by a drummer, a lute player, someone with a drum and a bullhorn, and the jostling rabble; in the foreground was a tiny man with a pair of gigantic white spectacles perched on his oversized nose, wearing a black suit hung with red tassels and flapping a noisemaker in our direction. You could almost hear the cacophony.

"Now that," Rich wrote to Kathryn and Peter, "is a *parade*."

By now we had abandoned any thought of going to Pompeii in favor of spending more time in Napoli. "Do we want to see any of the city's major landmarks?" Rich asked the next morning over a breakfast of coffee and croissants in our bed and breakfast's dining room. He flipped open the iPad and we put our heads together to peruse the list of the city's major POIs: a couple of castles, the national art museum, an archeological museum, the New Jesus Church (built in 1470) . . .

"The cathedral sounds kind of interesting," I said. I was reading about its most famous resident, San Gennaro (Saint January), who had served as bishop of Naples in Roman times and was now chief among the city's fifty official patron saints.

Back in 305, the Romans condemned San Gennaro to death by bear mauling (ouch!), but either it didn't work or somebody thought better of it, because in the end he was simply beheaded, thus depriving the Church of some rich iconography. Immediately after his death, a woman named Eusebia saved some of Gennaro's blood, which was placed in a glass vial now residing inside a reliquary in Napoli's cathedral. Several times a year it was brought out and placed near the saint's severed head, at which point the dried blood miraculously returned to its original liquid form. Kissing the reliquary had reportedly cured many dire illnesses, parading it through the streets had saved the city from the eruptions of Mt. Vesuvius and other disasters, and on the rare occasions when the blood had failed to liquefy, it was a sure sign that the city should brace itself for bad times.

Incredibly, some skeptics question the authenticity of this miraculous blood. They point out that the substance might be something else — a viscous gel, say, such as hydrated iron oxide, which is a rusty red, looks solid, and liquefies when shaken. Chemists have reproduced the results using materials and techniques known in medieval times, when the relic first appeared. Cynics suggest that artisans of the day were taking advantage of the hot market in holy relics, manufacturing this "miraculous" substance for profit. These naysayers note that twenty such vials of liquefying blood, attributed to seven different saints, all appeared in the Naples area at about the same time. Since then, all the "blood" has been debunked — except for San Gennaro's, which the Church won't allow to be opened for fear it could be damaged. The Vatican is officially neutral about "The Miracle of the Blood," but individual religious leaders such as Saint Alphonsus Liguori and Cardinal Newman have proclaimed it to be the real deal.

"When's the next miracle scheduled?" Rich asked.

"Well, we missed the one on September nineteenth," I said, reading on. "And unfortunately there won't be another one until December. Not much point in going to the cathedral if we can't see the main event." I passed the iPad over to Rich and sat back to drink my coffee.

Skimming further down the list of things to do in Naples, he said, "How about the catacombs?"

"There are *catacombs*?" I said, sitting up straighter and putting down my coffee cup. In the Catholic schools of my childhood, these underground labyrinths were described in the most mysterious and romantic terms. Dug deep into the ground just outside the walls of ancient cities, they were complex networks of narrow tunnels where saints (and others) were buried and Christians worshipped in secret to escape Roman persecution. "I've always wanted to see catacombs. Let's go there."

We chose the nearest and largest of Napoli's three underground burial labyrinths, the Catacombe di San Gennaro. It wasn't the first resting place for the saint's remains, nor was it the last, but he did spend four hundred years or so there, entombed in a very nice shrine. That all ended in the ninth century when Prince Sico arrived from Benevento, San Gennaro's home town, and tried to take Naples by siege. That didn't work out so well for him, but he did manage to make off with the saint's bones — at least the ones from the neck down. Somehow, in all the excitement, the skull was left behind in the catacombs. (And I'd like to see the assigned grave robber explaining *that* little mix-up to Prince Sico.) Eventually San Gennaro's skeleton and cranium were reunited and moved to various holy locations before coming to their final resting place in a special chapel in Napoli's cathedral.

The Catacombe di San Gennaro hadn't looked all that far away or difficult to find on the map, but after an hour and a half of brisk walking, we were well outside the old walls of the city, hot, tired, and not at all sure we were headed in the right direction. Clearly, we needed to stop somewhere and recombobulate.

Spotting a sidewalk café, we sat down gratefully at the tiny table and ordered fruit juice. Our waitress was a pretty girl with the kind of world-weary sophistication that only a teenager can project. On her left arm was a tattoo in English and beautifully rendered in a swirly script that flowed from elbow to wrist, reading "Nothing last forever." When she'd sauntered back inside the café to fetch our drinks, I whispered to Rich, "That is why I can never get a tattoo. Having a typo like that on my body would make me nuts."

"Karen, finding a typo like that on a *menu* makes you nuts. If there was one on your *arm*?" He shook his head. "Let's just say I'd hate to be the tattoo artist responsible for *that*."

"Death penalty offense," I said. "That's a given." The waitress returned, deposited the juice on our table, and went over to a motorcycle parked at the curb where she perched on the seat, smoking a cigarette and practicing looking decorative. I walked over and mimed a request to take a photo of her tattoo. She acquiesced, striving for the languid air of one who has learned to put up with paparazzi as the price of fame. But I could tell she was secretly pleased.

As we paid our bill, she gave us directions to the Catacombe di San Gennaro, explaining in a mix of Italian, fractured English, and hand signals that we needed to cross a bridge and climb to the top of the hill, where we would find a church called Madre del Buon Consiglio (Our Lady of Good Advice).

The church's unusual name came from a fresco that miraculously detached itself from the wall of an Albanian church and floated over to Italy in 1467, coming to rest in a church near Rome and performing all sorts of medical cures and other supernatural acts. Four hundred years later a young Neapolitan devotee painted a tribute copy of the famous fresco, and this newer work of art was soon performing its own miracles, such as stopping an outbreak of cholera and dispersing ash clouds from Mt. Vesuvius. Or so it was said . . .

At a ticket booth near the entrance of Our Lady of Good Advice, we were informed that the catacombs could only be visited under the auspices of a professional guide. Apparently by "professional" they merely meant "paid to do it" as opposed to "qualified" or "trained" or even "capable at the most basic level of fulfilling the expectations usually associated with the task." Our guide was meant to be multilingual, but when she attempted to speak in English her initial remarks, delivered in a monotone only slightly above the volume of a whisper, came out "Willcub mumble mumble alle catacomb di San Gerrano. Mumble tua guida. Please to rimaneri vicini e non esitate asking le question . . ."

It went downhill from there, figuratively and, of course, literally. We descended, a group of two dozen confused foreigners, following our "professional" guide down a series of stairs and ramps to the underground tombs.

Unlike Rome's catacombs, which I gathered were narrow and rather claustrophobic, these had wide aisles, high ceilings, and even a few sizable rooms. Most of the interments took place in narrow wall slits, but there were some larger niches decorated with frescos and tile, built to allow high-ranking clergy and the city's wealthier families to spend the afterlife comfortably ensconced in suitably luxurious real estate. All the bodies from the catacombs had long since been moved to another cemetery; the details of this transfer were a bit murky, and this being Napoli, I hesitated to probe too deeply.

The lighting in the long corridors and empty niches was dim and dramatic, the dirt underfoot soft as suede, and it would have been marvelously atmospheric except for one jarring note: someone had seen fit to turn the catacombs over to an art school, unleashing the students' creativity in a series of temporary installations that filled the former resting places of the dead with flickering televisions, piles of cunningly arranged burnt books, and other Original Commentaries on Death. It was like visiting the Louvre and discovering that the curators had invited graffiti artists to add their own flourishes — a pair of Google glasses on the Mona Lisa, amusing plastic mannequin arms on the Venus de Milo — to perk up the boring old artwork.

"This is *ghastly*," I whispered to Rich. "What were they *thinking*?"

We were destined never to know. Our guide shed no light on the subject, stammering and growing so painfully flustered over questions from non-Italian speakers that it seemed kinder to leave her alone. Rich and I dropped back to the outer edges of the group and soon slipped away altogether, moving deeper into the dark corridors to explore the catacombs on our own. As the querulous voice of the guide faded away and we left the art students' unsightly contributions behind, I was at last able to contemplate the catacombs in peaceful silence.

Burying the dead underground got its start at least a hundred thousand years ago, in the days when the ancients believed that the afterlife took place in an underworld beneath the planet's surface. I guess they thought it was courteous to give the dear departed a six-foot head start on the downward journey. While belief in a physical underworld has gone seriously out of vogue, we're still burying our dead out of respect, a desire to protect the body from predators, an equal desire to protect the community from any germs the deceased may be carrying, and to provide closure for those left behind.

There are dissenting views, of course; some Buddhists and Hindus, for instance, favor sky burials, believing the proper fate for the human body is to complete the cycle of life by becoming food for the birds. I could admire the concept intellectually, but having once come across some little human bones on a hillside in the Himalayas, I rather shrank from the reality of the practice. No, I was sticking with my desire for a nice, clean, done-and-dusted cremation. Rich and I had often talked about it—

That's when it struck me: I had managed to drag Rich to yet another cemetery! And here I'd vowed to avoid them for the rest of the trip. How could I have forgotten?

"Ready to head back?" I asked brightly.

"No, let's go on and see where this takes us."

"How far do you think it goes? Any idea how big this catacomb is?" I asked.

And for the next little while Rich was happily engaged in calculating how far we'd come and mentally matching that to maps he'd seen of the catacombs and the city to determine if we'd reached the probable limits of this section. He was still working on it when we found ourselves in a large, high-ceilinged space, and there on the far wall was just about the last thing I expected to see: an ordinary, modern door.

"Should we—?" I began.

"I believe Our Lady of Good Advice would tell us to go right ahead."

"What about alarms?"

He shrugged. "We can always play the dumb tourists. Besides, this is *Napoli*."

Enough said. *Rules*? What rules?

He tried the door, which opened at his touch, and I followed him through. We found ourselves in a large, dark, quiet space with light filtering through tall windows. It was an abandoned church. As far as I could tell in the twilight, it was clean enough if slightly musty, with the peculiarly heavy air you find in places that are rarely disturbed. Out of respect — and a sincere desire to avoid being required to explain our presence to any overzealous catacomb police who spoke no English — we tiptoed up the aisle to the main doors and slipped outside.

I stood blinking in the bright sunlight pouring down on a small parking lot. There were eight or ten cars, mostly battered Fiats, and high, gray walls rising on the right and left. I could just make out a sign that included the word *"ospedale,"* and I said slowly, "I think that means hospital." Our escape from the catacombs was taking on a distinctly surreal quality as we stumbled, like Alice, from one unexpected setting to another. "What next?" I wondered. "A mad tea party?"

"Curiouser and curiouser," Rich said, echoing my thoughts. "That church must have been the chapel for the hospital. I wonder why they abandoned it."

"Could they possibly have thought it was unhealthy to put sick people next to a bunch of dead bodies?"

We were still speculating on the fate of the abandoned chapel as we crossed the parking lot and stepped out onto the street, walking into a scene that was, if not a tea party, certainly a bit mad.

It was Napoli in full flower. After the muffled silence of the catacombs, the noise and color and motion were shocking. Vehicles and people zoomed about in all directions at top speed and maximum volume. Up ahead, an old woman leaned out of her third story window, shouted, and dropped a basket down on a rope, timing it perfectly to coincide with the arrival of the man strolling around the corner carrying her groceries. Beside me, a young girl finished crossing the intersection and stepped onto the curb a split second before a trio of Vespas tore around the corner. And that's when I realized that this wasn't chaos at all; in its own way, it was as choreographed as a dance, and everyone there knew the rhythm, the speed, and the steps. What made the Neapolitans different was that they were all dancing to a beat so wild and improvisational that it made the rest of us look as if we were plodding through a formal minuet.

It took us ten dizzying minutes to pass through the kaleidoscopic crowd. And then we arrived at the base of the bridge we'd crossed hours earlier to get to Our Lady of Good Advice. The bridge was as high overhead as the roof of a four-story building, and finding a way back up to it by surface roads would have required a long, complicated detour. However, by an extraordinary piece of good fortune, this was the site of one of Napoli's three free elevators, built to connect areas divided by severe topographical differences. To be honest it didn't look much newer or more reliable than the one in our building and I was afraid Rich would balk, but after watching several Neapolitans zip up and down in it without mishap, he shrugged, I said a prayer to St. Christopher, and we climbed on board. We made it up to bridge level without a hitch, and from there we retraced our steps back to the massage parlor we called home.

The following morning, strolling around after breakfast trying to decide how to spend our last hours in the city, Rich and I happened upon a narrow alley called San Gregorio Armeno. This was the famous street where all of Napoli and half of Europe shopped for their nativity scene figures every Christmas.

In the Mediterranean countries, a crèche scene wasn't just the Holy Family, angel, shepherds, Three Wise Men, and a few animals, like the ones I'd known in my childhood. Here, an event as important as the birth of God required a much larger entourage, usually the entire city of Bethlehem plus a legion of plumed Roman soldiers and often a desert section with the pharaoh's palace as a backdrop for the flight into Egypt. The caravan of the Magi required not just the three camel-riding kings but a full entourage with treasure-toting Nubians, jugglers, monkeys with parasols, snake charmers, and pet tigers.

Electric cords and batteries powered flickering fires and moving figurines, such as old women scattering corn to chickens, and butchers carving up pigs, their tiny, blood-stained cleavers rising and falling rhythmically. (Apparently nobody but me found anything incongruous about the presence of pork in this Jewish community.) There were stables topped by fluffy gray clouds that, at the press of a button, rained water down on the scene, often draining into a little stream that might hold live goldfish. People added to their collections every year, and the Italian artists were famous for the quality and inventiveness of their work.

One of the most popular figures was the little crouching figure of the *caganer*, traditionally placed behind the stable or a bush, clearly and explicitly defecating. The Italians and Spanish loved this character, insisting that he (or she, in today's more egalitarian times) added a much-needed touch of earthy realism. Celebrity *caganers* were hugely popular; online vendors offered such well-known faces as Bruce Springsteen, Kate Middleton, Albert Einstein, Rodin's the Thinker, Bart Simpson, Darth Vader, Santa . . . and just about everybody else. That day in San Gregorio Armeno, most of the celebrity *caganers* were Italian politicians and sports stars I didn't recognize. Although I didn't think to look for them at the time, no doubt they had Pulcinella and the rest of the *commedia dell'arte* there too.

I hadn't adopted this tradition myself, but I knew many people who found this to be the perfect finishing touch on their nativity scene at home, work, or church. Every December, as they tenderly tucked a little *caganer* into the shadows, they took pride in adding a humble touch to the awesome moment, reminding us that we didn't have to be perfect, or even respectable, to be part of something wonderful.

And that, I thought, was Napoli's gift to the world. They embraced the rough, flawed, and unseemly sides of themselves right along with the parts that were more socially acceptable. They did everything "wrong." They didn't obey the rules. People lived at full tilt and top volume, without apologies. They drove the wrong way down trolley tracks honking at the timid souls who stopped for red lights. I suspect the first thing they taught their kids was how to color outside the lines. And from what I could see, they would never clean up their act in order to become the next vacation playground for the cruise lines. Yet all these "wrongs" added up to something very right: a city that knew what it loved and lived as it chose. Napoli didn't try to seduce you, which was why it was so easy to fall in love with the city — not despite its faults, but because of them.

[CHAPTER 19]

Homecoming

Two days later, we were home.

The shock of stepping off a train into the familiar setting of our own Seville railway station was perhaps the most discombobulating of all my arrivals. Rich and I went to the same McCafé where we'd had coffee on the morning of our departure some eighty-two days earlier and sat at the same table with a cup of the same underwhelming brew. I couldn't be sure, but it tasted as if it had been sitting at the bottom of the pot since the day we left.

"We made it," said Rich, settling back with a sigh of contentment — at the achievement, certainly not the coffee.

"Won't Enrique be surprised."

We'd been traveling fast for the last forty-eight hours. From Napoli, we'd taken a northbound train to Civitavecchia, the port just above Rome, where we caught the night ferry across the Mediterranean to Barcelona. The voyage took nearly eighteen hours, but fortunately we'd managed to secure our own stateroom and the sea was smooth as glass. We arrived in Barcelona in time for dinner and left the next morning on the high-speed train for Seville.

And now there was just a twenty-minute walk left in a journey that had taken us nearly six thousand miles through thirteen countries.

I set down the McCoffee. "Let's go."

I stood, gathering up my things for the last time on this journey. We strolled out of the café, crossed the street, passed in front of the gymnasium where we'd worked out for years, and as we turned the corner I saw a familiar figure rushing toward us on his way to the train station.

"Enrique!" called Rich.

And Enrique stopped, dumbstruck. "You made it!" he cried. "You're back!" He threw his arms around me. "I can't believe it! Welcome home." He clapped Rich on the back. "This is incredible!"

"I *told* you we planned to survive the trip," I said, laughing.

He shot me a look that clearly meant, "Oh sure. You got lucky *this time* . . ." and said aloud, "I hope you're planning to stay put for a while."

"Absolutely."

"Thank God for that," said Enrique. And then he kissed me on both cheeks and ran for his train, and Rich and I continued our walk home.

As we passed the familiar shops, cafés, and churches, Rich said, "What's that quote? The one about going back where you started your trip and it's the same but it's not?"

Rich is notorious for his enthusiastic but wildly inaccurate use of famous quotations, butchering everything from Shakespeare to Christmas carols in ways that were almost as painful for me as misspelled tattoos. Before he could do anything worse to the lovely verse from T.S. Elliot's *Four Quartets*, I quoted hastily, "We shall not cease from exploration / And the end of all our exploring / Will be to arrive where we started / and know the place for the first time."

"Yeah, that one," he said. "I feel just like that."

Five minutes later we were standing in front of our building, with its slightly crumbling walls and peeling paint, the old green door with the lock that tended to stick, the worn stone stoop where so many courting teens from the nearby high school had sat canoodling. Everything had the exaggerated brightness of the strange and exotic, overlaid with the comforting familiarity of home. And then I passed, as the next line of Elliot's poem put it, "Through the unknown, remembered gate . . ."

The elevator carried us upward through the silent building, and then Rich had his key in the lock and the door was swinging open. The sub-letters were gone, the woman who cleans for us had scrubbed the place spotless, and our friends Simone and L-F had left us flowers and a welcome sign decorated by their young daughters. I was smiling as I rolled my suitcase into our room for its final unpacking.

Home at last. I felt lightheaded with relief and happiness — we'd made it! I was also a bit dazed and disoriented at the thought that my railway adventures were coming to a close (at least for now). We soon had our suitcases emptied, the laundry tossed in the hamper, and our travel gear tucked away for future use. But mentally unpacking took considerably longer.

For the next week, I still felt like a railway nomad. I woke every morning unsure of where I was, but certain that I should be packing my bag and heading to the train station. Every night I had to restrain myself from checking the mattress seams for bedbugs. I was constantly energized, the way I often feel on trips — awake, alive, and ready for action. We went to an InterNations gathering and dined out with various friends, plunging into our social lives at top speed.

The second week we crashed. We were so exhausted that we could barely drag ourselves out of bed in the morning. We hibernated like bears hunkered down in our cave, living on fruit and cheese and crackers, watching back episodes of *Game of Thrones* and *Downton Abbey*.

"It's train lag," said Rich. "We'll get over it."

I just yawned.

After a week of sloth and indolence, I woke up one morning feeling more alert, and before I knew it, Rich and I were back on our feet and out in the world again. That third week, I remember feeling a sort of euphoria. I had done an amazing thing and proved, to my own satisfaction at least, that I could still have the kind of spontaneous travel adventures that I'd had in my youth.

Our friends were wonderful, inviting us out for drinks and listening to our ramblings about the trip and how we were surviving the re-entry. I tried (not always successfully) to limit the amount of time I spent talking about my nomad days. While many of my Spanish and expat *amigos* seemed to get a tremendous kick out of hearing my travel tales, others soon lost interest, and I tried to stop yammering before their eyes glazed over and they actually started snoring. I had to keep reminding myself that the rail journey, writ large in my own life for so long, was barely a footnote to the rest of the world. I kept running into people I'd known for years who said, "That's right, I forgot, you've been away. Go any-place interesting?" And I'd try to condense my three-month adventure into a sentence or two, something that could be blurted out before they'd finished their beer and wandered off to fetch another round.

How to sum up the journey in a few sentences? If you asked Rich, and many did, he would rattle off the statistics he'd been tabulating.

We had traveled across 13 countries: Spain, Italy, Germany, Austria, the Czech Republic, Poland, Hungary, Slovakia, Romania, Bulgaria, Serbia, Montenegro, and Croatia. We covered just under 6,000 miles — 5,983, to be exact. We took 38 trains for a total of 4,627 railway miles, and traveled 668 miles on ferries, 190 miles in buses and taxis, 6 miles by horse-drawn cart, and 492 miles on foot. When Rich calculated our trip expenses — which we defined as the expenditures over and above what we'd have spent anyway on daily living — they came to $85 a day for the two of us, matching the $3,500 apiece that Rich had budgeted almost to the penny.

Of course, the numbers were only the beginning of the story. Some friends wanted to know how the trip had changed us.

"I feel as if I'm seeing everything with fresh eyes," Rich told them.

I had to agree. Even the most familiar neighborhoods seemed to take on the kind of luster they'd had when we first moved to Seville, the I-can't-believe-I'm-here wonderment.

T.S. Elliot was right. Arriving back where we started, I felt as if I knew my home for the first time.

I'd always viewed my home as the physical nucleus of my life: the kitchen where I baked birthday cakes, the sofa where I took siestas, and the table where I served Thanksgiving dinner. It was the base camp from which I scaled mountains, the port from which I embarked on careers and relationships, and the cave to which I retreated to lick my wounds.

I might not, like some I'd met on our railway journey, have roots extending back thousands of years, running nearly as deep as the earth's core. But I'd learned how to stake my temporary claim to one small spot on the planet's crust and build a life for myself there. In recent years, my idea of home as a single fixed point had begun to crumble due to dividing my time between Seville and San Anselmo. I had felt a faint, nagging concern that belonging to both might mean that I did not properly belong to either one.

Then I'd become a railway nomad, traveling for thousands of miles through more than a dozen countries. And instead of feeling adrift and disconnected, as I'd half expected, I had grown increasingly at ease with myself and at home in the world. I remembered how in August I'd glanced anxiously over my shoulder while disembarking in Genoa and how, months later, I'd found Napoli's rampant squalor and anarchy endearing rather than alarming. I had become more used to the world's antics; they might — did! — still surprise me, but they wouldn't necessarily make me feel out of place. Returning to Seville had made me realize that my sense of home was no longer firmly tethered to one or two fixed points on the map but was something I carried with me wherever I was.

And perhaps that is the lesson that the nomadic life is meant to teach us: going out into the world isn't about abandoning our home but expanding it.

I have friends who live in gated communities and exist in a state of constant, low-grade fear of everyone outside the walls. It's as if they had chosen to retreat to the mountain citadel in Veliko Tarnovo and worried, every time the drawbridge went down, that the woman delivering the dry cleaning or the guy mowing the lawn was in the vanguard of an invading force. These friends live in constant, barbarians-at-the-gate vigilance, trusting, it seems, fewer people every year, narrowing their definition of "us" to a very small circle indeed.

Getting out and meeting strangers is the best way I know to stop viewing the world through the distorting lens of "us" versus "them."

As Mark Twain put it, "Travel is fatal to prejudice, bigotry and narrow-mindedness."

That quote always reminds me of the time during my long-ago vegetarian phase when I was visiting friends in Alabama and happened to be seated next to an avid hunter at a dinner party. He talked in a sweet, lazy drawl about his father showing him how to stalk, kill, and skin animals in the woods and how he was now teaching the basics to his little girl. I sat there with a fixed smile and gritted teeth, simmering with unvoiced self-righteousness, knowing that murdering innocent creatures for sport was vicious, cruel, and utterly abominable behavior.

Then he added casually, "Of course, I eat everything I kill."

And I suddenly saw hunting from his point of view: as an honorable way to put food on his family's table, as taking *responsibility* for the killing that supported his life. Throughout most of my life I had eaten animals that other people had slaughtered, and I was sitting at that very dinner table wearing leather shoes. My misplaced sense of moral superiority evaporated in a split second, and I have been grateful to my dinner companion ever since. No, I haven't started stalking my Thanksgiving turkey in the woods with a bow and arrow, but I now understand why good people might.

Surrounding ourselves with nothing but kindred spirits and like-minded people is dangerous, making it entirely too easy to view everyone else with disdain and suspicion. On the railway trip I'd seen catastrophic examples of the consequences of dividing the world into "us" and "them": Auschwitz, the Palace of the People, and the Memorial to the Victims of Communism and the Resistance, to name but a few. Travel can show us the dangers of that kind of thinking and remind us how little our perceived differences matter.

My childhood was overshadowed with fear and hatred of enemies behind the Iron Curtain. I'd let go of that outdated ideology decades earlier, of course, but even if I hadn't, those prejudices would never have survived meeting the people of those former communist countries: Eva in Prague, gearing up to start a blog she found as daunting as Mt. Everest; Claudius and the White Witch dishing out gossip about Vlad the Impaler in Transylvania; and Calin, welcoming us into the circle of the Bucharest Hash House Harriers and pressing upon us a travel supply of homemade brandy. Were we really so different from one another? That's what we travel to discover. Often it turns out, as the comic-strip character Pogo so famously said, "We have met the enemy and he is us."

The shadows of many old divisions are dissipating in the electric glare of modern technology. With wifi floating through in the mountains of Bulgaria and smartphones nestled in the denim pockets of Transylvania teens, we're all connecting in new ways. And that is changing the way the world thinks and plays and works. Often our jobs are no longer confined to a single office or the hours from nine to five. How often do people you know answer work-related texts and emails during an evening out or while they're on vacation? How often do you do it? Being available wherever you find yourself is simply a part of doing business these days.

Like our definition of work, our concept of home has also expanded from a single, fixed geographic location to something much broader. Very, very few of us have all the people we love gathered in one spot anymore. Yet unlike our great grandparents' generation, who lived with the hard truth that moving away often meant saying goodbye forever, we can easily keep in touch with friends and family scattered across the country, even across continents. If home is where the heart is, then we are all citizens of the world.

But while being in a single physical location no longer defines who we are or what we do, it's still the way we experience the world. Returning to Seville gave me a deep and delightful sense of homecoming. After sleeping in thirty-six strange beds, I was overjoyed to be back in my own.

As the third week's post-trip euphoria faded, a sense of profound contentment lingered. My body reveled in the familiar comforts of the sofa with the faux-fur throw where I took siestas, my back-friendly desk chair, and my laptop with the larger screen. I loved having a whole closet full of clothes, although I noticed how much longer it took me to dress with so many nuanced options to choose from. The shoes alone required an absurd amount of deliberation. But most of all, I was happy to see friends and spend time with them, sitting in my favorite cafés, absorbing the fact that I was really back in Seville at last.

Rich began taking long walks through the city, rediscovering each neighborhood with those fresh eyes. His sciatica (or whatever it was) still troubled him, but doing exercises and visiting a physical therapist from time to time gave him good mobility and kept the pain at manageable levels.

"It will never be perfect," he said with a philosophical shrug. "But I can live with it. It won't stop me from doing what I want to do."

It didn't take long for friends to start asking us when and where the next big trip would be. For the longest time, I simply laughed and shook my head. I couldn't begin to think about it. I had just finished physically and mentally unpacking my bags; I needed more time to settle. I was still experiencing what author William Gibson calls "soul delay." My spirit needed time to catch up with my body's physical location.

And then one day in early December, when we'd been home about five weeks and had gone to watch Seville put up its holiday lights, Rich turned to me and said, "What would you think of taking off for a year and going around the world?"

What? No. I *really* wasn't ready to think about that. I said slowly, buying time, "A whole year on the road?"

Just that morning I had been looking at the map on the kitchen wall and idly thinking that someday, when we were ready to travel again, it might be fun to head to northeastern Europe. Estonia, Latvia . . . I knew less than nothing about those countries, but they seemed far enough off the main tourist routes to be intriguing. I'd been wondering whether it might be fun to travel a bit longer next time, maybe for four to six months. But now I was blindsided by Rich's question. A whole year on the road?

"I honestly don't know, Rich. I mean, it sounds like the grandest of all grand adventures. But I'm just not sure . . . At least not for a while . . ."

"I didn't mean this week," he said. "Just think about it."

It was a huge idea. Scary. Exciting. Dizzying.

I went home, lay down on the couch, wrapped myself up in my fluffy faux-fur throw, and thought about the last three months and the next five years.

During our railway journey, the only times I'd felt the urge to stop traveling was when I was in places I didn't like. Trundling around rural Transylvania in a horse cart, seeking out an underground bar in Belgrade, or careening madly through the streets of Napoli, I'd felt as if I could continue on forever. But when I found myself on the road more traveled, in places that had turned themselves into theme parks crowded with tourists standing in long lines for pre-packaged experiences, I would suddenly notice that I *was* a bit tired and wonder if it was time to be getting back to my "real" life.

And then there was the future. In six months, Rich would turn seventy. Even with his imperfect leg he showed no signs of slowing down, but the hard fact was that we did not have unlimited years of travel ahead of us. (Does anyone?) He had brought up the idea of an around-the-world trip before, and we'd always agreed to put it off. But if he was serious about it, the time was now — or at any rate, in the next few years — if we didn't want to risk losing the opportunity forever. Did I really want to stand in the way of his lifelong dream, even if it didn't perfectly match my own travel preferences at this moment?

What would Our Lady of Good Advice recommend?

I was still pondering this the next day as I walked through downtown Seville along a street filled with holiday shoppers and tourists checking out the latest fashions in the store windows. Glancing at a display in one of the chains selling cheap, trendy clothes for twenty-somethings, I saw a mannequin wearing a dark blue T-shirt that said, in slightly cheesy white lettering, "Out there is an adventure. Let's go."

And I thought, "Hell, yeah." What was I doing, hesitating about going around the world with Rich? Was I *insane*? What kind of fainthearted fool turns down *that* kind of opportunity?

I marched right in, bought that T-shirt, and went home to tell Rich that I was ready to pack my bag and go around the world anytime he wanted to.

"Really?" he said. "Because I've been thinking about it and it suddenly hit me that going around the world would mean a ridiculous amount of air travel. So maybe we should forget about a global grand tour. What would you think about six months in the remoter reaches of northeastern Europe?"

I started to laugh. "I think I just sold my hair to buy you a chain for your pocket watch, while you were out pawning the watch to buy me fancy hair combs." In the tradition of O. Henry's famous story "Gift of the Magi," we were working at cross-purposes, and my grand gesture just went out the window.

"Merry Christmas, darling," he said, grinning.

Rich and I are now exploring the idea of taking a long train trip through northeastern Europe — to Lithuania, Latvia, and Estonia, among others. Of course, we'd need to steer clear of countries in political turmoil because, as I've mentioned before, I don't want to wind up dead — or in a Ukrainian prison, for that matter. Rich is keeping tabs on the U.S. State Department travel warnings for the region and has begun to research possible destinations, train routes, and of course, more apps. In odd moments, we find ourselves standing at the map on the kitchen wall, tracing routes from Estonia to Finland and from there to St. Petersburg (Санкт-Петербург), just a short ferry ride across the Baltic Sea.

Of course, we may end up choosing another destination altogether — China? Cuba? New Zealand? There's a lot of world out there that we haven't seen.

Whatever direction we think we're headed, I know to expect delays. Our next nomadic adventure could be derailed at any moment by a crisis in our health, our family, world politics, the global economy, flesh-eating zombies from outer space, or some unimaginable event so cataclysmic that it wakes Good King Wenceslaus and tumbles the dragon bones from the wall of Kraków's castle at last.

Whatever happens, I know I'll encounter a few surprising turns in the road, taking me *out there* into the unknown, probably when I least expect it. There will always be missed trains, but — with luck — there will also be a pastry to eat while I'm waiting for the next one.

A nomadic railway journey is like a favorite niece or nephew, the one who likes to hide behind the sofa ready to leap out with a roar, hoping to surprise you into remembering that life is supposed to be fun.

I may not travel in precisely the same way that I did when I was nineteen, but I hope that I never stop saying, "Out there is an adventure. Let's go."

THANKS

I'm so glad you decided to join me on this journey and that you stuck with us all the way to the end. If you enjoyed *Adventures of a Railway Nomad*, writing a review on Amazon or sharing it on Facebook or Twitter would go a long way toward helping others find the book.

BUT WAIT, THERE'S MORE!

Please visit my webpage, EnjoyLivingAbroad.com, to see

Photos of places we visited

An interactive map of the route

Links to Rich's favorite apps and gear

ABOUT THE AUTHOR

An award-winning journalist, author, and blogger, Karen McCann has been living in Seville, Spain, since 2004. Wanderlust has taken her to more than forty-five countries, including many developing or post-war nations where she and her husband volunteered as consultants to struggling microenterprises. A fourth-generation Californian, she lived in Cleveland, Ohio, with her husband for two decades before the couple moved to Seville "for a year" and decided to make it their home.

The story of the move to Seville is chronicled in her book *Dancing in the Fountain: How to Enjoy Living Abroad*. More adventure stories and travel tips can be found in her blog Enjoy Living Abroad and in her short guides *Pack Light* and *101 Ways To Enjoy Living Abroad*. *Adventures of a Railway Nomad* is her most recent book. She and her husband are currently planning another, longer, less structured adventure, which may decide to turn itself into a book.

Made in the USA
San Bernardino, CA
26 July 2015